NEW TESTAMENT THEOLOGY

NEW TESTAMENT THEOLOGY

BY

HENRY C. SHELDON

PROFESSOR IN BOSTON UNIVERSITY
AND AUTHOR OF "UNBELIEF IN THE NINETEENTH CENTURY,"
"SACERDOTALISM IN THE NINETEENTH CENTURY," ETC.

WIPF & STOCK · Eugene, Oregon

Wipf and Stock Publishers
199 W 8th Ave, Suite 3
Eugene, OR 97401

New Testament Theology
By Sheldon, Henry C.
Softcover ISBN-13: 978-1-7252-9764-7
Hardcover ISBN-13: 978-1-7252-9765-4
eBook ISBN-13: 978-1-7252-9766-1
Publication date 1/19/2021
Previously published by The Macmillan Company, 1911

This edition is a scanned facsimile of
the original edition published in 1911.

PREFACE

It has been our endeavor to prepare a book which, on the one hand, shall be sufficiently free from scholastic formality to be fairly acceptable to the general reader, and, on the other hand, sufficiently compact in statement, logical in arrangement, and fundamental in its treatment of the subject-matter, to be fitted for service as a text-book. The conviction that there is room for a treatise which seeks to exemplify these characteristics is our principal excuse for presenting the volume to the public.

The reader will easily discover the critical standpoint of the book, and will notice that it is not to be ascertained by mere reference to the names of critics which occur in the volume. We have been quite free to cite judgments, which seemed to us to be on the side of a sound consensus, from writers whose general standpoint is rather emphatically contrasted with our own.

BOSTON UNIVERSITY,
December, 1910.

CONTENTS

CHAPTER I

SOURCES BACK OF THE NEW TESTAMENT WRITINGS.

		PAGE
I.	General Glance at these Sources	3
II.	Pharisaism, or the Later Jewish Orthodoxy, and its Contributions	8
III.	Alexandrianism, and its Contributions	20
IV.	Questions as to the Indebtedness of Certain Special Portions of the New Testament to Post-Canonical Judaism	36

CHAPTER II

THE SYNOPTICAL GOSPELS AND THEIR TEACHINGS.

I.	The Characteristics of these Gospels and the More Probable Theory as to Their Interrelations	39
II.	The Story of the Nativity	56
III.	The Self-Consciousness of Christ as a Subject of Development and a Source of Teaching	59
IV.	Some Distinguishing Characteristics of Christ's Teaching.	68
V.	The Trend of Christ's Teaching Respecting the Nature of the Kingdom of God and the Conditions of Entrance.	73
VI.	Leading Conceptions of God as Set Forth by Christ.	87
VII.	Leading Conceptions of Man and the World	93

CONTENTS

		PAGE
VIII.	The Witness of Christ Respecting His Own Person and Office	99
IX.	Christ's Teaching on the Progress and Consummation of the Kingdom	107

CHAPTER III

PORTIONS OF THE NEW TESTAMENT MORE OR LESS AKIN TO THE SYNOPTICAL GOSPELS IN THEIR REPRESENTATION OF A PRIMITIVE TYPE OF CHRISTIAN TEACHING.

I.	Consideration of the Proper Compass of the Chapter.	123
II.	The Teaching of the First Part of the Book of Acts.	140
III.	The Teaching of the Epistle of James	153
IV.	The Teaching of the Apocalypse	158

CHAPTER IV

THE PAULINE THEOLOGY.

I.	The Several Groups of Pauline Epistles.	172
II.	The Sources of the Pauline Theology	188
III.	General Conceptions of God, of the World, and of the Rational Creation, which Underlie the Pauline Epistles	199
IV.	The Chief Pauline Antitheses — Flesh and Spirit, Law and Grace	213
V.	The Person of Christ	219
VI.	The Holy Spirit	226
VII.	The Reconciling Work of Christ	228
VIII.	Justification and Regeneration.	235
IX.	The Unfoldment and Manifestation of the New Life	243
X.	The Church and the Sacraments	252
XI.	The Second Advent and the Related Events.	258
XII.	The Teaching of the Pastoral Epistles	266

CHAPTER V

MODIFIED PAULINISM — HEBREWS AND FIRST PETER.

		PAGE
I.	Introductory Considerations	270
II.	The Conception of God in Hebrews and First Peter	278
III.	Hints on the Nature and Rank of Men and Angels	280
IV.	The Person of Christ	284
V.	The High-Priestly Work of Christ	286
VI.	Christian Life, Individual and Collective	293
VII.	Eschatology	297

CHAPTER VI

THE JOHANNINE THEOLOGY.

I.	The Question of Authorship	300
II.	Sources and Peculiarities	318
III.	Johannine Antitheses	325
IV.	The Doctrine of the Father and the Son	331
V.	The Holy Spirit	340
VI.	The Work of Christ	343
VII.	The Initiation and Unfoldment of the New Life	347
VIII.	The Christian Brotherhood	353
IX.	Eschatology	356
X.	Conclusion	358
	Index	361

NEW TESTAMENT THEOLOGY

NEW TESTAMENT THEOLOGY

CHAPTER I

SOURCES BACK OF THE NEW TESTAMENT WRITINGS

I. — General Glance at These Sources.

The distinctive character of Biblical Theology makes it appropriate to devote specific attention to the subject of sources. As distinguished from Systematic Theology it is very largely a historical discipline. While the former directs attention to the outcome of revelation, and seeks an orderly presentation of the doctrines which are demanded by a preponderance of biblical and rational evidences, the latter is interested in the stages of revelation, and seeks to exhibit the peculiarities of different doctrinal types in the Bible together with the historical conditions by which their rise and development were influenced.

In a full survey of the theme of this chapter it will not be overlooked that the foremost source was the consciousness of Jesus Christ, viewed as the spring of His words and deeds. This consciousness, unique in itself, had a unique power to generate the new order of life and thought which is mirrored in the apostolic literature.

A source only second in importance to that named was

the Scriptures of the Old Testament, the books of the Hebrew canon. These furnished in no small degree content and coloring to the consciousness of Christ, and supplied a background to the religious thinking of all the New Testament writers. Such foundation ideas of the New Testament edifice as the absolute supremacy of God, His distinct personality, the intensity of His ethical life, and His purpose to build up a perpetual kingdom of righteousness, belonged to the great inheritance which was transmitted by the Hebrew oracles.

A third source may be described as post-canonical or extra-canonical Judaism. Very likely it would be no mistake to affirm a certain analogy between the standpoint of the primitive representatives of Christianity and that of the Protestant reformers. As the latter sought to break through the overgrowth of ecclesiastical tradition, and to get back to Christian originals, so the former felt an incentive to disengage religion from Judaic traditionalism and to appeal directly to the Old Testament Scriptures as containing the more incorrupt deposit of truth. The analogy suggests, nevertheless, that the developments of later Judaism may have exercised considerable influence upon New Testament doctrine. The Protestant reformers, notwithstanding their inclination to go back to the primitive springs of Christian truth, were unquestionably influenced by the results of patristic and scholastic thinking. A system which had leavened the intellect of generations could not suddenly be renounced at every point. If antipathy to some of its features drove into counter tenets of a specially pronounced character, other features remained unchallenged and entered into the new theological structure which was designed to take the place of the old. It seems, therefore, in the light of the historical parallel, to be probable that post-canonical Judaism was somewhat of a factor in shaping the theological conceptions which have come to expression in the New Testament, and that it wrought in the way of attraction as well as of repulsion.

Further illustration of the obligations of the New Testament to the first two sources will be left to be brought out, as occasion may arise, in connection with the various subdivisions of our theme. As repects the third source, since its consideration is somewhat off the track of the more ordinary theological study, it will be well to give it specific attention in this connection.

In post-canonical Judaism the principal factors of which note needs to be taken were the Pharisaic and Hellenistic systems. The latter of these had its culminating expression in the Jewish community of Alexandria. We may say then in brief terms, that post-canonical Judaism made its principal contributions to New Testament theology through Pharisaism and Alexandrianism. This statement implies that the Sadducean and Essenic schools exercised a subordinate influence upon Christian thinking. There is no reason to doubt that this was the case with the former, and our conviction is that it was true, though in a less emphatic sense, of the latter.

The Sadducees were more largely an aristocratic and political party than a theological school. They had place only so long as Judaism played a political rôle. Nothing was heard of them after the complete overthrow of the Jewish people had cancelled opportunities for diplomacy and political management. Doubtless the Sadducees had somewhat of a special theological interest, but it was not intense enough to exercise any appreciable influence beyond their own limits. If on one side their position was acceptable to the Christian standpoint, namely as respects their rejection of the traditions with which the Pharisees had supplemented the written law, on another side, that is, in their negative attitude toward the future life, they came into sharp collision with Christian sentiment. On the whole, the connection of the Sadducees with the rise of Christianity was simply external. It did not reach to doctrinal content.

A much greater religious earnestness belonged to Essenism than to Sadduceeism. In some of its teachings, also, phases more or less parallel to gospel precepts may be specified. If Christ reprobated the taking of oaths, taught His disciples to foster peace as opposed to warlike violence, inculcated an unworldly temper, spoke a word of commendation of those practicing continence for the sake of the kingdom of heaven, and strongly emphasized the duty of unselfish and brotherly ministering, He set forth features of an ideal that was recognized in the maxims of the Essenes. Some writers have supposed that Christ had a special connection with this Jewish association, and that His discourses show the tinge of its tuition. But this conclusion is to be regarded as doubtful for the following reasons: (1) Most of the points mentioned as having their counterpart in the teaching of the Essenes were the dictate of Christ's fundamental views of God and man. There was a sufficient source for them in the clear and balanced religious intuition with which He was so richly endowed. (2) The formal resemblance between precepts does not exclude at all points material differences in conception. For example, if Christ, as reported by the evangelist, spoke favorably of some who had made themselves eunuchs for the sake of the kingdom of heaven, He could not have done so in the interest of the ascetic standpoint which dictated the opposition of the Essenes to marriage; for the general tenor of His teaching is emphatically opposed to that standpoint. (3) In central and fundamental respects the system of Christ's teaching is opposed to the Essenic. The governing point of view of the latter was purity in the legal and ceremonial sense; on this line it was a species of high Pharisaism. The former placed absolutely no stress on ceremonial purity as compared with interior morality and religion. Again, the one was monastic and separatistic in spirit, seeking for holiness by isolation from a contaminating world; the other was animated by a spirit of world-embracing sympathy, and welcomed communication with all classes and conditions of men who needed to be benefited. These are important contrasts. In the light of them it does not seem too much to say with Wellhausen : " The Essenes were not forerunners of Christianity, to which this kind of esoterism and of separation from sinners was originally entirely foreign."[1] While claiming this much it is not necessary to affirm that no sort of stimulus, no element of religious

---

[1] Israelitische und Judische Geschichte, p. 296. Compare H. J. Holtzmann, Lehrbuch der neutestamentlichen Theologie, I. 118; Harnack, What is Christianity? p. 32; Schultz, Grundriss der christlichen Apologetik, p. 146.

conception or work, came from Essenism. As a part of the environment inclosing an incipient Christianity it may have had its effect. Our contention is that there is insufficient ground for regarding it as a prominent factor in shaping Christian thought.

II. — Pharisaism, or the Later Jewish Orthodoxy, and its Contributions.

Pharisaism stands for the characteristic development of post-exilian piety in Israel. It names the great central channel in which earnest religion flowed from the days of Ezra. As a distinct party the Pharisees may not have antedated the Maccabean crisis. But the tendency, of which they represented the matured stage, or rather the exaggerated development, went back to the era of that national rebuilding which was undertaken by the returned exiles. This tendency did not dominate the entire national life, at least for any considerable interval; nevertheless, it was central to the religious movement, especially of Palestinian Judaism, from Ezra to Paul. The natural outcome of that movement was the identification of Jewish orthodoxy with Pharisaism.

In judging of the dogmatic contents of Pharisaism in the first century it is legitimate to make much use of the Talmud. For, while this great compendium of Jewish legal and religious lore was not completed till some centuries later, the traditions which it incorporates and the type which it exhibits were doubtless in large part extant by the time of Christ's public ministry. This conclusion is strongly supported by the correspondence between the image of Pharisaism which it mirrors and that which is given in the Gospels. In addition to the Talmud we may properly employ a number of writings, mostly pseudepigraphic, which were written between 170 B.C. and A.D. 100. Here belong the Book of Enoch, the Psalms of Solomon, the Assumption of Moses, the Apocalypse of Baruch, the Fourth Book of Ezra, the Book of Jubilees, and some of the Sibylline verses.

The adverse associations which go with Pharisaism should not blind us to the fact that at the start it represented a doctrine of the law which in large part was the dictate of a praiseworthy zeal for righteousness, and that it always acknowledged many excellent points both in practical ethics and in religious doctrine. Its fatal error was that it ultimately went on to such an exaggerated and particularistic stress upon the law as brought life under bondage to positive rules, and left little place for a consideration of the demands of interior piety.

It is an almost incredible externalization of religion which is ascribed to Pharisaism in some of the strictures of Christ. Doubtless His strong words cannot justly be applied in all their length and breadth to every man who was enrolled among the Pharisees. But as regards the controlling animus of Pharisaism, it cannot be said that they savor of oratorical exaggeration. The sources confirm the conclusion that in its progressive evolution Pharisaism reached such a pass, that it could fairly be described as legality run mad. As is clearly shown in Weber's learned treatise on the later Jewish Theology,[1]

---

[1] Judische Theologie auf Grund des Talmud und Verwandter Schriften.

the resources of language were exhausted in enforcing the importance and sanctity of the law. The Scriptures containing it were represented as written with the highest degree of inspiration. It was often identified with the heavenly wisdom, and was therefore viewed as preexisting in God before the foundation of the world. It was described as an image of God's spiritual essence, or as the daughter of God. All things necessary to salvation, it was asserted, are contained in it. To supplement it is impossible; it is complete and is valid for all time, yea, for eternity. The study of it takes precedence of all other duties. Everything closely associated with it derives from the relation honor and sanctification. The Hebrew, as the language of the law, is the preferred speech, the tongue employed by angels. All the mountains contended for the honor of being the theatre of the proclamation of the law. All the world was hushed into complete silence when God spoke the sacred code. As the people of the law Israel has a character of special holiness. The outside peoples are unclean; they make no part of the kindom of God, and are not destined to eternal life. The ministry of angels is confined to Israel, while the heathen world constitutes the proper field of demons. The course of nature is sustained for the sake of the people of the law.[1] Were it not for them, God would not think it worth while to give either rain or sunshine. The study of the law is not unbecoming even to the majesty of God. Says one rabbi: "The day has twelve hours; in the first three the Holy One sits and

---

[1] Compare Fourth Ezra, vi. 55–59, vii. 11.

busies Himself with the law." Very likely some of these statements go beyond the average sentiment of Pharisaism, but they indicate the goal toward which it tended, and reflect with approximate fairness the spirit by which it was ruled.

Somewhat of a deistic character evidently pertained to this way of thinking, which recognized little else in God but the lawgiver, and made the way of approach to Him a long line of legal performances. It does not appear, however, that Pharisaism was formally deistic in its theory. It inculcated a strong view of divine providence. According to the representation of Josephus, the Pharisees believed both in the divine ordering of events and in the free will of men.[1]

The Pharisaic conception of personal salvation corresponded to the dominance which was given to the legal point of view. The ruling idea was legal performance in the sight of God, rather than transforming fellowship with God. Repentance, it was taught, secures indulgence for past sins, while performance of the works prescribed by the law creates a title to positive rewards. In this relation a vicarious function was admitted. It was conceived that in virtue of the solidarity of Israel the sufferings of a righteous man, and especially his undeserved death, might serve to expiate the sins of the people, and that in general the merits of the forefathers might help to enlarge the credit of a later generation.

It does not appear that the doctrine of a vicarious expiation of sins through suffering was applied in later

---

[1] Antiq. Bk. xviii. chap. i; Wars of the Jews, Bk. II. chap. viii, § 14.

Judaism, at least in its more characteristic teaching, to the Messiah. The references to a suffering Messiah are not of sufficient weight, in comparison with representations of an opposite nature, to stand in the way of the conclusion that later Jewish orthodoxy gave little place in its Messianic forecast to such a picture as is contained either in the fifty-third chapter of Isaiah or in the gospel story of the cross.[1] Some scholars have supposed that it was in particular a disinclination to refer to the Messiah the Old Testament texts descriptive of suffering and death that led to the introduction of a subordinate Messiah of the house of Joseph, to whom the more sombre element in prophetical anticipation could be applied.[2] The information, however, respecting the genesis in Jewish thought of the Messiah Ben Joseph is very scanty.[3]

The conception of the nature and rank of the Messiah appears to have been a somewhat wavering one in post-exilian Judaism. In some of the apocalyptic writings, notably in the second section of the Book of Enoch (chapters xxxvii–lxxi) and in the Fourth Book of Ezra (vii., xiii., xiv.), the Messiah is described in language which imports that he was regarded as a superhuman and heavenly being, in a peculiar sense the Son of God. Especially in the Book of Enoch is this high rank dis-

---

[1] Schurer, Geschichte des judischen Volkes im Zeitalter Jesu Christi, § 29; Weber, Jüdische Theologie, §§ 79, 80; Stanton in Hastings' Dictionary of the Bible, III. 354; Lagrange, Le Messianisme, pp. 236 ff.

[2] Baldensperger, Das Selbstbewusstsein Jesu, pp 143–155.

[3] A mention occurs in the Talmud, Tract Succah, chap. v, Rodkinson's translation. See also the references in Weber, § 80.

THE QUESTION OF SOURCES 13

tinctly asserted. According to its representations the name of the Messiah was named on high before the sun and the signs were created, and before the stars of heaven were made. He is to be a staff to the righteous, a light to the Gentiles and the hope of all the troubled of heart. Before him all the dwellers on the face of the earth are to bow. The sum of judgment is to be committed to him, and the secrets of wisdom will stream forth from his mouth. Thus the Book of Enoch approaches the New Testament point of view respecting the position of the Christ. And it has a further point of comparison with the New Testament in that it employs in part the same descriptive titles, such as the Elect One, the Righteous One, the Son of Man.[1]

---

[1] The measure of confidence with which this high conception of the Messiah can be regarded as a mirror of Jewish thinking will of course depend appreciably upon the evidence for the pre-Christian origin of the Similitudes, as the second section of the Book of Enoch is called. It is possible to surmise here an infusion of Christian thought, in case the origin of Christianity preceded the composition of the Similitudes. On the question of date scholars are divided. A majority consider that the Similitudes contain too little of specifically Christian matter to make it at all probable that they came as a whole from a Christian hand, even if it be supposed that they include aught from that source. The most recent editors find no insuperable difficulty in the way of the supposition that this entire portion of the Book of Enoch originated before Pompey's invasion of Jerusalem. Such is the judgment of R. H. Charles in his translation and commentary; also of Georg Beer in Kautzsch's Apokryphen und Pseudepigraphen des Alten Testaments, II. 230–232. On the basis of this chronology the recurring phrase "the kings and the mighty" is made to refer to the Asmonean princes and their Sadducean allies. Bousset prefers to find in this phrase a reference to foreign rulers, and thinks that the composition of the Similitudes occurred in the troubled era between the fall of the Asmonean line and the reign of Herod (Die Religion des Judentums im neutestamentlichen Zeitalter, p. 13).

On the other hand there are descriptions in the later Jewish writings which do not carry the rank of the Messiah above that of an exalted human potentate. The tendency within the circle of Pharisaic or orthodox Judaism may be judged to have been in the direction of the latter view. This was the current theory in the second century, if we may draw a conclusion from the words which Justin Martyr put into the mouth of the Jew Trypho, for they express the belief that the Messiah was to be simply a man sprung from men.[1] Perhaps, as Holtzmann suggests, the fact that Christianity took up and propagated the higher view of the rank of the Messiah, may have helped toward its general renunciation within the bounds of Judaism.[2]

The office of the Messiah was given very largely an eschatological relation. It appears that from the Maccabean period to the end of the first century of the Christian era Jewish theological thinking was concentrated in no small degree upon eschatology. The Book of Daniel was followed by a line of apocalyptic effusions which present in dramatic colors the events of the last days. Two of these, the apocalypse of Baruch and the Fourth Book of Ezra, written, it is supposed, not far from the year 70 of the Christian era, may be regarded as giving the outlines of the matured eschatology of later Judaism. The time of their composition makes it indeed possible that Christian thinking may have influenced at one point or another their representations; but, on the other hand, the antipathy of Jewish writers of that era to Chris-

---

[1] Dial. cum Tryph. xlix.
[2] Lehrbuch der neutestamentlichen Theologie, I. 84.

tianity stood in the way of borrowing from its contents. Moreover, the two treatises named are congenially related to other Jewish writings which deal with the subject of eschatology. Accordingly, there is no reason to doubt that they represent with substantial fidelity the trend of Jewish orthodoxy in that era. Their scheme of eschatology, as summarized by Schurer,[1] embraces the following points: (1) A final season of stress and confusion; (2) the coming of Elijah as forerunner; (3) the appearance of the Messiah; (4) a final attack of hostile powers; (5) destruction of the hostile powers; (6) renewal of Jerusalem; (7) gathering of the dispersed; (8) the kingdom of glory in Palestine; (9) renewal of the world; (10) the general resurrection of the dead; (11) the final judgment and eternal salvation and damnation. As regards the resurrection, it may be noticed that the earlier view confined it to the righteous. The Psalms of Solomon, composed probably near the time of Pompey's invasion of Jerusalem, seem to favor this view,[2] and it is ascribed to the Pharisees in the sketch of their beliefs by Josephus.[3] The same limitation appears in some sections of the Book of Enoch.[4] In certain instances the resurrection of all Israel, but with a possible exclusion of the Gentiles, was assumed.[5] Several writings, aside from those representative of the Alexandrian

---

[1] Geschichte des judischen Volkes im Zeitalter Jesu Christi, § 29, pp. 440-464.

[2] Psalms of Solomon, iii. 13, 16, xv. 1.

[3] Antiq. xviii. 1; Wars of the Jews, II. viii. 14.

[4] Book of Enoch, xci. – civ.

[5] Book of Enoch, li. 1, 2; 2 Maccabees xii. 42-44.

theology, apparently contemplate only a resurrection of the *spirits* of the dead.[1]

The foregoing exposition affords a basis for estimating the influence of Pharisaism upon New Testament theology. That it wrought as a developing force by way of repulsion is quite evident. Its overstrained legality gave occasion to a distinct and energetic exposition of the deep interior demands of true piety. It drew from Christ the most intense protest against allowing the form to usurp the place which belongs to the spirit, and served as the background against which he set forth clearly defined and imperishable images of a spiritual religion. With Paul also Pharisaism was a motive-power to intense stress upon the subjective demands of religion. Had not the apostle lived within the system and realized in the depths of his soul its incompetency to bring emancipation and true peace, he would not have been prepared to champion with such marvellous and untiring fervor the cause of evangelical freedom against the rôle of legal servitude.

As regards positive influences coming from Pharisaism, it is not easy to measure them exactly through the whole range of doctrinal topics, since there is room for the question whether given aspects of teaching are to be reckoned as outgrowths of Old Testament principles, or as showing the imprint of contemporary Jewish orthodoxy. On various points, however, there are grounds for a fairly satisfactory inference.

---

[1] Psalms of Solomon; Book of Jubilees; Assumption of Moses; 4 Maccabees. See R. H. Charles, Eschatology, Hebrew, Jewish, and Christian.

It was noticed that in the sketch by Josephus the Pharisees are represented as holding, on the one hand, a strong view of divine sovereignty over events, and on the other contending for the fact of free will in men. As to whether they had any way of reconciling these contrasted views, or made any attempt to show their congruity, the historian says nothing. Commentators have discovered a like uncancelled antinomy in the New Testament. Especially has this been observed in the writings of Paul. There are sentences in his epistles which seem to place no limit upon the divine ordering, and there are sentences which clearly enough assume the free and responsible agency of men. Was Paul in this matter exhibiting points of view which he had inherited from Pharisaism? It is quite easy to suspect that to have been the case. But two things may serve to check a confident conclusion in that direction. In the first place, the double view in question — the profound stress upon divine ordering and the acknowledgment of man's free agency — was no exclusive property of Pharisaism, but very largely characteristic of the Old Testament. In the second place, it belongs intrinsically to the mode of earnest religious oratory both to accentuate in strong terms God's overruling wisdom and might, and to address men as free and responsible. It lies outside the plane of oratory to reconcile the opposing views. To do that is the function of philosophical reflection. It seems to follow, therefore, that Paul, simply as the Old Testament student and the religious orator, could very well have been led to use the forms of expression under consideration. It is to be granted, nevertheless, that it might not have been so natural for him to use them had he been reared as a Sadducee instead of being trained in the school of the Pharisees.

The same order of remark applies to the Pauline stress upon the connection of the Adamic trespass with the prevalence of sin and death in the world. That stress is fully paralleled in Fourth Ezra and the Apocalypse of Baruch, books which indeed were of later origin than the Pauline writings, but which may be supposed to represent at least a considerable current of thought in the Pharisaism of an earlier time.[1] There is, therefore, a certain probability that Paul's Pharisaic training had something to do with his strong view of the results of Adam's sin; though, on the other hand, it is quite conceivable that he may have gained the major part of the incentive to his representations from Old Testament suggestions and his own earnest contemplation of the contrast between Adam and Christ.

As respects the person and work of the Messiah, the Pharisaic view appears far more in contrast than in affinity with the New Testament teaching. The one contemplated preeminently a national deliverer and ruler; the other pictures the redeemer of the human race. The one supposed that the Messiah's reign would be realized mainly through visible earthly instrumentalities; the other makes large account of invisible spiritual agency

---

[1] Fourth Ezra, iii. 7, 21, 22, iv. 30, vii. 118; Apocalypse of Baruch, xxiii. 4, xlviii. 42, liv. 15. Compare Ecclesiasticus, xxv. 24. In contrast with these sources, the Book of Enoch and the Book of Jubilees emphasize the corrupting agency of apostate angels. For a survey of the subject see Bousset, Die Religion des Judentums im neutestamentlichen Zeitalter, pp. 384-391.

and of the efficacy of heart association with an ideal personality. The one tended toward a simple humanitarian conception of the Messiah; the other, while giving a much purer and more beautiful ideal of the humanity of Christ than was grasped by its rival, exhibits unequivocal tokens of faith in his superhuman dignity and unique connection with the divine. The idea of vicarious atonement appears in both; but, as has been noticed, this idea in the Pharisaic system was given a very faint association with the Messiah, and reduces to the conception that in virtue of the solidarity of Israel the doing or suffering of one member may serve as a ground of indulgence toward a less deserving member. It is possible, as Pfleiderer supposes,[1] that Paul proceeded from this conception as a starting-point when he undertook to construe the work of Christ. However this may be, it is not to be overlooked that Paul's total theory is pretty broadly contrasted with the Pharisaic conception. Not only does the former give a central importance to the atoning work of the Christ which was quite unknown to the latter; it joins with the notion of an objective atonement the idea of a mystical union with Christ, and makes this no less than the other part and parcel of the divine plan of salvation. This idea, it does not need to be said, was quite beyond the Pharisaic circle of thought. On the whole, the Pauline theory of Christ's work cannot be regarded as making any very distinct revelation of the disciple of the Pharisees. Even as regards the elementary conception of a vicarious atonement, or meritorious doing and

---

[1] Das Urchristenthum, p. 171, edition of 1887.

suffering on behalf of another, suggestions enough could have been found by the apostle in the Hebrew Scriptures.

As regards eschatology, it must be granted that the later Jewish orthodoxy seems to have given considerable coloring, not to say content, to the New Testament. The reader of the New Testament cannot fail to notice that in one connection or another nearly all the points which have been mentioned as characteristic of the Pharisaic eschatology come into view. The representations of the former have of course less of a Jewish outlook than those of the latter. The two, however, picture much the same succession of unfoldments. The germs may be found in the Old Testament, but it is known that eschatology was a vital part of the dogmatic thinking of Judaism in the post-Maccabean period, and it is probable that its general framework was well intrenched in the minds of those who penned the New Testament writings. It may be added in this connection that on the subjects of angelology and demonology the New Testament reflects very largely post-exilic developments. That a difference, however, goes with the resemblance will not be overlooked by one who reflects on the warm and intense view of the divine immanence which is characteristic of the New Testament. Angelic mediation in connection with such a view naturally assumes less importance than was given it in later Judaism with its relatively distant God.

III. — ALEXANDRIANISM AND ITS CONTRIBUTIONS.

Alexandrianism, as the term is used here, denotes Judaism under the influence of Greek philosophy and animated by a pronounced ambition to show the entire harmony between itself and the best content of that philosophy. It found literary expression especially in the book entitled the Wisdom of Solomon and in the writings of Philo. The former very likely originated in the century preceding the Christian era. The latter were written within the first half of the first Christian century. Attempts have been made to discover signs of the distinctive Alexandrian style of thinking in some earlier writings, more especially in Ecclesiasticus, in the Septuagint translation of the Old Testament, and in the Third Book of the Sibylline Oracles. But the signs are too faint to afford anything more than a doubtful warrant for associating these writings with the peculiar philosophy which found in Philo its culminating expression.

In its attitude toward the law Alexandrianism was characterized by a much freer spirit than that which ruled Pharisaism. As represented by Philo it taught indeed that the prescriptions of the law ought to be literally fulfilled; but evidently it did not regard them as possessing in themselves the importance which they had for the eyes of the Pharisaic doctors. A principal reason urged by Philo for the literal fulfillment was its adaptation to prepare one to understand better the deeper meaning of the law.[1] It was mainly the ethical and philosophical truth which the pentateuchal system was regarded as shadowing forth that interested Philo and the men of his school. We find him speaking in the best vein of Jewish prophecy on the worthlessness of sacrifices apart from

---

[1] Migration of Abraham, xvi. Works, II. 64, Yonge's translation.

the appropriate inner disposition. "In the eyes of God," he says, "it is not the number of things sacrificed that is accounted valuable, but the purity of the rational spirit of the sacrificer ... The altar of God is the grateful soul of the wise man."[1]

As respects biblical interpretation, Alexandrianism cannot be regarded as having resorted to an altogether exceptional course in its espousal of allegory. In the later Jewish exegesis generally the door stood open to allegorical interpretations. The rabbis entertained the notion that the Scriptures, as the product of an infinite author, have no such limited significance as pertains to an ordinary human composition, but contain even in their individual statements manifold meanings.[2] From this standpoint there was no check upon allegorizing aside from convenience and custom. The peculiarity of Alexandrianism was, on the one hand, its extraordinary industry in drawing out the mystical or allegorical sense of Scripture, and, on the other, the degree to which it made allegorical interpretations a means of satisfying its ambition to represent Judaism as embracing much of the content of the Gentile philosophies.[3]

---

[1] On those who offer Sacrifice, iv., v. Works, III. 233-5.

[2] In a Talmudic comment on Jer. xxiii. 29 it is remarked: "As a hammer divideth fire into many sparks, so one verse of Scripture has many meanings and many explanations." (Sanhedrin, fol. 34, col. 1, cited by Hershon, Talmudic Miscellanies, p. 11.)

[3] As specimens of Philo's allegorizing we note the following: "By the green herb of the field Moses means that portion of the mind which is perceptible only by the intellect" (Works, I. 57). "He means by Abraham's country the body, and by his kindred the outward senses, and by his father's house uttered speech" (II. 44). "By his saying of Ishmael,

THE QUESTION OF SOURCES

Like other Jewish schools of the age, the Alexandrian regarded the Scriptures as an out and out communication from God, and took practically no account of the conditioning agency of the human recipients of the revelation. "The prophet," says Philo, "even when he appears to be speaking, is silent, and another being is employing his vocal organs, his mouth and tongue, for the explanation of what things he chooses."[1]

In the Alexandrian conception of God and of His relation to the world a tinge of transcendentalism and dualism may be noticed. God is represented as exalted in the mystery of His being far above man's power of insight, so as to be incapable of being defined in any positive manner. While His presence in the world of sense is not denied, statements are made which imply a feeling that the world is not worthy of immediate contact with God. If we may judge from the trend of reference both in the Book of Wisdom and in the writings of Philo,

---

'His hand shall be against every man, and every man's hand against him,' he means to describe the design and plan of life of a sophist, who professes an over-curious scepticism, and who rejoices in disputatious arguments" (II. 237). "The five cities of the land of Sodom are a figurative representation of the five outward senses which exist in us." (II. 426). "The same relation, then, that a mistress has to her handmaidens, or a wife, who is a citizen, to a concubine, that same relation has virtue, that is Sarah, to education, that is Hagar" (II. 162–7). "It is not without a particular and correct meaning that Joseph is said to have had a coat of many colors, for a political constitution is a many-colored and a multiform thing, admitting of an infinite variety of changes in its general appearance, in its affairs, in its moving causes, in the peculiar laws respecting strangers, in numberless differences respecting times and places" (II. 460).

[1] On Who is the Heir of Divine Things, liii. Works, II. 147.

God is not conceived to be altogether responsible for the sphere of material being. He is represented as creating only its form, not its substance. The initial act in the process of creation is described as the reduction to order of a formless matter.[1]

To provide for relating God to the world thus conceived to be scarcely worthy of His presence, the Alexandrian theology made much account of an intermediate agent, a kind of vicegerent of the Most High in the visible universe. This agent is described in the Book of Wisdom under the name of "Wisdom," and is represented as "all-surveying," "pervading and penetrating all things," "a breath of the power of God," "a clear effluence of the glory of the Almighty," "an effulgence from everlasting light," "an unspotted mirror of the working of God," and "an image of His goodness."[2] In the writings of Philo the favorite term for designating the agent of mediation is the Logos, a term which, as used by him, embraces the gist of the Platonic doctrine of ideas and of the Stoic doctrine of an immanent reason in the world. It is the reason of God viewed as taking a worldward direction. As such it is the image of God, the archetype of the world, the instrument for fashioning all things, the dividing and arranging power in the universe and the bond of union therein. While an intercessory function in behalf of men is not denied to this image and instrument of the Divine Being, it is in general pictured by Philo in its cosmic relations. To predicate

---

[1] Wisdom, xi. 17, Philo, The Planting of Noah, i. Works, I. 416. Compare James Drummond, Philo Judaeus, I. 188, 299–301.

[2] Book of Wisdom, vii. 22–30.

an incarnation of the Logos after the pattern of the Christian conception was entirely foreign to his point of view.[1]

In the circle of Alexandrianism the Messianic expectation seems to have been of the palest kind. Philo, in common with his co-religionists, looked forward to a time when the scattered Israelites should be gathered into their own land, and the race at large, won to righteousness, should enjoy the blessings of peace and plenty. In this sense he believed in a Messianic kingdom. But if by a Messianic hope one means the centering of expectation upon the appearance of a glorious and ideal personage bearing a special divine commission, and destined to work with marvellous efficiency as the visible leader and king of God's people, then it must be said that the writings of Philo do not show any proper trace of a Messianic hope. As Drummond remarks, "Philo preferred moving in the region of abstract ideas, where there is more elevation of thought than warmth of personal affection."[2] The cosmic Logos rather than the personal Messiah was before his mind. It cannot be seen that he in anywise connected the former with the common Jewish conception of the latter.

Among the features of the Alexandrian anthropology which show the influence of Hellenic thinking the doctrine of the preexistence of souls and a disparaging estimate of the body as a clog or fetter to the spirit may be mentioned. The former is intimated in the Book of Wisdom in the representation of the writer (who assumes

---

[1] Compare Sheldon, History of Christian Doctrine, I. 67–70.
[2] Philo Judaeus, II. 322.

the rôle of Solomon) that, being a good soul, he had the privilege of coming into an undefiled body.[1] Philo's teaching is quite as distinctly on the side of preexistence. "All the wise men," he says, "mentioned in the books of Moses are represented as sojourners, for their souls are sent down upon earth as to a colony."[2] This view appears not to have been confined to the Alexandrian school. Notwithstanding the utter lack of warrant for the notion of preexistence of souls in the Old Testament, later Jewish thought as embodied in the Talmud leaned decidedly to that notion.[3] With Philo the idea of emanation seems to have been conjoined with that of preexistence. "Every man," he says, "in regard to his intellect is connected with divine reason, being an impression of, or a fragment or a ray of that blessed nature."[4] We find also with Philo the distinction between the generic man and the concrete man. The former was antecedent to the latter, perfectly immaterial, neither male nor female, the heavenly archetypal man.[5] As regards the other feature of the Alexandrian anthropology, the slighting estimate of the body, it was sufficiently pronounced to serve naturally as a basis for Gnostic asceticism. The sensuous nature may not indeed have been formally denounced as intrinsically evil.[6] Still the body was characterized as an undesirable incumbrance,

---

[1] Book of Wisdom, viii. 19, 20.
[2] Confusion of Languages, xvii Works, II. 17
[3] Weber, Judische Theologie, § 46.
[4] Creation of the World, li. Works, I. 43, 264.
[5] Creation of the World, xlvi, Allegories of the Sacred Laws, I. xii. Works, I, 39, 60.
[6] See Drummond, II. 297–301.

a hindrance to the true life of the soul. "It is not possible," says Philo, "for one who dwells in the body and belongs to the race of mortals to be united to God, but he alone can be so whom God delivers from that prison house of the body."[1]

Both the lack of a vivid Messianic hope on the part of the Alexandrian school and its disparaging estimate of the body naturally affected its eschatology. The idea of a great crisis, to be inaugurated and led on to its consummation by the Messianic king and judge, passed out of view. The thought of a bodily resurrection, as also that of a great physical catastrophe, was ignored or discountenanced. In place of the concrete representations which ruled the central current of Jewish belief and expectation, the Alexandrian school presents us with the general notion of an immortal life of disembodied souls.

In considering the influence of the Alexandrian theology upon the New Testament writings it behooves us to remember that parallelisms almost always can be found in writings which belong to the same general class, ethical, speculative, or mystical, and that accordingly they do not prove the fact of borrowing except on the score of being very specific in character or extraordinary in measure. On account of the wide range of Philo's writings it might be expected that some points of resemblance could be pointed out between them and any Christian book belonging approximately to the same age. With or without a basis in actual historical connections, resembling items were bound to appear. In fact they

---

[1] Allegories of the Sacred Laws, III. xv. Works, I. 118. Compare I. 80, 92, 125, II. 208, 209.

have been discovered in writings as remote in spirit from the speculative and mystical system of Philo as are the Synoptical Gospels and the Epistle of James.[1]

The New Testament books in connection with which the question of Alexandrian influence is most appropriately raised are undoubtedly the Epistles of Paul, the Epistle to the Hebrews, and the Johannine books. As respects the first, it is generally conceded that their historic background was formed more largely by Pharisaic Judaism than by Alexandrianism. It is also admitted, if not so generally, still by eminent critics, that there is no decisive evidence that Paul had access to the chief despository of Alexandrianism in the writings of his older contemporary, Philo. From this point of view it is natural to conjecture that, if the apostle actually came into contact with Alexandrian thinking, so far as this was not consummated through personal communication with Apollos and men of his stamp, it was brought about largely through the Book of Wisdom. Pfleiderer decides very confidently both for the fact of such contact and for its effectuation in particular through this writing. He considers it to be of great historic significance that the elements at once of Pharisaic Judaism and Hellenic thinking should have had place in Paul's mind, this combination having afforded a natural means of transition to a system at once transcending the particularism of Judaism and offering a needful complement or corrective to Hellenism. In his view the influence of the Book of Wisdom may be discerned in a number of Pauline particulars. It may be seen in the description of the natural

---

[1] Siegfried, Philo von Alexandria, pp. 310–317.

man as incompetent to receive divine verities[1]; in the judgment passed upon the Gentile world, partly indulgent and partly severe;[2] in the thought of the continued existence of the soul in a heavenly dwelling, which thought in 2 Cor. v. 1. ff. takes the place of a bodily resurrection;[3] and in sentences bearing on the subject of predestination.[4] As to the merit of this contention, we see nothing in the way of the probability that Paul was acquainted with the Book of Wisdom. At the same time, when we measure the active and fertile mind of Paul against the mind of the unknown Alexandrian, and note that the passages from the two which are brought into comparison show only a vague and general resemblance to each other, we are far from sharing the impression of Pfleiderer as to the distinct obligations of Paul to the Book of Wisdom. It may have been a factor in Paul's mental furnishing, but we do not find sufficient evidence for concluding that it was a prominent factor.

In the exegesis of the Apostle to the Gentiles an occasional sentence may undoubtedly be found which smacks of post-exilian methods of interpretation. It is not clear, however, that herein Paul was following the Alexandrian school rather than the Pharisaic or rabbinic. His singular rendering of the promise to Abraham's seed (Gal. iii. 16) was not without parallel in the custom of the latter school to extract special meanings from single words.

---

[1] Wisd ix. 13-17, 1 Cor. ii. 6-16.
[2] Wisd. xiii. 1-9, xiv, 21-28, Rom. i. 18 ff , 1 Cor. xii. 2, Gal. iv. 8 ff.
[3] Wisd. ix. 15.
[4] Wisd. xv. 7, xii. 10-12. See Otto Pfleiderer, Das Urchristenthum, pp. 161, 162, 305, edit. of 1887.

There was also, as has been noticed, a warrant in Pharisaic custom for allegorizing. That Paul was not borrowing specifically from Alexandrianism in the instances of allegorical interpretation to which he resorted may be regarded as intimated by the fact that the mystical sense which he attached to Old Testament characters and incidents is quite different from that assigned to them by Philo. For example, while Paul (Gal. iv. 22–31) construes Hagar and Sarah as emblematic respectively of the state of legal bondage and of evangelical freedom, Philo makes them typical respectively of education and of virtue.[1]

It has been supposed by some that in the Pauline anthropology the influence of Alexandrian teaching is discernible. Especially has this alleged influence been discovered in the strong antithesis between flesh and spirit which is drawn by the apostle. His language, it is claimed, is in the line of the Hellenic dualism which was appropriated by Philo. But it is to be noticed that Paul, unlike Philo and the Greeks, is on record as a believer in the resurrection, that is, in the perpetuity of embodied existence, and that in one connection or another he spoke of the body, or more specifically of the flesh itself, as a subject of possible sanctification. These facts show at least that he was not clearly and consistently committed to the platform of Hellenic or Alexandrian dualism, and afford ground for the suspicion that his disparaging references to the flesh are not to be taken in the proper sense of that dualism. This order of references, it must

---

[1] On Seeking Instruction, ii., iii. Works, II. 158–160.

be granted, is not in the vein of the Hebrew Scriptures. But then Paul may have found the principal incentive to them in experience and observation rather than in the maxims of Hellenic philosophy on the incompatibility of the body with the higher life of man. It is certain to our mind that the latter source did not control his thinking; that to some extent it may have tinged his thought, and especially his speech, can be admitted.

On the subject of christology it is particularly the contents of the epistles to the Colossians and the Ephesians that have given rise to the surmise that Paul was influenced by the Alexandrian theology. It is true that in these epistles Christ, as the Son of God, is depicted as holding a general cosmic relation, and that He is styled the image of the invisible God and the first-born of the creation — representations which have their parallel in Philo's characterization of the Logos. But it is to be noticed, on the other hand, that these christological items had been touched upon in the earlier epistles of Paul,[1] and that he was only fulfilling the existing occasion to combat an incipient Gnosticism if he gave them in the later instance a special emphasis. These facts legitimate the conclusion that he was not diverted from his earlier standpoint in christology by Alexandrian influence. There remains, of course, the possibility of contending that his earlier standpoint was itself indebted to this influence. It must, however, be acknowledged that the further back a point of view can be traced in the mental vision of the converted Pharisee, the less likelihood is there that it was

---

[1] 1 Cor. viii. 6; 2 Cor. iv. 4; Rom. viii. 29.

furnished in whole or in part by a contemporary, or even by a predecessor, belonging to the Alexandrian school. Having said this much against giving too large a credit for Paul's christology to the Alexandrian speculation, we admit the possibility that in respect of form something may have come to the apostle from this storehouse.

Whatever may be the verdict respecting the indebtedness of the Pauline epistles, it cannot reasonably be disputed that the Epistle to the Hebrews exhibits distinct obligations to Alexandrianism. The conclusion is unavoidable that the mind of the writer had been well furnished with its characteristic thoughts and forms of expression before he undertook the task of Christian authorship. In the opening passage of the epistle there are phrases which remind of the description of wisdom in the Book of Wisdom and of the exposition of the Logos in the writings of Philo. The way in which the epistle introduces citations from the Scriptures, as being the words of God rather than the language of such and such a sacred writer, corresponds to the custom of Philo. The typology with which the spirited composition is so largely occupied is quite in the Alexandrian vein, the author conceiving of the Old Testament institutions not merely as shadows or types of realities brought to view in a later and more perfect dispensation, but as copies of patterns preexisting in heaven. Several individual items in the epistle have very distinct parallels in the Alexandrian literature. Thus the representation that God made oath to Abraham by Himself because he could not swear by a greater is found in Philo,[1] as is also the character-

---

[1] Allegories of the Sacred Laws, III. lxxii. Works, I. 161.

ization of Melchizedek as king of peace and righteousness and unconnected with father or mother.[1] The phrase "a great high-priest" is found in the epistle and in Philo alike. Both exceed in like manner the distinct warrant of the Old Testament in representing the high-priest as *daily* offering sacrifice. Both speak of Moses as "faithful in all his house."[2] In short the evidences of the influence of the Alexandrian writings upon the Epistle to the Hebrews are unmistakable.

On the other hand, it is not to be overlooked that there are wide contrasts between the two. The author of the epistle keeps closer in general than did Philo to a biblical basis, and avoids the fanciful extreme in allegorizing to which a speculative temper enticed his predecessor. The representation of the former respecting the incarnation of the preexisting Son, His partaking of flesh and blood and His thorough identification with man in lot and experience, is entirely alien to Philo's conception of the Logos. Scarcely less remote from that conception is the stanch view taught in the epistle respecting the atoning sacrifice of the Mediator. In truth, it can be said that the Alexandrianism of the Epistle to the Hebrews pertains more largely to the domain of color and form than to that of dogmatic substance.

As respects the Johannine writings — that is, the fourth Gospel and the epistles of John — criticism commonly affirms a certain affiliation with the Alexandrian

---

[1] Allegories of the Sacred Laws, III. xxv., xxvi. Works, I. 128, 129.
[2] See other items as cited by Siegfried, Philo von Alexandria, pp. 321–330; also by Ménégoz, La Théologie de l'Épître aux Hébreux, pp. 187–217.

literature. In the prologue to the Gospel the author gives evidence of acquaintance, direct or indirect, with the Logos doctrine of Philo. The conclusiveness of the argument for a direct acquaintance can be called in question; still it is not improbable that the writer, whoever he may have been, taking up his pen forty or fifty years after the works of Philo had been completed, in a time when a bent to speculative and constructive thought had begun to manifest itself in the circle of Christianity, should have looked into the writings of the celebrated Alexandrian. Another point of comparison with the Alexandrian literature is discoverable in the predilection shown in the Johannine books for a typical sense in the forms and events of sacred history. A still further point of comparison may be noted in the antithesis which is drawn between the world, this present sphere of time and sense, and the realm of invisible and eternal realities. In some instances the Johannine characterization of the world is verbally as disparaging as that which is given forth in the dualistic representations of Philo.[1]

Too much account, however, is not to be taken of any one of these resembling features. The Johannine Logos, while conceived in His preexistence and general world-relation somewhat after the fashion of Philo, is assigned to relations and experiences altogether foreign to the Philonian view. The Johannine typology, while exhibiting a leaning to mysticism akin to that of Philo, does not

---

[1] Philo says, "It is as impossible that the love of the world can coexist with the love of God, as for light and darkness to coexist at the same time with one another" (Fragment, Works, IV. 244). John says, "If any man love the world the love of the Father is not in him" (1 John ii. 15)

cover the same range as the Alexandrian. The latter makes much account of the patterns or archetypes of things preexisting in a divine or celestial sphere. The former, omitting this distinctive feature, contemplates the events of sacred history and the facts and relations of nature as means of shadowing forth the spiritual truths of the new dispensation. Finally, the apparent dualism between the two worlds seems, when the total references of the Johannine writings are taken into account, to differ from the Philonian, as depicting not so much an essential opposition as a contrast of actual ethical condition.[1]

We conclude, therefore, that while the Johannine type reflects in a measure the Alexandrian, there is no good reason to suppose such a fusion of the substance of the latter into the former as some writers have assumed. The degree of dependence shown by the fourth Gospel

---

[1] For further points of a possible comparison see Siegfried, Philo von Alexandria, pp. 317–321, also Grill, Untersuchungen uber die Entstehung des vierten Evangeliums, pp. 106–138. The list of resemblances between the Johannine and the Philonian sentences, as presented by these writers, is at first sight quite impressive; but, as Drummond remarks, a scrutiny of the parallels brings to view marked differences in style and phraseology, as well as striking contrasts in thought. In respect of vocabulary John seems to have been influenced by Philo in a very scanty measure. "Philo is fond of compounds with δυς-, having twenty-eight words of this kind; the fourth Gospel has none. Philo has forty compounds with εὐ-; the Gospel has only two common words. Philo has seventy-three compounds with ἐκ-, not one of which is in the Gospel, though the latter has fourteen such compounds, nearly all very common words. Philo has sixty-seven compounds with ἐπι- which are not in the Gospel, the Gospel having eleven ordinary words." (James Drummond, article "Philo," in Hastings' Dict. of the Bible, v. 207, 208.) So far then as the evidence of vocabulary goes, there is reason to conclude against the supposition of any protracted and absorbing study of Philo's writings by the author of the fourth Gospel.

NEW TESTAMENT THEOLOGY

upon the school of Alexandria is less than that revealed by the Epistle to the Hebrews.

IV. — Questions as to the Indebtedness of Certain Special Portions of the New Testament to Post-Canonical Judaism.

The foremost questions respecting the influence of post-canonical developments upon the New Testament literature have now been considered. But some points relating to individual books and passages deserve a few additional words. The extent to which Pharisaism supplied, or anticipated, the framework of the ordinary New Testament eschatology involves evidently a measure of indebtedness on the part of the Apocalypse to post-canonical Judaism. Beyond this general indebtedness it is supposed by some critics that this book was influenced by specific specimens of apocalyptic literature which came forth in later Judaism.

In the Epistle of James a close mental association with the "wisdom literature" has been detected. It has been claimed also that the epistle shows a closer affiliation with the Hellenistic literature of this order than with the Hebrew. Some have thought that the language and ideas of James bear evident traces of the maxims of Ecclesiasticus. A comparison, however, of the two writings does not reveal any such detailed resemblance as to make it appropriate to emphasize very strongly the dependence of the epistle.[1]

---

[1] In particular compare James i. 2 with Ecclesiasticus ii. 1–6; i. 27 with iv. 10; i. 19, ii. 14–26 with iv. 29; iii. 2 with v. 13; i. 12–15 with xv. 11–20; ii. 13 with xxviii. 1, 2; iii. 5–8 with xxviii. 13–26; v. 2, 3 with xxix. 10.

In proportion to its length, the Epistle of Jude is especially distinguished by borrowing post-canonical matter. Not only does it cite directly from the so-called Book of Enoch, but it also introduces a legendary account of a contest between the archangel Michael and the devil over the body of Moses. In 2 Tim. iii. 8 we have similarly, in the names given to the Egyptian sorcerers, an item which has no ground in the Hebrew Scriptures. It has the appearance of being a traditionary addition to history. The peculiar reference in 1 Cor. x. 4 to a rock that followed the Israelites in the wilderness has its counterpart in the rabbinic notion of a literal rock that mercifully kept along with the host in the wilderness and refreshed it with the stream that gushed from its side. It is not impossible that Paul had this notion in mind when he referred to the rock as Christ. At any rate it is difficult to surmise what should have prompted him to introduce the figure of a moving rock, were not that figure already at hand in the traditional representation. Little account, however, is to be made of this item, since Paul gives no sanction to the tradition, and seems to bring it in only by way of literary device to emphasize the function of Christ in ancient Israel. Once more, reference may be made to 1 Cor. xi. 10 where Paul instances a consideration of the angels as a reason for the veiling of women. The supposition of some commentators is that the apostle was thinking of Gen. vi. 2, and considered the incident there recorded as implying that it is a matter of prudence for women to cover up their beauty from the gaze of angels. On the side of this supposition is the indubitable fact that in a widely current interpretation Gen. vi. 2 was understood to teach that the daughters of men became a source of temptation to the angels.[1] It should not be overlooked, however, that many exegetes have preferred to find a different meaning in the apostle's reference. No more should it be overlooked that the natural sense of Gen. vi. 2 is that which Jewish interpretation near the beginning of the Christian era currently attached thereto, and that accordingly the appropriation of that interpretation would not make the verse in Corinthians an instance of a postcanonical opinion as opposed to a canonical.

The discussion shows, as the very reason of the case would teach one to anticipate, that Christianity was not isolated from the theological thinking of contemporary Judaism. Both Pharisaism and Alexandrianism supplied moulds in which the thought of one or another New Testament writer was cast, not to say influenced the thinking of one or another writer. It does not follow, however, that Christianity did not have in general a distinctly closer affinity with the higher levels of Old Testament thought than with the cardinal phases of the later Judaism. Neither does it follow that Christianity was not profoundly original. The contrary must be asserted in both relations. In the summit of Jewish prophecy, as recorded in the canonical Scriptures, Christianity had its most congenial antecedent. In spirit and in subject-matter the New Testament message represented an immense advance beyond the plane of postcanonical Judaism, though the latter, by the inevitable working of the law of historical connections, has left its traces.

---

[1] Book of Enoch, vi, vii., x., xii., xv., lxix.; Book of Jubilees, iv., v., vii., x.; Apocalypse of Baruch, lvi.

CHAPTER II

THE SYNOPTICAL GOSPELS AND THEIR TEACHINGS

I. — THE CHARACTERISTICS OF THESE GOSPELS AND THE MORE PROBABLE THEORY AS TO THEIR INTERRELATIONS.

AN exposition of New Testament Theology properly begins with the Synoptical Gospels. They embody the most primitive type of Christian teaching. As compared with the fourth Gospel their antecedent position will not be disputed. They were earlier in point of actual composition, and in subject-matter they show a more primitive cast. The fourth Gospel combines a large measure of theological reflection with the life-story of Christ. In the Synoptical Gospels the element of theological reflection may not be wanting, but it is certainly less conspicuous. Their treatment of the gospel history is more objective in tone. At least, their general agreement in form and content, as opposed to the singular cast of the fourth Gospel, argues for the relatively objective character of their representations. In the absence of distinct evidence to the contrary, the three concurring witnesses must be regarded as repeating the dominant tradition of their time respecting the sayings and doings of the Master. If we ask for the verdict of criticism on this point, it is given with entire unanimity for the conclusion that the fourth Gospel is relatively of a subjective cast, and approaches less closely to a verbal reproduction of Christ's discourses than do the Synoptical Gospels.

If the comparison be made with the Pauline epistles, it must be granted that in one point the antecedent position of the Synoptical Gospels is subject to denial. It is not established that any one of them was extant in its present form when those epistles were given to the Church. But the mere temporal priority of the epistles does not of course necessarily bespeak for them a logical priority. Christ lived and taught before Paul preached and wrote. Unless then the Synoptical Gospels were dominated by Paul's line of teaching rather than by the impression coming from the life and words of Christ, they represent the prior doctrinal type. Now we have no hesitation in saying that it is quite certain that in the composition of the Synoptical Gospels the Christ influence was decidedly preponderant over the Pauline influence. The latter may have wrought to some extent. Certainly it would be rash to affirm that neither Mark nor Luke derived anything in the way of thought or terminology from their companionship with Paul. On the other hand, several considerations advise against magnifying the apostle's influence on the composition of the Gospels. In the first place it is to be noted that general affinities with Pauline teaching are no sufficient proof of borrowing specifically from Paul. No one has ever proved that Christ did not anticipate in important respects the essentials of Pauline doctrine, so that a correct report of His sayings could not be given without including more or less of the distinctive features of that doctrine. In the second place it is to be observed that it is about as easy to detect Pauline substance in one Synoptical Gospel as in another. It is indeed theoretically conceivable that all the evangelists may have derived a strong doctrinal bias from the apostolic theologian. But will any one count it probable that Pauline influence should have overmastered the primitive evangelical tradition in the mind of every expositor of the same and caused in every instance an interpolation of Pauline dogmatics at the expense of the original type? It is decidedly improbable, and the fact that Paulinism of the pronounced type of Galatians and Romans appears to have been already in the sub-apostolic age well-nigh out of the field of vision is right in line with this improbability. In the third place, it must be contended that the unsophisticated reader does not naturally discover a specifically Pauline coloring in the Synoptical Gospels. He fails to find there a single sentence that recalls the technical Pauline exposition of the theme of justification and reconciliation, or the peculiar Pauline manner of putting the antithesis between law method and gospel method. On the other hand, he is forced to observe how the distinctive lines of synoptical representation respecting the "Kingdom" and the "Son of Man" are wanting in the Pauline epistles. Indeed, he cannot escape the conviction that the notes of independence in the Gospels greatly exceed those of dependence.[1]

---

[1] As to any alleged influence of Pauline thinking on the historical substance of the Synoptical Gospels, Somerville well remarks: "That the value of the record as a source of historic truth has been impaired to any extent by theological bias proceeding from the school of Paul, is

Of the three Gospels, it is generally confessed, the first has most of a Judaic impress. In various relations the Jewish background in the writer's mind is made to appear. It is seen especially in his forwardness to exhibit the unity of the two dispensations by specifying how the whole line of events in the one is prophetically intimated in the other.[1] It is seen in the ease with which he slides into the use of the Jewish order of theocratic terminology, as when, for example, he speaks of Jerusalem as the holy city, or styles it the city of the Great King.[2] It is seen, furthermore, some have contended, in the stress which, in a given connection, is laid upon the fulfillment of the law up to its least item,[3] and in the distinct enunciation of the principle that every man is to fare at the hands of the Judge according to his deeds.[4] But it is not to be overlooked that Matthew's Gospel has an offsetting aspect. If, on the one hand, it shows Jewish coloring to a special degree, on the other hand it does not fall below any one of the Synoptical Gospels in the measure in which it transcends Jewish provincialism and particularism. It presents many glimpses of a spiritual and world-wide

---

what scarcely any one will admit who feels the power of life depicted in the Gospels. The harmony of the character of Christ as there delineated, the intermingling of the divine and the human in such a way that 'the lowly and human never degrade Him in our eyes, nor His power and greatness remove Him out of our sympathies and understanding,' is inconsistent with the supposition. That such a picture was or could have been the growth of unconscious theologising is far more incredible than that it is what it professes to be, the record of a sublime reality." (St. Paul's Conception of Christ, pp. 225, 226.)

[1] Matt. i. 22, 23. ii. 15, 17, 18, 23, iv. 15, 16, viii. 17, xii. 17–21, xiii. 14, 15, xxi. 4, 5, xxvii. 9, 10.

[2] Matt. iv. 5, v. 35.   [3] v. 17–19.   [4] xvi. 27.

religion. It pictures the Gentile world in the person of the magi as first recognizing and worshiping the Christ.[1] It minifies the exclusive advantages of race connection by recording the declaration that God is able from the stones to raise up children unto Abraham.[2] It pictures Christ as setting forth a higher rule than that of the olden time,[3] and as claiming to be lord over such a sacred institution as the Sabbath.[4] It bespeaks tolerance and consideration for new elements in religion by protesting against the folly of putting new wine into old wine-skins.[5] It represents the little one in the new kingdom as greater than the most stalwart representative of the old.[6] In express terms it declares that many shall come from the east and the west to occupy a place in the kingdom which Israelites will be found unworthy to occupy,[7] and that as a people they shall be dispossessed of the Lord's vineyard and see it let out to other husbandmen.[8] It records a formal injunction for the preaching of the gospel not simply within Jewish boundaries, but to all nations.[9] So far is it from resting in a mere legal plan of gaining divine benefits that it invites to the confidence that the best gifts of God may be obtained by simply asking in the spirit of childlike faith and sincerity.[10] In short, it is quite plain that, whatever inheritance came over from Judaism into Matthew's Gospel, it did not prevent the distinctive spirituality and universalism of Christianity from gaining emphatic expression therein. It is possible, however, that the intimacy of the writer's mental associ-

---

[1] ii. 1, 2, 11.
[2] iii. 9.
[3] v. 21–49.
[4] xii. 8.
[5] ix. 17.
[6] xi. 11.
[7] viii. 11, 12.
[8] xxi. 33–45.
[9] xxviii. 19.
[10] vii. 7–11.

ation with Judaism may in part account for the fact that this Gospel more than any other of the three contemplates Christianity as an institution, in other words, gives more place to the churchly element. In virtue of this characteristic the first Gospel supplied a congenial basis for the early Catholic tendency — the tendency to the unification and organization of Christian society.

In Mark's Gospel a special dogmatic interest is not prominent. At least, such interest is not likely to be manifest to the reader who has not decided beforehand as to what type of christology is historically credible. The writing of the second evangelist is essentially a descriptive Gospel. Its aim is a vivid reproduction of the life of Christ, a picture of the Master in His deeds. With the single exception of the prophetic exposition of the "parousia" it introduces no lengthy discourses. In the exercise of its pictorial art it passes rapidly from scene to scene, giving however such events as it attempts to delineate with about as much detail as does either of the companion Gospels.

As compared with Matthew's Gospel that of Luke shows less of Judaic coloring. The writer seems either to have had a less vital reminiscence of Judaism, or else to have kept it purposely in abeyance as not being likely to edify the Gentile readers whom he more particularly contemplated. It cannot be said that he pushes Christian universalism beyond the point of view of Matthew; for the latter, as has been noticed, passes well-nigh to the limit; but his universalism is more largely disengaged from adjuncts which remind of Jewish antecedents.[1]

---

[1] For examples of universalism in Luke see ii. 30–32, iii. 8, xiii. 29, xxiv. 47.

That Luke, as a disciple of the free spirited apostle to the Gentiles, naturally gave this cast to his composition need not be denied. At the same time, there is little occasion to find in his Christian universalism a specific token of his Paulinism. When Luke wrote, Christian universalism was no party shibboleth. With inconsiderable exception it was the thoroughly accepted maxim of the community of believers. As a special trait of Luke we may notice his predilection for the gracious side of Christ's personality and teaching. He abridges the anti-Pharisaic polemic, and adds to the matter furnished by his fellow evangelists not a little that is illustrative of divine tenderness and compassion.

As to order of composition, criticism may be said to have established a probability in favor of the priority of Mark's Gospel among the extant records of the life of Christ. In the first place, so far as simplicity is a token of primitiveness, this Gospel has an unequivocal claim to be placed first in the list. In the second place, it is very difficult to suppose that certain narratives contained in the other Gospels would have been omitted by Mark had they been before him in written form at the time that he drew up his history. Doubtless a problem remains in respect of omitted matters, whatever order of composition may be assumed; but this problem is more easily dealt with on the supposition of the priority of Mark than on the opposing hypothesis. In the third place, the Gospels of Matthew and Luke bear distinct evidences of a composite character, such as are not observable in Mark. Luke's Gospel begins with an acknowledgment of acquaintance with documentary sources. In line with this acknowledgment there is a token of contact with a plurality of documents in the occurrence of a considerable number of doublets, that is, repetitions of the same or closely similar sentences. Among the sources which contributed to Luke, a prominent place evidently belonged to Mark. Thence were taken almost entirely the contents of three extensive passages, namely iii. 1–vi. 19, viii. 4–ix. 50, xviii. 15–xxiv. 10, comprising in all about eleven chapters. This matter, too, is given very largely in Mark's order. Quite as distinctly as Luke's Gospel that of Matthew gives evidence of a composite character. An indication of a plurality of sources is found in the number of doublets which the latter incorporates, this number being quite as great as that contained in Luke.[1] A further indication of the same fact is discovered by some critics in the union which, as was noticed above, this Gospel exhibits between a pronounced affiliation with Judaism and an equally pronounced leaning to Christian universalism. The contrasted features are regarded as due to the differing standpoints of the contributors. It is claimed also that a token of the composite character of Matthew appears in the fact that some citations from the Old Testament give evidence of reference to the Septuagint version, while others show the influence of the Hebrew. To some of these considerations, especially the second, we are not able to attach any great weight; but when taken together, and sup-

---

[1] Compare Matt. x. 21 with Matt. x 35; xii. 31 with xii. 32; xiii. 12 with xxv. 29; xvi. 4 with xii. 39; xvi. 24 with x. 38; xvi. 25 with x. 39; xviii. 8 f. with x. 29 f.; xix. 9 with v. 32; xxi. 21 with xvii. 20; xxi. 22 with vii. 8; xxiv. 23 with xxiv. 26

plemented by the fact of the superior simplicity and homogeneity of Mark's Gospel, they certainly favor the conclusion that Matthew's Gospel is to be esteemed a composite production, and as such having had in Mark a source instead of serving as a source to Mark. That one of the two made contribution to the other is indicated by approaches to identity in matter and phrase.

While the Gospels of Luke and Matthew incorporate the larger part of the narratives of Mark, they appear to have originated in independence of one another. Several facts point to this conclusion. The number of narratives which they have in common over and above those in Mark is small compared with the narratives that are special to each. Though they agree in going back of the story of the second evangelist to the birth and infancy of Jesus, they are far from exhibiting an identical content in these introductory portions. It is to be noticed also that they differ in respect of the order in which they reproduce the matter which they have in common with Mark. Moreover, they give in textual or verbal respects different renderings of this matter, such as are well explained on the supposition that each, independently of the other, worked over the text of Mark. Specially noticeable variations from Mark's dialect do not appear to have passed over from one to the other.

In addition to finding a common source in Mark's narratives, it is believed that Matthew and Luke drew in common from a collection of sayings, or discourses. The two evangelists appear to have incorporated an identical body of the sayings of Christ, giving these in some instances with a close approach to verbal identity, and in others diverging quite appreciably in respect of form. In individual instances a fair explanation of these facts of correspondence might be found in the supposition that one of the Gospels supplied the original text, and that the other reproduced this with more or less freedom. But a supposition of this kind collides with the evidence along various lines for the mutual independence of the two Gospels. The only satisfactory conclusion, therefore, seems to be that the resembling discourses were taken from a source no longer extant, from a collection of the sayings of Christ to which the two evangelists independently had access. The first evangelist is estimated to have derived one-sixth of his matter from this source, and the third nearly as large a proportion.

A reference to this collection — which is suggested, if not established as an historical reality, by a comparative study of the Gospels — may possibly be contained in this sentence of Papias : " Matthew composed the 'Logia' (τὰ λόγια) in the Hebrew tongue, and every one translated it as he was able."[1] Appeal may be made to the Septuagint, to the New Testament, and to early patristic usage in favor of understanding by the " Logia " sayings or discourses. A certain support is thus given to the inference that Papias could not have referred to the complete Gospel of Matthew, with its narrative portions, but rather to a collection of discourses, the composition of which was antecedent to the Gospel of Matthew as known to us. We are warned, however, not to make too much of the significance appropriate to the term " Logia," since we find that Papias himself in referring to Mark's

---

[1] Eusebius, Hist. Eccl. iii. 39.

Gospel seems to have included the record both of the words and deeds of Christ under the phrase οἱ κυριακοὶ λόγοι.¹ The ground is consequently wanting for an adequate assurance that in referring to Matthew's Logia he did not intend to designate the complete Gospel as known to history.² In that event it must be said that he was mistaken in supposing it to have been written primarily in Hebrew. Criticism does not grant that our Matthew as a whole could have been a translation from Hebrew into Greek. We are thus left without any indisputable historic testimony for connecting the Logia, as a collection of discourses, with the Apostle Matthew. The actual existence, however, of the supposed collection of sayings is not made improbable by the uncertainty of the reference of Papias. The common content of Matthew and Luke is a token of a source, other than Mark, to which both Gospels were indebted; while the lack in them of a common content, aside from that supplied by Mark, in their narratives of Christ's passion and resurrection, is a sign that the source in question was adapted to furnish sayings rather than narratives of events.

In using Mark's Gospel the author of the first Gospel proceeded in some instances more conservatively than did the third evangelist. The difference in this respect, however, is not wide. Both used the earlier narrative of Christ's life with a freedom which implies that, while they attached to it a high value, they did not regard it as a strictly authoritative rendering of the Christian tra-

---

[1] Eusebius, iii. 39.
[2] Compare Jülicher, Einleitung, p 239; Lightfoot, Essays on the Work entitled Supernatural Religion, pp. 175, 176.

dition. Matthew's reproduction of the "Logia" very likely comes nearer to the original text than does Luke's; but the latter offers a compensation in the more probable association with historical situations which he gives to the "Logia." It is commonly admitted that Matthew's Gospel exhibits considerable freedom in massing the discourses of Christ.

It is quite possible that the composition of the "Logia" preceded that of Mark's Gospel. Some scholars suppose that there is sufficient ground for concluding that the second evangelist made use of that source. But, apart from the eschatological discourse in chapter xiii, there is little evidence in Mark of the use of any source that assumed to report the words of Jesus. The borrowing from the "Logia" remains therefore a problematical point. Still more open to question is the theory of an original Mark (Ur-Marcus) back of the canonical.[1] According to an early tradition, Mark depended largely in his writing upon Peter's testimony[2]. While positive proof is wanting, the tradition is entirely credible. If, then, we suppose the "Logia," as is eminently probable, to have been based on apostolic reminiscence and testimony, we must recognize an apostolic basis as underlying the greater part of the whole group of the Synoptical Gospels; for, while some other sources made contribution to the first and third Gospels, these two were derived in large part from Mark and the "Logia."[3]

---

[1] Julicher, Einleitung, pp. 256, 257; Moffatt, The Historical New Testament, p. 264. [2] Eusebius, iii. 39.

[3] For convenient summaries of the evidence bearing on the interrelation of the Synoptical Gospels see Paul Wernle, Die Synoptische Frage; John C. Hawkins, Horae Synopticae; Harnack, The Sayings of Jesus; Stanton, The Gospels as Historical Documents, Part II.

Means for determining the precise date of any one of the Gospels are wanting. Harnack concludes that Mark was written between 65 and 85 A.D., probably between 65 and 70; that Matthew was later than Mark, though probably written between 70 and 75; and that the origin of Luke is to be placed between 78 and 93.[1]

While the Synoptical Gospels cannot properly claim the character of contemporary records, it may still be urged that they were written at an advantageous date. The character of Jesus and the significance of His work and message could be viewed at a little distance from the historical theatre in a truer perspective than would have been attainable from a contiguous standpoint. As has been said, "The Gospels in reality do more for us, written between 65 and 105, than they would have done if composed before 35. . . . It needed the four decades between 30 and 70 to render the period before 30 luminous."[2] The actual interval was long enough to give to reflection and experience a chance to bring about something like a fair understanding of the evangelical history. At the same time the interval was not so long as to effect a forfeiture of the benefit of the vital reminiscence of those who had been the companions of the Master during the period of His public ministry. The impress of that reminiscence is stamped upon these writings. In the quality and trend of their teaching they so clearly attest a unique individuality as to enforce the conviction that they were generated by a historical reality, and on the whole kept

---

[1] Die Chronologie der altchristlichen Litteratur, I. 653-655. Julicher prefers somewhat later dates.

[2] Moffatt, The Historical New Testament, pp. 14-16.

close to that reality. The peculiarity of their language, too, is quite in accord with this conviction. "The Greek language lies upon these writings like a diaphanous veil, and it requires hardly any effort to retranslate their contents into the Hebrew or Aramaic. That the tradition here presented to us is, in the main, at first hand is obvious."[1]

The survival of the Synoptical Gospels (not to speak here of the fourth Gospel) is a token that in respect of trustworthiness and value they could claim a primacy among the early attempts to record the words and deeds of Christ. To be sure it is conceivable that adventitious causes might have worked to suppress worthy rivals. But what is known of uncanonical Gospels does not lead us to believe that any of them had an equal title to survival with the Synoptical. The majority of those whose titles have come down to us are quite outside the field of comparison. In the present connection there is scanty occasion to mention any of them except the Gospel according to the Hebrews, the Gospel according to the Egyptians, and the Gospel of Peter.

The references of Clement of Alexandria, of Origen, of Eusebius, and especially of Jerome, to the Gospel according to the Hebrews may be taken as indicating that in its general tenor this version of Christ's life could not have been very remote from the Synoptical Gospels. Had it contained much matter adapted to provoke a sharp antipathy in Catholic minds, the references to it would naturally have been characterized by a different tone. Still its title to rank with the Synoptical Gospels

---

[1] Harnack, What is Christianity? p. 21.

as a treasury of primitive tradition is open to question. Several of the citations which make up the scanty remains of this Hebrew Gospel are not favorable to the assumption of parity. A dogmatizing element enters into its account of Christ's baptism both in the broaching by Him of the subject of His sinlessness, and in the characterizing of Him as the Son, the firstborn, of the Holy Spirit, and the sought-for resting place of that Spirit. The superior simplicity and sobriety of the Synoptical representation suggest that it is the more original version of the baptismal incident. In still more unfavorable contrast with the Synoptical narrative is the fantastic statement that the mother of Christ, that is, the Holy Spirit, transported Him by a single hair of His head to Mount Tabor. Finally a Judaizing preference for James crops out in the affirmation that the risen Lord first of all appeared to James — a representation which contradicts Pauline testimony as well as the Synoptical records. Items like this certainly justify the very general disposition which has been manifested by scholars to place this writing in a rank distinctly secondary to that of the Synoptical Gospels.[1]

It might be judged from the title of the Gospel according to the Egyptians that this writing at one time had wide currency in Egypt. But too large a conclusion ought not to be built upon a mere name. It is quite possible that the title contained an element of exagger-

---

[1] For a full view of the data which pertain to the topic see Handmann, Das Hebraer-Evangelium; Harnack, Die Chronologie der altchristlichen Litteratur, I. 625–651; Stanton, The Gospels as Historical Documents, Part I. pp. 250–264.

tion. Then, too, it is probable that it was designed to cover only native Egyptians as distinguished both from those of Jewish and those of Greek descent; and no one knows what proportion of the Christians in Egypt was included in the first of these parties when the title "according to the Egyptians" was attached to the Gospel. The lack of any reference to it by Eusebius is an indication that in the sight of the Church at large it obtained little prominence. As to its content, the means of judging are scanty. Origen simply mentions it among heretical Gospels.[1] From Clement of Alexandria we learn that it was associated, whether fairly or unfairly, with the teaching of the Encratites,[2] and Epiphanius informs us that it was a chief source of a Sabellian or modalistic christology.[3] On the whole the extant data quite decidedly fall short of accrediting it as having any just claim to take rank with the Synoptical Gospels. The Sabellian feature is certainly the reverse of a sign of primitiveness. At least critics who are disposed to regard an Ebionite christology as a sign of early origin cannot consistently attach a like significance to a Sabellian christology, for the two were wide apart in dogmatic intention.[4]

The Gospel of Peter is mentioned by Eusebius as being quite outside the circle of Catholic recognition.[5] Notice, however, was taken of an item in it by Origen.[6]

---

[1] In Luc. i.
[2] Strom. iii. 9, 13
[3] Panar. lxii. 2
[4] See Harnack, Chronologie, I. 612–622; Stanton, The Gospels as Historical Documents, I. 264–268.
[5] Hist. Eccl. iii. 3.
[6] In Matt. x. 17.

THE SYNOPTICAL TEACHING

Back of Origen it is not certainly known to have been mentioned by any other writer than Serapion. It has indeed been conjectured that Justin Martyr referred to this Gospel under the title "Memoirs of Peter";[1] but the point is in dispute.[2] The extant portion of the Gospel of Peter relates to the passion and resurrection of Christ. From this portion it is made quite evident that the author wished to propagate docetic views. Somewhat of an occasion for discounting his narrative is also found in the singular account which he gives of the authority and agency of Herod in connection with the trial and crucifixion of Christ. Possibly the Gospel of Peter may have recorded some extra-canonical items that were based on genuine tradition; but what is known about its contents is not adapted to foster a very high opinion of its merits. Its fraudulent claim to have emanated from the Apostle Peter is justly reckoned as a ground of limited confidence in its trustworthiness.

As respects sayings which may with any fair degree of probability be imputed to Jesus, the Apocryphal Gospels, or more broadly speaking, all extra-canonical sources together, make a very meagre addition to the content of the New Testament.[3] Scholarship must doubtless regret that better means of acquaintance with these Gospels are not available. Still there is little reason to modify

---

[1] Dial. cum Tryph. cvi.

[2] Compare Harnack, Bruchstucke des Evangeliums und der Apokalypse des Petrus; Swete, The Akhmim Fragment of the Apocryphal Gospel of St. Peter; Stanton, The Gospels as Historical Documents, I. 93 ff.

[3] Ropes, Die Spruche Jesu; also in Hastings' Dict. of the Bible, V. 343 ff.

this judgment of Jülicher: "The Apocryphal Gospels of the second century, several of which are known to us — such as that according to the Hebrews, that according to the Egyptians, and the Gospel of Peter — are the result of working over the canonical Gospels or the sources used by them, in conformity to sectarian or heretical tendencies. Accordingly some individual items of a primitive character may have found lodgment there. But Luke and Matthew stand already at the point where the production of Gospels ceases to be a gain for the Church, and begins to signify only a peril."[1]

II. — THE STORY OF THE NATIVITY.

The special theological item which meets us here is that of the supernatural conception as taught by Matthew and Luke. An examination of the story of the nativity given by these evangelists respectively must convey the impression that they made up their versions independently. Interesting particulars which are put in the foreground by the one are entirely passed over by the other. It follows then, since neither copied from the other, that we have here the testimony, not of one, but of two representatives of early Christianity, to belief in the supernatural conception or virgin-birth of Christ. Joining this fact with the probable date of the Gospels as noticed above, we are brought to the conclusion that the item of the supernatural conception has a pretty fair claim to be regarded as an apostolic item. It seems to have had a right of way close upon the border of the apostolic age,

---

[1] Einleitung in das Neue Testament, p. 301.

not to say within the limits of that age. In the absence then of a dogmatic motive for denying the historical character of the item, one can rationally be tolerant of the verdict that it stands for the simple truth.[1] At the same time, from the standpoint of biblical theology there is no occasion for great stress upon the item of the supernatural conception. The New Testament treats it almost exclusively as a matter of history, the one exception being the remark which Luke puts into the mouth of the angel of the annunciation: " wherefore that which is to be born shall be called holy, the Son of God." These

---

[1] An adverse consideration has been found in the fact that a Syriac manuscript of the Gospels (the Sinai-Syriac), which is supposed to be relatively very early, makes Matt. i. 16 to read " Joseph begat Jesus." A decisive weight, however, need not be given to this fact for the following reasons: (1) Joseph was in the sight of the law the father of Jesus. So far as the latter was a subject at all for a genealogy after the Jewish pattern He was to be located in the line of Joseph. In the stereotyped form of the genealogical table the statement of this fact of being legally in the line of Joseph might run " Joseph begat Jesus," though of course a little reflection on the matter would elicit within the company believing in the supernatural conception a demand for mending such a phrase. A pretty close approach to this inexact way of speaking may be observed in Luke. Notwithstanding his unequivocal declaration of the supernatural conception, the evangelist so far accommodates himself to the current and natural style of reference as to speak of Joseph as the father of Jesus, and of Joseph and Mary as the parents of Jesus — a form of expression which, curiously enough, Mark has avoided (vi. 3), whether with or without design. (2) Jesus was commonly reputed to be the son of Joseph. Supposing the verity of the supernatural conception we must still conclude that *at first* it was recognized only by a select circle. But this circle is not necessarily to be deemed an unreliable witness on account of its limited compass. It is quite possible that the Catholic faith in the supernatural conception may have rested back upon more competent testimony than that underlying the contrasted opinion. Surely it would take something more than a single instance of an early

words indicate a belief that the supernatural conception was to Jesus a source of extraordinary sanctity and dignity. It is quite too much, however, to find in them a demonstration that the writer regarded the supernatural conception as the sole basis of the special sonship of Jesus. Luke certainly could not have thought thus if his companionship with Paul had any effect upon his

---

text verbally in line with the ordinary popular conviction to demonstrate that belief in the supernatural conception was destitute of a substantial historic basis (3) All extant manuscripts of Matthew and Luke, not excepting that which contains the special version of Matt. i. 16, assert the fact of the supernatural conception. There is some ground, therefore, for suspecting that the form of Matt i. 16 in the Sinai-Syriac manuscript represents the mistake or caprice of a copyist (4) There are reasons for thinking that, prior to the composition of the first and third Gospels, written embodiments had been given to belief in the supernatural conception. "The story as given by our Matthew and Luke," says C. A. Briggs, " does not come from these writers, but from their sources. They briefly remark upon it and interpret it, but they do not materially change it. These sources are poetic in form and also in substance, and have all the characteristics of Hebrew poetry as to parallelism, measurement of lines, and strophical organization. They evidently came from a Jewish-Christian community and not from Gentile Christians. They are therefore ancient sources, different from and yet to be classed with the Gospel of St Mark and the Logia of St. Matthew, rather than with our Gospels of Matthew, Luke, and John" (Introduction to the Study of Holy Scripture, p. 523). Thus the memorials of faith in the supernatural conception go back to a point which may reasonably be regarded as falling within the domain of apostolic tradition.

It is noticeable that Lobstein, though distinctly challenging the fact of the supernatural conception, fully agrees with the conclusion that Matthew and Luke recorded upon this point a belief which had been current for a considerable period. " Matthew and Luke," he says, "only received and set down in writing far older traditions." (The Virgin Birth of Christ, pp. 77, 78). It is to be observed also that Lobstein thinks it imprudent to make any special account of the exceptional reading in the Sinai-Syriac manuscript (p. 121)

christology. Apart from this incidental and somewhat indeterminate item, the New Testament builds nothing upon the postulate of the supernatural conception. In the more constructive portions it receives no mention. The supposition, therefore, that the postulate was introduced to meet a dogmatic demand belongs essentially to the sphere of the historic imagination, and needs a much better substantiation than it has yet received. A like judgment is to be passed on the supposition that a lively expectation, current among the Jews, was the source of belief in the supernatural conception. Proper traces of such an expectation are not discoverable.[1] On the contrary there is distinct evidence of its non-existence in the known belief of the stricter party among the Judaizing Ebionites and in the testimonies of Justin Martyr[2] and Hippolytus.[3]

III. — THE SELF-CONSCIOUSNESS OF CHRIST AS A SUBJECT OF DEVELOPMENT AND A SOURCE OF TEACHING.

As Christ was born into the visible estate and relations of a child, it is natural to suppose that He had a progressively unfolding self-consciousness, such as is essentially characteristic of the child. A human life not

---

[1] "The Jewish common people," says Dalman, "never expected the Messiah to be born of a virgin; and no trace is to be found among the Jews of any Messianic application of Isaiah's words (vii. 14) concerning the virgin's son, from which by any possibility — as some have maintained — the whole account of the miraculous birth of Jesus could have derived its origin" (The Words of Jesus, p. 276).

[2] Dial. cum Tryph., xlix. 1.

[3] Philosophumena, ix. 25.

subject in its psychical experience to the law of growth would be human only in the most superficial sense, that of mere outward semblance. Unless then we are to impeach the candor and reality of the gospel revelation, and to justify a pronounced docetism, we must suppose Christ to have been a subject of development in His inner consciousness, as well as in outward or physical respects. If there is any motive at all for denying this development it must be on the score of a theoretic Christology, a supposed necessity that special union with the divine should have cancelled, on the part of Christ, all limitation of knowledge, all natural occasion for growth in the understanding of Himself and of the universe. Now in response to this theoretic Christology it is to be said, in the first place, that it is by no means certain that it is sustained by any cogent theoretical demand. Being and consciousness are never commensurate in us, and least of all are they so at the beginning of our career. We are born into relations which are far above the plane of our cognizance in early childhood. The analogy suggests that in the Christ-child and the Christ-youth consciousness may not have been by any means commensurate with being and essential relations. Granting that from the start there was an organic bond with the divine, perfectly unique, never duplicated in creaturely history, still it might be that in the consciousness of the Son of Mary this should be unrevealed until some favored moment should afford an initial glimpse of it, and that advance to a full understanding of it should be along the path of a widening and deepening experience. Again it is to be replied to the theoretic christology in question that it is not privileged to put aside facts in the interest of mere theory.

Turning to the gospel narratives we find their implication unmistakably on the side of a progressive unfoldment of the consciousness of Christ, or of His understanding of Himself and the divine kingdom. In the first place it is to be noticed that one of the evangelists as much as definitely asserts progressive unfoldment. "Jesus advanced," says Luke, "in wisdom and in stature" (ii. 52). In the second place it is to be observed that all three of the Synoptists distinctly represent Christ as subject to temptation. Now temptation is properly the experience of a growing subject and not of one who occupies the standpoint of omniscience. In the presence of the absolutely unlimited vision any solicitation to defection from the perfect way should no more be able to subsist than is a piece of cotton gauze in the intensest flame. Moreover, the nature of the temptations which are detailed by the evangelists is suggestive of an experience of growth or inward clarification. They seemed to have concerned especially the method of carrying out the high vocation to which Christ knew Himself to be called as he passed from the baptismal scene. Should popular desire and expectation be gratified by a resort to the method of power and display, or should the humble and cross-bearing method be undeviatingly pursued?— that appears to have been the question with which He was called to wrestle. His spirit was quick to see the affinity of the former alternative with the kingdom of evil, and to repel it as a misleading or Satanic suggestion; but who can doubt that He passed out of this experience with a clearer and intenser view of Messianic method than that which previously had been entertained by Him? His being tempted was not a mere spectacle for outsiders to contemplate. It was in all probability a stage in the unfoldment of His own sense of the requirements of His peculiar vocation. Again, the evangelists use language which naturally implies that Christ's experience included the unexpected, that He was capable of the emotion of surprise. He marvelled, it is said, at extraordinary instances both of faith and unbelief.[1] Once more, in disclaiming knowledge of a particular future event[2] Christ showed that the order of mental life to which He was subject admitted of an increasing content. We conclude, then, that the sacred biographies invite us to believe that Christ had a real childhood, and a real youth, and a real manhood, as being under the human law of growth and as advancing not merely from the forseen to the actual but from the unknown to the known as well. In making this statement we speak, obviously, only of the consciousness in our Lord which was immediately back of His communication with the world, the consciousness expressed in such conceptions and forms of speech as belong to the time sphere in which man lives. How this consciousness was related to the timeless life of the eternal Son, the Divine Logos, it is not attempted in this connection to determine. That is rather a question for speculative dogmatics than for biblical theology.

In considering the unfoldment of Christ's self-consciousness it ill becomes us to assume that we can gauge its

---

[1] Matt. viii. 10; Mark vi. 6; Luke vii. 9.
[2] Matt. xxiv. 36· Mark xiii. 32.

progress with anything like precision. The subject has never been directly reported upon, and the indirect tokens are not abundant; for there is no adequate warrant for supposing that the moment when a truth relative to Himself was first declared was also the moment of its first emergence into His own consciousness. Religious discretion may have put a seal upon His lips for long intervals. Possibly the visit to Jerusalem at the age of twelve, when He put the puzzling question to His parents, "Wist ye not that I must be in my Father's house," or "in the affairs of my Father," marked a special stage of inward premonition as to His unique relation and calling. The τοῦ πατρός μου of that question was certainly quite foreign to the ordinary dialect of the Jewish child, and indicated the dawning of a peculiar sense of intimacy with the Father in heaven. It is not ascertained, it is true, that in uttering these words He spoke a sentiment which had just come into His consciousness. Still there is nothing improbable in the supposition that the special occasion was providentially utilized as a means of special inner revelation. That this was the case in the next recorded scene of his life, the baptism in the Jordan, there is no reason to doubt. It is to be noticed that in the report of this scene by both Matthew and Mark the manifestation from heaven is represented as directed to Jesus personally, and not to the bystanders; also that Luke agrees with Mark in representing the voice owning Jesus as the well-beloved Son to have been addressed to Him rather than to the people. We are thus invited to believe that, whatever light was already upon the spirit of Jesus in divine relations, He reached here a new stage in His advance toward a perfectly luminous self-consciousness. As already indicated, the testing to which He was subjected in the great initial temptation, was probably also a means of clarifying and settling His conviction respecting the extraordinary office which He was to fulfill. Beyond this stage there is in our view, little ground for attempting to specify, though it is quite credible that the events of His ministry may have contributed to a full-orbed consciousness of Himself and His position. Some have argued that His foresight of the cross was stimulated by His discovery of the utter hopelessness of receiving aught but sharp hostility from the ruling party in His nation. But this is unverifiable conjecture. No one can determine in such a matter what was due to external conditions and what to inward revelation. We may suppose the inward and the outward to have wrought together, but we shall do poor justice to the personality of Jesus unless we make large account of the former. The singular openness of His spirit toward heaven is rationally emphasized as being the medium of extraordinary illumination.

In the self-consciousness of Christ two cardinal distinctions may be noticed. The first is the utter absence of any shadow of sin. The tenor of the Synoptical Gospels is in accord with the categorical declarations by the apostles of Christ's perfect sinlessness. These Gospels do not indeed make a formal declaration on the subject. The evidence they afford is indirect, but it is not scanty. In the first place there is no sort of indication that Christ ever uttered a prayer for forgiveness or cherished an emotion of penitence. In the second place He is exhibited as possessing such an extraordinary balance of the highest positive virtues that the lack of expressed penitence cannot reasonably be imputed to a blind self-inflation or to any sort of mere eccentricity. Thirdly, Christ associated Himself with the impartation of divine benefits in a way implying that He felt no need of any friendly offices in His own behalf, but rather was qualified to fulfill such in behalf of all others.[1] Fourthly, Christ placed Himself outside the rank of sinners in declaring His blood to be shed for the remission of sins. Fifthly, He equally exalted Himself above the plane of a common sinful humanity in describing Himself as destined to sit upon the throne of judgment and to hold in His hands the awards of eternity. In short, the Synoptical representation plainly invites to faith in a Christ free from every stain and trammel of sin. It is not impossible indeed for the one who is bent upon finding a flaw to read it into two or three items in the report of Christ's words or deeds. But there is no reason to suppose that the evangelists themselves had the slightest misgiving over these items. It is the stainless Master whom they understood themselves to be picturing.

The second great distinction of Christ's self-consciousness is His luminous sense of sonship in relation to God. This is to be regarded as closely related to the foregoing. Just because there was no ground of self-reproach in Christ, no shadow of condemnation on His spirit, He was qualified to exemplify the filial character as it was never exemplified by any other member of the race. He had no cause for faltering or abashment in His approach to

---
[1] Matt. xviii. 19, 20.

the Father. Not merely in some moment of special exaltation, but habitually, He dwelt in the light of the Father's face, and knew that He was the recipient of His complacent love. In the Synoptical account there may not be, it is true, so direct an assertion of unbroken union and fellowship as is embodied in the Johannine words, "I and my Father are one." But there is an implication of the same truth in the strong words recorded by both Matthew and Luke: "All things have been delivered unto me of my Father; and no one knoweth the Son, save the Father; neither doth any know the Father, save the Son, and he to whomsoever the Son willeth to reveal Him."[1] This consciousness of an exclusive prerogative to reveal the Father argues a perfectly unclouded assurance of moral unity with Him. It testifies to a sense of perfect sonship.

This was the source of Christ's teaching. Christianity was born in this holy of holies — the consciousness of Christ as the stainless Son, having the full-orbed sense of sonship. He could give an authentic exposition of God because He was so perfectly in touch with the Father. He could set forth in clear outlines the kingdom of heaven, for He was the ideal citizen of that kingdom, and fulfilled its aim and end in His perfect harmony and loving fellowship with the Father. He could point out to men the way of life, for He knew by inner possession what is the true life of man's spirit. Here was the source of His matchless confidence. He could teach with authority because He had authority in Himself. The constituents of His self-consciousness were His credentials.

---

[1] Matt. xi 27, Luke x. 22.

No spiritual dynamic, no mere afflatus from without, could have taken the place of these. The luminous personality was the spring of the illuminating utterances. He gave of His own, and that is why He spoke with such freshness and simplicity. He had no need of the compiler's art. The truth was in His spirit, and He had but to express it in the intelligible images which His eye was quick to discover in nature and human society. As Beyschlag remarks, " His speech is all directness, living perception, pure genius; everything in it flows, not from any mediated or artificial world of ideas, but from native spiritual wealth, from the fullness of His inner life."[1] This is a truth which merits to be profoundly emphasized. Christ was and is the religious teacher of mankind because of the habitual and ideal realization of the highest truths in His own consciousness. Doubtless He deferred to and took from the Old Testament. It was matter of the plainest discretion in dealing with an Old Testament community to move not a little in the field of Old Testament imagery. But Christ, at least at the stage of His public ministry, really appropriated from the Jewish oracles only because their best was in harmony with His moral and religious intuition. The superior standard was in Himself, and He had no hesitation in setting maxims of His own above the ancestral code. Were we to judge from His silence, we should be led to conclude that there were broad tracts of the Old Testament which had a very subordinate significance to His mind.

---

[1] New Testament Theology, I. 32.

IV. — Some Distinguishing Characteristics of Christ's Teaching.

We have just mentioned one of these in specifying the intimate connection which subsisted between the teaching of Christ and His unique consciousness as the Son who enjoyed perfect communion with the Father. A second characteristic is not undeserving of being placed alongside of this, namely, the inseparable union which the words of Christ from first to last assume to subsist between morality and religion. The misadjustment into which the historical religions generally have run, mostly in the line of subordinating the ethical to the formally religious, but occasionally also, in the line of a relative slighting of the properly religious, has no counterpart in the scheme set forth by Christ. The most casual perusal of the Synoptical Gospels cannot fail to reveal with what absolute decision the notion is repudiated that any performances in the name of religion can take the place of a conscientious and straightforward discharge of duty to one's fellows. Stress upon the ethical appears at every turn. It appears in blessings pronounced upon the merciful and the peace-makers; in the strong condemnation uttered against anger and intemperate railing; in the requirement to be first reconciled, so far as possible, with one's brother before approaching God's altar; in the demand for a chastity which imposes full restraint even upon the thoughts and the desires; in the inculcation of a charity and good-will which are broad and earnest enough to do good not merely to friends but to enemies also; in the instruction that consistent and effectual prayer for divine forgiveness must be accompanied by the spirit of forgiveness towards those who have trespassed against us; in insistence upon transparent sincerity and singleness of purpose; in reprobation of that haste in judgment which leads one to rebuke the faults of his fellows before taking time to discover his own; in emphasis upon the duty to order conduct towards others as one would wish to have conduct ordered toward himself; in lifting up the requirement of equal love to the neighbor to a place of honor beside the supreme obligation of a man. It appears, moreover, in the whole attitude of Christ toward the Pharisaic model. Upon nothing did He so fix the imprint of scornful reprobation as upon the disposition to rate ceremonial scrupulosity above carefulness to fulfill the common duties springing out of the relations of man to man. To His mind this was a shabby, whitewashed substitute for religion, a lying semblance deserving the very acme of righteous indignation.

On the other hand, Christ was very remote from substituting simple ethics for religion. His point of view was not that of Confucius with his pale regard for the thought of the Divine Being. Still less was it that of Gautama with his virtual exclusion of the Divine Being altogether from the sphere of practical consideration. As clearly as He held in view the ethical province, so clearly He held in view the all-encompassing presence of the divine. The thought of the heavenly Father was to Him as the sun in the sky. Divorce from fellowship with Him was equivalent in His conception to doom to outer darkness. Spiritual victory He regarded as dependent upon cleaving closely to God; and the pathway to true peace and superiority to earthly trouble which He set before men was the path of self-delivery to God, and of simple trust in His minute unceasing care. From first to last in the teaching of Christ there is no suggestion but that the true life for man is one insphered in the thought of God and in the grateful consciousness of His presence. In short, religion in no wise falls behind morality as a subject of profound emphasis. The two are combined in beautiful unity.

Another characteristic of Christ's teaching is the union of simplicity and elevation which it exemplifies. The ideal which He sets forth is very lofty, but at the same time it is thoroughly human. This is especially true of His teaching in the Synoptical representation. In the fourth Gospel a mystical element finds place, and if we accept the substantial fidelity of this Gospel to history we shall be led to conclude that Christ did not wholly avoid those mystical aspects which in fact pertain to the spiritual world and to man's connection therewith. But it accords with our view of the relatively objective cast of the Synoptical Gospels to suppose that they reflect the dominant tone of Christ's teaching. We conclude then that Christ kept the mystical element within bounds, and occupied His discourse mainly with the more intelligible aspects of truth. He sketched an ideal which any one who contemplated it might feel was made for a real world and real human beings, adapted rather to lead on to the attainment of manhood than to put something unknown and strange in its place. Nowhere in His words do we find a hint that union with God implies a swamping of self-consciousness, a species of annihilation such as is involved in the Neo-Platonic doctrine of ecstasy and the Brahmanical doctrine of reabsorption. Nowhere do we hear a summons to lose self save in the sense of a rational absorption in the pursuit of great, holy, and benevolent ends. The call is homeward. The marked tendency of Christ's teaching is, in truth, to make the man who truly appropriates it at home both with himself and with God. It rebukes nothing that is purely and truly human. Equally free from false asceticism and fanciful mysticism, it is sane and practical without being prosaic or commonplace.

In respect of form the teaching of Christ was in the line of genial address, as opposed to formal disquisition. It partook of the qualities of vivid, poetic, imaginative conversation. With scholastic elaboration it had no affinity. It was popular oratory, discourse adapted in respect of its terms to penetrate to the understanding of the average man. As being in the line of popular oratory, Christ's speech was necessarily distinguished by a measure of accommodation. Speech that falls under that category can never be in an unknown tongue. At whatever new conception it may aim, it must make large use of current expressions and forms of thought. In following the path of this rational accommodation Christ simply chose the effectual way to get his message into the world. Not otherwise could he have secured for it the needful lodgment in the minds and the hearts of men. Doubtless it is possible to push the notion of accommodation too far; but it may legitimately be given a considerable scope. In picturesque, popular discourse it was practically necessary for Christ to weave into His speech numerous items from the intellectual and religious environment. Matters of this kind often served as a framework or scaffolding for setting forth His proper message, and the design which went with their use is better described as pictorial or rhetorical than as dogmatic. No one supposes that Christ meant to teach astronomy when He spoke of the rising of the sun, or to meddle with questions of geographical location when He spoke of laying up treasure in heaven. With little better right can a dogmatic intent be imputed to His use of customary forms in citing Old Testament literature, or to His casual employment of popular conceptions on such themes as angelology, demonology, and eschatology. Sober interpretation of Christ's teaching requires, therefore, careful discrimination between the main truth elucidated and the simple accessory. The latter may indeed belong within the province of revelation, but a merely incidental use of it in a given connection is inadequate ground for assigning it to that province.

The popular form of Christ's discourse may explain an occasional resort to hyperbole. A principle embodied in a clear-cut, unqualified aphorism was better suited to seize hold of the attention of men and to enlist memory and interest in its behalf than a principle wrapped up in limiting clauses. What way of setting forth the duty of avoiding the vengeful spirit could be more striking and effective than to speak of offering the other cheek to the smiter? How could the duty of uniting simplicity with transparent sincerity in speech, as opposed to an artificial and arbitrary scheme of oaths, be more vividly impressed than by an injunction to swear not at all? Instructions of this kind picture the ideal spirit which ought to rule conduct. It is not necessary to suppose that they were designed to be fulfilled with strict literalness, or with unbending refusal of accommodation to modifying conditions beyond the control of the individual. Indeed, if we may trust the testimony of the fourth evangelist, Christ Himself intimated as much by the rebuke which He ministered to the one unlawfully smiting Him when arraigned before the high priest.

V. — THE TREND OF CHRIST'S TEACHING RESPECTING THE NATURE OF THE KINGDOM OF GOD AND THE CONDITIONS OF ENTRANCE.

The kingdom of God, or the kingdom of heaven, as Matthew, differing herein from Mark and Luke, preferred to call it,[1] appears undoubtedly as a central theme of the Synoptical Gospels. Jesus is represented as beginning His ministry by preaching the gospel and declaring to the people that the kingdom of God was at hand.[2] He is said to have put the like message upon the lips of His disciples, instructing them in every city they should enter to proclaim, "The kingdom of heaven is at hand," "The kingdom of God has come nigh unto you."[3] In many of His parables and discourses Jesus directly occupied Himself with expounding the kingdom and setting forth the relation of men thereto. What his own preferred phrase was, whether "kingdom of heaven" or "kingdom of God," is not determined, and is of no

---

[1] Instances in which Matthew uses the former phrase are xii. 28, xix. 24, xxi. 31, 43.
[2] Mark i. 14, 15. [3] Matt. x. 7; Luke x. 9.

consequence. It is not improbable that He used the two interchangeably. Their sense is evidently identical; for the "kingdom of heaven" is not indicative of location, but rather of kind or origin.[1] It is the kingdom in which the will of God rules and which has its possibility of growth in His gracious presence. It comes to earth when He is obeyed on earth as in heaven. It is simply, therefore, the kingdom of God, the theatre of His moral sovereignty, as realized in particular through the mediatorial work of the Son.

A full review of the references in the Synoptical Gospels to the kingdom must give an impression of two contrasted aspects. These may be designated respectively the spiritual and the apocalyptic. On the one hand is a line of statements which presupposes that the kingdom is a present and an essentially interior reality. On the other hand is a line of statements which implies that the kingdom is a future reality, and is to come to manifestation, or be inaugurated, by a great crisis. As between these two orders of views there is no reason to doubt that popular thinking inclined to the latter. The current conception of the kingdom was apocalyptic, and with the apocalyptic aspect a very decided political coloring was associated. The dominant view of the Messianic time was that of an era when a powerful external intervention, a putting forth of divine might, should

---

[1] Bousset regards Matthew's expression as illustrating a tendency which had grown up among the Jews to substitute an abstract term for the name of God. "*Heaven* is here simply an equivalent conception for *God*." (Die Religion des Judenthums im neutestamentlichen Zeitalter, pp. 307, 308.)

crush the hostile forces of the world and exalt the people of Israel to a ruling position.

The teaching of Jesus was at least in form so far correspondent to popular conception that it gave a place to a future crisis. It practically discarded, however, the political associations which ruled ordinary Jewish anticipation at that day. The idea of a proper national supremacy cannot be seen to have entered into the eschatalogical discourses of Jesus. Thus the apocalyptic phase, as admitted by Him, had its manifest point of distinction from the popular version. But the greater distinction in Christ's teaching lay in the qualification which His very decided stress upon the spiritual aspect of the kingdom, as a present and interior reality, virtually put upon the apocalyptic aspect. Some recent critics, it is true, have contended that the apocalyptic was the ruling point of view in Christ's mind. But evidence to the contrary is interwoven with the gospel narratives. In the first place, Christ seems to give a present and spiritual character to the kingdom when He says, referring to the still living John the Baptist, "He that is little in the kingdom of God is greater than he."[1] A like implication of a present and spiritual realm is contained in the connected words representing the attainment of the kingdom as the result of eager pursuit: "From the days of John the Baptist until now the kingdom of heaven suffereth violence and the men of violence take it by force."[2] A present reality is also given to the kingdom when Christ says to the Pharisees, "The

---

[1] Luke vii. 28; Matt. xi. 11. [2] Matt. xi. 12; Luke xvi. 16.

publicans and harlots go into the kingdom of God before you,"[1] or when He charges against them, "Ye shut the kingdom of heaven against men; for ye enter not in yourselves, neither suffer ye them that are entering in to enter."[2] The same inference belongs to Christ's approving response to the scribe, "Thou art not far from the kingdom of God."[3] It is by no means to be supposed that proximity in the sense of time or place is mentioned here. The evident reference is to inner disposition, and so the kingdom is conceived as a present and spiritual reality. This character is likewise very distinctly assigned to the kingdom in the condition that is specified for entrance, that of being converted and becoming as little children.[4] A parallel significance belongs to the injunction and promise, "Seek ye first His kingdom and His righteousness; and all these things shall be added unto you."[5] Here it is the one who seeks, and presumably gains the kingdom, that is represented as authorized to put aside anxiety about temporal necessities. The kingdom therefore is placed under the category of a personal and present possession — an inference which is supported, so far as Matthew's version is concerned, by the coupling of righteousness with the kingdom as an object of pursuit. As little is the coming of the kingdom put off to a future crisis in the words with which Christ replied to a Pharisaic calumny, "If I by the Spirit of God cast out devils, then is the kingdom of God come unto you."[6] This imports that a driving out of devils, an abridgment of the evil kingdom, is equivalent

---

[1] Matt. xxi. 31.   [3] Mark xii. 34.   [5] Matt. vi. 33; Luke xii. 31.
[2] Matt. xxiii. 13.   [4] Matt. xviii. 1–4.   [6] Matt. xii. 28; Luke xi. 20.

THE SYNOPTICAL TEACHING 77

to that extent to an introduction of the divine kingdom. Again the list of parables in which the kingdom is likened to the mysterious sprouting and growth of grain sown in a field, to the development of a mustard seed into a large plant, and to the working of the minute substance of leaven through whole measures of meal,[1] distinctly favors the thought of the kingdom as a present and gradually unfolding reality. Likewise the comparison of the kingdom to a treasure hid in the field, for which a man gladly barters all his possessions,[2] or to a goodly pearl which the merchantman values above his whole stock besides,[3] manifestly makes the kingdom a present means of personal enrichment, an essentially spiritual treasure.[4] Once more, the collocation of petitions in the Lord's prayer implies that the coming of the kingdom is identical with the doing of God's will on earth as it is done in heaven. Finally, the sentence of Luke xvii. 20, 21, "The kingdom of God cometh not with observation; neither shall they say, Lo, here! or There! for lo, the kingdom of God is within you," is decidedly on the side of the spiritual as opposed to the apocalyptic sense of the kingdom. It is true that the expression ἐντὸς ὑμῶν ἐστίν can be translated "is among you" or "in your midst." But the rendering given is

---

[1] Mark iv. 26–29; Matt. xiii. 31, 33.   [2] Matt. xiii. 44.

[3] Matt. xiii. 45, 46.

[4] On the substance of the parabolic teaching Gould well says: "The teaching of the parables is the clearest teaching in the New Testament in regard to the manner of establishing the kingdom, and this teaching is clearly at variance with the supposition of a sudden or early winding up of the world's affairs." (Biblical Theology of the New Testament, p. 47.)

quite as agreeable to the antecedent statement. It is to be noticed, moreover, that the alternative translation does not eliminate from the passage a spiritual conception of the kingdom. If the kingdom was among those addressed by Christ, and yet undiscovered by them, the inference would be that it was rather a spiritual dominion than an external visible kingdom ushered in by power.[1] Our conclusion then is that it is a decidedly faulty exegesis which supposes that the spiritual aspect was overshadowed in Christ's thought or teaching by the apocalyptic. So strongly is the former inculcated in the Gospels that consistency can be given to Christ's teaching as a whole only on the supposition that He meant to indicate by the apocalyptic picture the fact that the ethico-religious process going on in the world is to reach a decisive consummation and have its results perfectly manifested.

So comprehensive a theme naturally provided for a variety of representations. Viewed as to its source and central principle, the kingdom is the realized moral rule of God; viewed as to the relations of its subjects, it is an ideal society. Regarded as a sum of spiritual goods which accompany or result from the realized rule of God, the kingdom can be spoken of as a treasure to be received; regarded as the domain where a divine and heavenly regime obtains, it can be described as a province or sphere which is to be entered. As already inaugurated and in process of development, the kingdom is here and

---

[1] Compare Klopper, Zeitschrift fur wissenschaftliche Theologie, 40th year, 3d number; Bacon, The Beginnings of Gospel Story; Sharman, The Teaching of Jesus about the Future.

now; as awaiting a great consummating stage it is yet to come. Obviously these various aspects need not be regarded as necessarily involving any contradiction.

With the spiritual character of the kingdom, as recognized in Christ's thought, there was naturally associated a free attitude toward the Mosaic law, a qualifying of the distinction between Jew and Gentile, a bent to religious universalism. He did not indeed make any formal declaration that the time had come for setting aside the Mosaic law. Nevertheless He gave a distinct stress to the new cast of the kingdom, as in the parables on the wine-skins and the garment. Moreover He enumerated principles which as good as abrogated parts of the ancient code. If what He said about the powerlessness of things external to defile a man were to be accepted, then a considerable section of the Levitical legislation[1] must seem to have a very slight ground for continued subsistence. If his instructions on the subject of divorce were to be taken as authoritative, then Deut. xxiv. 1, 2 must needs be reckoned as obsolete. The lordship which He claimed over the Sabbath may also be regarded as a hint that to His consciousness the legal system of Israel did not possess finality. An outlook passing quite beyond an exclusive Judaism was moreover indicated in the specification in the parable of the sower, that the Son of Man is the sower, and the field is the world.[2] With this sentence may be joined many others which are in like manner indicative of a transcendence of Jewish boundaries. We need not repeat them here, for we gave a list of them while attempting in the first section

---

[1] Lev. xi.–xv. [2] Matt. xiii. 37, 38.

of this chapter to establish the Christian universalism of Matthew's Gospel. There is one passage, it is true, which might be thought to make for the perpetuity of the Mosaic law in all its details. In the sermon on the mount Christ is reported to have said that He came not to destroy the law but to fulfill, and that not one jot or tittle of the law shall pass away till all be accomplished.[1] But an isolated passage like this cannot be allowed to nullify the force of multiplied statements. If the words are to be accepted as correctly reported, it is necessary that they should not be taken in their bald verbal sense. We shall not be at fault perhaps in construing them as a strong rhetorical expression for the twofold truth that Christ had no intention to carry on His reform by the method of excision from the ancestral code, and that the real intent of that code, its essential religious purpose, should have complete fulfillment in the kingdom proclaimed by Himself.[2] Christ's declaration is not that everything in the law will perpetually be obligatory in the letter, but that nothing in the law shall fall short of fulfillment. That the fulfillment was actually achieved will not be denied by anyone who duly considers how the whole ideal aim and striving of the Old Testament dispensation came to realization in the truth and grace of which Christ was the bearer and the expression.

---

[1] Matt. v. 17–19. Compare Luke xvi. 17.

[2] "He fulfills," says Bruce, "by realizing in theory and practice an ideal to which Old Testament institutions and revelations point, but which they do not actually express. Therefore in fulfilling He necessarily abrogates in effect, while repudiating the spirit of a destroyer. He brings in a law of the spirit which cancels the law of the letter, a kingdom which realizes prophetic ideals, while setting aside the crude details of their conception of the Messianic time." (The Expositor's Greek Testament, I. 104.)

THE SYNOPTICAL TEACHING

The conditions of entrance, as laid down in the Gospels, correspond with the spirituality and universality of the kingdom. Repentance is clearly indicated as one of the foremost conditions. The disciples of Christ going forth under His instructions are said to have preached that men should repent.[1] Christ described it as a part of His vocation to call sinners to repentance,[2] and declared that there is joy in heaven over one sinner that repenteth.[3] Not less distinctly he indicated the necessity of faith. His initial message as reported by Mark was "repent ye, and believe in the gospel."[4] To the woman who washed His feet with her tears He said, "Thy faith hath saved thee, go in peace."[5] To the Syrophœnician woman, to blind Bartimæus, and to the woman with an issue of blood He gave a gracious response according to their faith,[6] bestowing indeed in these instances temporal benefits, but certainly conveying an impression by His emphatic words that no sort of divine benefit would be denied to faith, and that it must be the key to the kingdom. As much as this is signified in His pithy declaration, "All things are possible to him that believeth."[7] And what else is it than the method of faith which He commends for gaining what God has to give, when, He says, "Ask and it shall be given you?"[8]

The Synoptical representation, then, makes repentance and faith the principal conditions of entrance into the kingdom, and the major stress seems to be placed upon

---

[1] Mark vi. 12.
[2] Luke v. 32.
[3] Luke xv. 7.
[4] Mark i. 15.
[5] Luke vii. 50.
[6] Matt. xv. 28, Mark x. 52; Matt. ix. 22.
[7] Mark ix. 23.
[8] Matt. vii. 7.

faith. The fact that where the two are named in conjunction repentance stands first is no token that it has a logical priority. The order followed in the gospel statements may be regarded as the homiletical order. Under certain conditions the preacher may very properly begin with insisting upon the need of repentance. Still in the logical order faith is the prius of repentance. It is the positive side of the total transaction of which repentance is the negative. The latter is the turning away from the soiled and imperfect. But no one gains any effective incentive to this turning away except through an appreciative vision of something better. He must perceive and give at least initial assent to a higher ideal in order to motive and strength for parting from the lower. Now this initial assent, or inner movement toward self-committal, is faith begun. The positive force, or motive-power, is thus with faith, and repentance is logically secondary.

No definition of faith is recorded to have been given by Christ. But if He does not define He describes, and He leaves no doubt as to the true character of faith as a religious potency. The *a fortiori* argument which He builds on the willingness of earthly parents to give good gifts to their children, His stress upon the right and the duty of untroubled reliance upon the heavenly Father's care when once His kingdom has been made the first concern, His commendation of the publican's prayer, and His insistence upon the childlike disposition, clearly imply that by faith He meant a filial, humble, earnest spirit of self-committal to God. It is legitimate to add that He regarded the message of which He Himself was the bearer as especially inviting and obligating to this self-committal.

The kingdom which Christ proclaimed was not formally styled a kingdom of grace. It is not difficult, however, to discover that it was conceived to be of that character. Doubtless not a little was said by Christ about work and reward. As reported by Matthew, He declared in so many words that the Son of Man would render to every man according to his deeds,[1] and in His picture of the great assize He described the awards as being made according to this principle.[2] But in all this there is no denial of grace or gratuitous favor. In all earnest religious oratory a like strain ever recurs. It is found with Paul notwithstanding his vehement repudiation of salvation by works. The truth is that deeds are tokens of the character upon which destiny hinges, and that a wholesome incentive to the formation of a right character is imparted to the average man by the disclosure that at the end of one order of deeds great reward lies, and at the end of another dire loss and punishment. In popular address, therefore, it is natural to put emphatically the notion of work and reward. So Christ did. Nevertheless His total representation is far from paying tribute to the servile and legal conception of salvation. He imposed no system of austerities, leaving such a matter as fasting to the option of His followers.[3] He commended no strained scheme of self-denial, no form of self-imposed hardship as having saving virtue in itself.[4]

---

[1] xvi. 27.   [2] Matt. xxxv. 34–45.
[3] Matt. ix. 14, 15; Mark ii. 18–20; Luke v. 33–35.
[4] The requirement which Christ laid upon the rich young man, to

He represented the acquisition of spiritual goods as the result simply of using a treasure primarily committed by the Lord to men and not gained by their activity.[1] He excluded boasting over one's doings by instructing His disciples to still reckon themselves unprofitable servants after having done all that was commanded.[2] He spoke of the kingdom as a gift bestowed by the Father's good pleasure.[3] In His stress upon faith and His indication of its nature He as much as inculcated that it is the child, not the hireling, that God wants and is ready to bless. By the parable of the prodigal son He made it as clear as the day that it is the Father's love and not man's merit which is the great source of benefits, and that this love only asks for the receptive subject. By His own practice of consulting only the need and receptivity of the wretched and the outcast he illustrated most vividly the truth that the kingdom which He represented was a kingdom of grace. His picture therefore of work and reward, when viewed in the light of His entire teach-

---

sell all his property and give to the poor, is obviously not to be taken as a sign of a legal or monastic point of view. The requirement was of the nature of a special test such as was suitable to the moral condition of that individual. No similar test, so far as we know, was imposed upon Zacchaeus or any other. Jesus had an acute sympathy with the poor; but He did not discountenance private property or magnify the virtue of its renunciation. The blessing which in Luke's version of the beatitudes is pronounced upon the poor, if it is taken as the original, must be regarded as signifying not that the poor have the kingdom of heaven because of their poverty, but that in spite of all the distresses of poverty they are to be counted blessed, inasmuch as the kingdom of heaven is so fully accessible to them in answer to their humility and faith.

[1] Matt. xxv. 14-30.   [2] Luke xvii. 10.   [3] Luke xii. 32.

ing, is seen to have no affiliation with a mercenary type of piety. Back of it is the understanding that the one who works and is rewarded must have the spirit of the child and not of the hireling, and that above and behind all work and reward is the benevolent will of the heavenly Father.

A few sentences in Christ's discourses might seem to favor the notion that grace makes an independent or arbitrary choice of subjects. This is more especially true of Mark iv. 11, 12, where Christ says to His disciples: "Unto you is given the mystery of the kingdom of God; but unto them that are without all things are done in parables; that seeing they may see, and not perceive; and hearing they may hear and not understand; lest haply they should turn again, and it should be forgiven them." In respect of this passage it is to be noticed in the first place that the parallel verses in Matthew represent Christ's method of speaking as chosen not for the purpose of producing blindness, but because of already existing blindness. "Whosoever hath," it is said, "to him shall be given, and he shall have abundance; but whosoever hath not, from him shall be taken away even that which he hath. Therefore speak I to them in parables; because seeing they see not, and hearing they hear not, neither do they understand."[1] According to this version there is no purpose expressed to withhold a real treasure from any party, but simply a declaration that men are dealt with according to their receptivity. In the second place it is to be observed that if Mark's version be accepted, the purpose which it records must be

---

[1] Matt. xiii. 12, 13.

regarded as proximate rather than ultimate. Retribution for insensibility may be indicated, but as respects the great mass of those referred to it is incredible that anything more than a temporary forfeiture of the proper gospel benefit could have been meant. Christ's teaching respecting His mission to seek and to save the lost, and respecting the value to the heavenly Father of even one straying soul, makes it unthinkable that He wished any company of men to be given over to permanent blindness and obduracy. Moreover, we seem to be required by the tenor of the New Testament to conclude that His disciples were being educated to serve, after His departure, as the bearers of His gracious message to the general body of the Jewish people, and therefore to the multitude contemplated by the words in question. Thus the conditions exclude the thought of an arbitrary or irreversible rejection which might be suggested by the form of words in Mark's version. It should be noted, too, that in Mark's account of the speaking in parables there is a hint of benevolent intent. Jesus spoke the word, it it said, to the people in parables, "as they were able to hear it."[1]

The sense in which Christ acknowledged the notion of election is clearly indicated in the parable of the marriage feast.[2] At the close of that parable it is said, "few are chosen;" but it is said also that "many are called," and the tenor of the story shows plainly that it was nothing but lack of response to a cordial invitation which kept the majority from participation in the feast. In fine it empties out substance and sincerity from the

---
[1] Mark iv. 33.   [2] Matt. xxii. 1-14.

gospel message to suppose that Christ conceived the grace of the kingdom which He proclaimed to be under the bonds and fetters of an arbitrary election. The elect in His view were elected not merely to personal salvation, but to the office of extending salvation as far as possible, called to be the light of the world and the salt of the earth.

We mentioned among the distinctive features of Christ's teaching the inseparable union which it inculcates between the ethical and the religious, a union which does not permit the former ever to be sacrificed in the name of the latter. This truth is pertinent to the present connection, as reminding us that the doctrine of the gracious character of the kingdom has no sort of affinity with the notion of indifference on the divine side, but subsists in the gospel scheme right alongside of a mighty stress upon the ethical ideal. These two elements, the unbending ideal, on the one hand, to which a man is solemnly bound to conform, and the grace, on the other hand, which appeals to confidence, saves from despair, and rescues in spite of ill-desert, are in their close union and reciprocal action distinctive of the gospel and principal sources of its virtue. Neither can be put out of sight without detriment. As Sabatier has said, "To decompose the gospel salt is to destroy its savor."[1]

VI. — LEADING CONCEPTIONS OF GOD AS SET FORTH BY CHRIST.

Old and new were combined on this theme. Out of

---

[1] Outlines of a Philosophy of Religion, p. 164.

the treasury of Jewish thought came such lofty elements in the conception of God as His absolute supremacy, His distinct personality, and His ethical intensity. The teaching of Christ in the Synoptical Gospels, while remote from formal theologizing, distinctly implies every one of these elements. He represented God as One with whom all things are possible, and evidently conceived that everything both small and great in nature rests in His hand. To Christ's consciousness nothing was more thoroughly certain than the reality of fellowship with the Father as of one person with another. Not one trace of pantheistic vagueness can be found in His speech. No more does His point of view show any affiliation with deistic remoteness and indifference. It is a God thoroughly alive to the conduct and character of men, ethically intense, that His discourse pictures.

But with all this appropriation of conceptions from the higher ranges of law and prophecy, the teaching of Christ makes a decided impression of newness. It seems to transport one into an atmosphere and a territory quite other than those of the Old Testament. The explanation of this impression lies in the fact that Christ's exposition of the thought of God flowed out of His unique consciousness of sonship. No sage or prophet in Israel ever had anything like an equivalent of that conciousness. As has been noticed, He knew Himself as the well-beloved Son, having unhindered access to the Father, and dwelling habitually in the light of His complacent love. Dowered with a supreme sense of sonship He was prepared to be in a supreme way the expositor of divine fatherhood. His exposition was not a specula-

THE SYNOPTICAL TEACHING 89

tion but a shining forth of the light that was within Him.

This was the view with which Christ illuminated the religious landscape — this vivid, warmly-colored representation of God as the Father in heaven. The name of Father, it is true, had long had a place among the terms with which Israelitish thought described the Divine Being. But in the usage of the Hebrew Testament the name was descriptive rather of a national than an individual relation. It was the nation to which Jehovah stood in the character of Father, or possibly the king as the representative of the nation. Seldom did the thought gain expression that the individual is privileged to address the Holy One as Father. A suggestion of such a privilege was indeed contained in one and another sentence, especially in the words of the Psalm, "Like as a father pitieth his children, so the Lord pitieth them that fear Him." [1] A step beyond this, at least as regards verbal approach to the gospel, is observable in the Apocrypha. In Ecclesiasticus occurs the appeal, "O Lord, Father and Master of my life," [2] and in the Book of Wisdom it is intimated that the righteous man may be termed a son of God. [3] Still the adequate, unequivocal, inspiring assur-

---

[1] Psalm ciii. 13. Compare Hos. i. 10; Isa. i, 2, lxiii. 16; Mal. ii. 10.
[2] Ecclesiasticus xxiii. 1, 4.
[3] Wisdom ii. 18. (Compare Psalms of Solomon, xiii. 9.) This logically implies that God stands in a fatherly relation to the individual. The direct appeal to God as Father is nevertheless wanting. Instances of such appeal were evidently very rare till after the appearance of the New Testament. "In Palestinian circles," says Dalman, "in harmony with the Old Testament view, it is generally the *Israelites* as such who have God in relation to themselves as 'their father.' . . . In the

ance of the fatherly relation of God to the individual first came when Christ out of the fullness of His own filial consciousness talked of the Father. This name stood in his speech for a thoroughly individual relation. It lies in the whole tenor of His teachings, as well as in the verbal expression which He put into a formula of prayer for the disciple, that He had no thought but that each and every man should come to God as Father, and cultivate toward Him the spirit of the confiding child.

Some discussion has been expended on the question whether Christ taught the universal fatherhood of God — that is, His paternal relation to men generally, whether spiritual or unspiritual, obedient or disobedient. It must be granted that the Synoptical Gospels do not formally proclaim such a relation. Still it must be claimed that the Synoptical representation is decidedly on the side of the meaning which naturally goes with the phrase "universal fatherhood." It pictures God as ready to act toward men universally as though He recognized a paternal relation toward them. Christ as much as assumed to know thoroughly, and truly to represent, the mind of God. When therefore He declared His vocation to be the seeking and the saving of the lost, and showed how His compassion and solicitude went forth to the sinful and the outcast, He was giving an object lesson on the essential attitude of God to the underserving. By the whole tenor of His ministry He enforced the

---

Pseudepigrapha the name of father is nowhere used as a designation of God. The dicta of the Rabbis, from the end of the first Christian century onwards, are the earliest source of instances." (Words of Jesus, pp. 184–189.) Compare Bousset, Die Religion des Judentums, p. 357.

lesson which is to be gathered from the story of the prodigal son and the related parables. It matters little, then, that the formal affirmation of universal fatherhood is wanting. God is revealed as having fatherly compassion and goodwill toward the least worthy, and so by necessary inference toward every man. He is the generous being whose example of gratuitous kindness to the unjust perpetually invites men to love and bless their enemies. He is the absolutely good, the ἀγαθός, whose benevolence is without stint. This does not imply that He makes small account of distinctions of character. The Christ who pictured so strongly the consequences of unrepented sin, and urged the cutting off of the right hand that offends, had obviously no place for such a notion. As was stated above, He imputed to God the full measure of ethical intensity. It made no incongruity for His mind to suppose fatherly compassion and ethical intensity to coexist. Nor can it be seen that this point of view was illogical. Next to the actuality of sonship a potentiality of sonship is the most precious thing that the eye of God discovers among men. It is not inappropriate then for God to exercise fatherly forbearance and pity toward the sin-stained and unworthy man who still has in himself this potentiality. It is worth while to use some pains to prevent this pearl of great price from being lost.

The proper correlate to God's fatherhood is of course man's sonship. Still an affirmation of the one does not amount precisely to an affirmation of the other. By reason of human sinfulness a distinction is necessarily made between the fact and the potentiality of sonship.

In the Synoptical Gospels there is an implicit recognition of this distinction. In common with the rest of the New Testament they assume that it is through conformity to the divine pattern that men gain the title to be called in the full and proper sense sons of God.[1] While God in His disposition is constantly the Father, men need to attain to true sonship.

The dominant representation of God in the gospel gives the standard for the conception of prayer. It is consistently regarded as the trustful approach of the child to the supreme Father. So Christ represented it, not only in the form of prayer which He gave to His disciples, but also in the distinct appeal to the parental relation which he employed when He sought to inspire them with undoubting confidence in the presentation of their petitions. As may be judged from His reprobation of vain repetitions,[2] He considered it a senseless profanation of prayer to use it as a piece of magic or a merit-winning performance. He regarded it rather as the simple, unsophisticated expression of desire and need, the humble approach of the dependent member of the great spiritual household to the supreme and gracious Head of that household.

God as the prayer-hearing Father could but be conceived as exercising a minute and comprehensive providence. Christ took special pains to lighten up this aspect of divine relations. No more charming piece of optimism has ever been embodied in human speech than that contained in the word-pictures of Christ, which reveal the heavenly Father as noting the fall of the sparrow,

---

[1] Matt. v. 45; Luke vi. 35, xx. 36.   [2] Matt. vi. 7, 8.

numbering the very hairs upon the heads of His children, and exercising for them a loving foresight which makes it unnecessary to borrow an anxious thought about the events of the morrow. Doubtless Christ was perfectly aware that the appearance of divine providence is not always friendly. Perhaps in the parables of the selfish neighbor[1] and the unjust judge[2] He meant to give a suggestion that at times God may seem to take the unheeding attitude. In His own experience even, for at least one dark moment of overwhelming anguish, He illustrated how this cheerless appearance may dominate the outlook. But His unequivocal teaching was that God's notice and care extend to the minutest item of human interests, and He invited to a faith vital and buoyant enough to triumph over every adverse appearance.

In the postulate of universal fatherhood there is evidently latent a postulate of universal brotherhood. In fact Christ distinctly indicated that the two were closely related in His mind when He pointed to the merciful Father who bestows His gifts upon the undeserving as a model for the conduct of men. Furthermore in His interpretation of the requirement of equal love to the neighbor, as given in the parable of the good Samaritan, He plainly signified that the spirit of brotherly love should reach out to race-wide limits.

VII. — LEADING CONCEPTIONS OF MAN AND THE WORLD.

In sketching Christ's view of the kingdom and of the

---

[1] Luke xi. 5–9.   [2] Luke xviii. 1–8.

Father in heaven we have already intimated the most essential elements in His teaching respecting man. To His contemplation man was above all a child of God and a subject of His kingdom of righteousness. This was the ideal which He regarded as at least potential in every man, and in the light of which he estimated man's worth.

Among the tokens which Christ gave of His sense of man's worth was the stress which He placed upon the individual considered by himself, or stripped of all extraneous recommendations. No poverty or social abjectness removed a man in the least degree beyond the pale of His sympathy. Any one, however circumstanced, who was disposed to do the will of God, He received into cordial fellowship and pronounced worthy to be owned as mother, sister, and brother. To lose the individual in the mass He regarded as diametrically opposed to divine procedure. However great the number in the fold, the one straying sheep must be sought after and the finding of the lost one makes the most fitting occasion in the world for a jubilee.

Again, Christ expressed His sense of man's high place and worth by setting before him as the goal of attainment an image of divine perfection. "Ye therefore shall be perfect as your heavenly Father is perfect."[1] As the context indicates, it is especially the generous, overflowing, diffusive love of God that is to be copied. Similarly what is said of the obligation of the disciple to forgive trespasses and to seek occasion for ministering, rather than for being ministered unto,[2] contemplates him

---

[1] Matt. v. 48. [2] Matt. xx. 28.

as an associate and imitator of the perfect Father in heaven.

Still further, Christ attached a high worth to man in distinctly contemplating him as a candidate for immortality. His conception of the interrelation between God and man as that of Father and child naturally carried with itself a vital impression of the vocation of man to live an immortal life. This is essentially the point of His argument against the Sadducean negation. It flashes out the truth that the God who revealed Himself to Moses as the God of Abraham, Isaac, and Jacob, manifested thereby that He had received these fathers into sympathetic fellowship with Himself, and that the relation between Him and them was too intimate and real to allow the supposition that they had lapsed into the estate of remote nonentities. Those whom the paternal God recognizes as His own must survive the stroke of death. Corresponding to the living Father there must be living children, subjects of immortality.[1]

There is then no reason at all to doubt that the ideal which was recognized in Christ's habitual thought of man was a very lofty one. He gave unequivocal testimony on this subject. If we ask what was His estimate of the actual condition of men, we find the data for a conclusion somewhat less distinct. Not a statement can be found in the Synoptical Gospels which sounds much like the definite specifications of later times on original sin or innate depravity. Indeed were the words of Christ, which affirmed respecting little children, "of such is the kingdom of heaven,"[2] to be taken unquali-

---
[1] Matt. xxii. 32; Mark xii. 26, 27; Luke xx. 37, 38.   [2] Matt. xix. 14.

fiedly, the conclusion would be that birth into this world brings no entail of sin or depravity. But the warrant is not clear for taking the words in so large a sense. Christ saw in the simplicity and unsophisticated trustfulness of little children beautiful traits which ought to characterize mature life, and he undoubtedly regarded such subjects as embraced in God's kindly thought and standing within the bounds of the kingdom rather than outside. But that does not necessarily imply that He regarded these innocent and uncondemned citizens of the kingdom as having no tendencies by birth which would jeopardize their continuous standing in the kingdom and their unfoldment in harmony with its standard. He might have used just the words that He did, and still have held the conviction that man is so far by birth inclined to sin that he needs to be met on the threshold of moral activity by the regenerating agency of the Divine Spirit. The author of the fourth Gospel quite distinctly imputes to Him this conviction. The Synoptical representation, too, if falling short of an affirmation, contains at least a suggestion that Christ's thought took account of an element of moral infirmity and bondage in man's natural condition. In the line of this suggestion is the contrast which is drawn between the divine and the human in the question: "If ye then, being evil, know how to give good gifts unto your children, how much more shall your Father which is in heaven give good things to them that ask Him?"[1] This language seems to take for granted that those addressed admitted the common sinfulness of men. A like implication may

---

[1] Matt. vii. 11.

be discovered in what is said of the facility with which men enter into the broad as opposed to the narrow way.[1] The same may be said of the stress put upon repentance and upon the necessity of turning or being converted in order to gain entrance into the kingdom of heaven.[2] It is true that in each of these instances Christ pictured the actual moral state which is characteristic of grown men, and did not definitely assert that any part of the evil in that state is a matter of birth or inheritance. Still when we consider the trend both of Jewish and apostolic thinking, the more natural supposition is that Christ thought of the proneness of men to go astray as being in some measure an inborn tendency. His conception was not of the sombre Augustinian order. Neither was it of the Pelagian type. He regarded man as a mixed subject, having in himself the potentiality of a lofty ideal, but possessed also of wayward impulses, needing to pray habitually for forgiveness, and to watch incessantly against the wily assaults of evil.

It may be noticed, in respect of Christ's terminology as reported in the Synoptical Gospels, that it less definitely associates the moral evil in men with the flesh than is characteristic of the Pauline and the Johannine representation. The nearest approach to the phraseology of these later types is contained in the sentence, "Watch and pray that ye enter not into temptation: the spirit indeed is willing, but the flesh is weak."[3] This is as much as saying that the characteristic infirmity of man, or his susceptibility to temptation, is closely associated with the flesh as tending under certain conditions to

---

[1] Matt. vii. 13, 14.   [2] Matt. xviii. 3.   [3] Matt. xxvi. 41.

lassitude. On the other hand, however, it is not to be overlooked that Christ strongly accentuated the truth that the heart, as the centre of the moral personality, is the source of all the varieties of wickedness that come to manifestation in conduct.[1] This is the distinctive point of view in the Synoptical Gospels. The association of sin with the flesh is decidedly subordinate.

For the Christ who admitted so much of brightness into His thought of God and man in their mutual relations it was not natural to take a dark view of the world. He regarded it with a measure of sympathy and appreciation for which there was scanty precedent in Jewish thought and representation in the times proximate to His own age. Many touches in His discourses show that nature had to Him the worth of visible poetry. He saw upon it the light of His Father's countenance, and recognized in its varied forms tokens of His care and painstaking. The gospel representation, it is true, suggests that Christ's vision of the world was not without its shadowed side. He recognized the presence of an enemy who sows tares in the Lord's field. His language implies that He confessed that there was much of truth in the current Jewish conception respecting the working of Satan and his minions. But this recognition of a hostile force did not interfere with a predominant cheerfulness in His outlook upon the world. He knew the hostile force as one that quailed before His own word of authority, and viewed it as doomed to certain and utter defeat. In most striking and graphic expression of this

---

[1] Matt. xv. 18, 19; Mark. vii. 20-23.

confidence He exclaimed, "I beheld Satan fallen as lightning from heaven."[1]

VIII. — THE WITNESS OF CHRIST RESPECTING HIS OWN PERSON AND OFFICE.

An element of testimony is contained in the titles by which Christ preferred to designate Himself, among which "Son of Man" is the most frequently recurring. It is used in more than fifty distinct instances in the sayings of Christ as reported by the Synoptists. It has often been urged, and with a good degree of probability, that Dan. vii. 13 afforded an influential precedent as respects the use of this name. In that passage, it is true, no distinct individual is certainly specified. "One like a Son of Man," it is said, "came with the clouds of heaven" — that is, one in a human form, and therefore representing a kingdom of a higher order than those symbolized by the animal forms previously pictured.

---

[1] Luke x. 18. As was intimated in another connection, on such a theme as the agency of angels and demons it might be expected that Christ, to a considerable extent, would accommodate Himself to current forms of representation. Just how far He went in this accommodation is a question that is difficult to settle. Opinion is divided, but leans increasingly to the conclusion that very little dogmatic content ought to be put into the words of Christ in this relation. A writer as little given to adventurous criticism as Professor Stevens remarks: "The language of Jesus is pictorial and His purpose in speaking on such topics always terminates on ethical and spiritual instruction, and not on giving information respecting the acts of superhuman spirits. . . . Whether demon-possession be in reality a fact or a superstition, the authority of Jesus cannot fairly be cited for either the one or the other view of it." (The Theology of the New Testament, pp. 90, 91.)

But in proportion as a vital Messianic expectation wrought in Israel it was natural that the picture of a son of man should be made to denote a specific personality, the ideal king who was to come. If we may trust the conclusions of eminent investigators as to the pre-Christian origin of the middle portion of the Book of Enoch, the picture of Daniel had already been construed in this sense, at least by individuals, before Christ began His public ministry. Still there is no reason to suppose that in popular thought the term Son of Man was clearly understood to be an equivalent of Messiah. It might be understood in that way; at the same time it was not so well naturalized in this significance as spontaneously and uniformly to be so interpreted.[1] Accordingly it was admirably adapted to the use of Christ. His discretion warned Him against an open proclamation of His Messiahship at the beginning of His public teaching. The current notion respecting the office of the Messiah was decidedly unlike His own. An open assumption of the name, therefore, would at once have brought upon Him the pressure of a clamorous expectation which He must needs disappoint to the certain embarrassment of His ministry. The term Son of Man was indicative of a special vocation, but its sense was so far veiled that men were left to query whether it stood precisely for the Messiah. It was suggestive without being too openly declarative.[2]

---

[1] Compare Dalman, Words of Jesus, p. 306.

[2] Professor Charles concludes that the Book of Enoch served as the more immediate source of Christ's characterization of Himself as the Son of Man, but also that an altered signification was given to the term

From this exposition it follows that in calling Himself the Son of Man Christ was employing a modest and prudent form for the expression of His Messianic consciousness. The central meaning of the name, as He used it, was Messianic. It was not chosen specifically as a means of attesting His sense of complete partnership in human nature. Nevertheless in a negative way it does bear evidence to that truth. Christ could never have been partial to a name which was distinctly contrary to his self-consciousness. His habitual use of the term "Son of Man" shows at least that there was no opposition in his thought or feeling to the idea of genuine implication in the human race.[1]

---

by importing into it Isaiah's conception of the Servant of Jehovah. "Whilst, therefore, in adopting the title 'the Son of Man' from Enoch, Jesus made from the outset supernatural claims, yet these supernatural claims were to be vindicated not after the external Judaistic conceptions of the Book of Enoch, but in a revelation of the Father in a sinless and redemptive life, death and resurrection" (Book of Enoch, pp. 314–316). The direct borrowing on the part of Jesus from the pseudepigraphic writing may be doubted, but His use of the title in question does in truth remind both of the lofty personality depicted in the Book of Enoch and of Isaiah's suffering servant of Jehovah.

[1] A few words on an eccentric theory may be in place, the theory, namely, that Jesus never used the term *Son of Man* " either to claim Messiahship in any sense, or to hint that He was a ' mere man,' or 'the true man,' but in some pregnant utterances used it in reference to 'man' in general, his duties, rights, and privileges" (Nathaniel Schmidt, The Prophet of Nazareth). The ground for the theory is the contention that Son of Man (*bar nasha*) in Aramaic is a generic term for *man*. The contention may be admitted, and still the conclusion based upon it be regarded as decidedly incredible. Indeed it is vastly easier to believe that Jesus gave such connections to the generic term as to make plain His design to apply it in a specific sense to Himself than either that He uttered some general statements about *man*, or that the evangelists

In applying to Himself the complementary term "Son of God" (or at least "the Son" in connections where the sense requires the name of God to be understood) Christ undoubtedly meant to claim a relation of special fellowship and moral identity with the Father in heaven. He could not have meant less than this. The tone of His teaching implies, it is true, that it is the common privilege of men to be the sons of God. But it is to be noticed that in no instance does He place Himself on a parity with men in general in respect of sonship. On the contrary, the unmistakable import of the connections in which he names himself the Son is that He enjoys singular intimacy with the Father and has singular prerogatives over the divine kingdom. It may not be capable of proof from the Synoptical accounts that He meant by this title to claim sonship in the metaphysical sense. What is certain is that His use of the title in the Synoptical Gospels indicates a consciousness of an unique and lofty union with God, and that a union so exceptional, even though the primary stress be upon its ethical character, is a congenial basis for the idea of a metaphysical sonship.

Beyond the use of these titles Christ gave manifold illustrations of the order of self-consciousness which

---

represented Jesus as customarily using a form of self-designation which he never employed. The entire New Testament outside of the Gospels testifies by its mode of referring to Jesus that the early Christians had no inclination on their own account to name their Master the Son of Man, and thus supplies a cogent reason for inferring that the report of the evangelists about the employment of the term by Jesus rested on a vital tradition. As respects the verdict of New Testament scholarship, while several names are cited in favor of the theory in question, it is emphatically repudiated by the majority of critics.

dwelt in Him by the position which directly or indirectly He assigned to Himself. A review of His words compels the conclusion, that, with all the tokens He gave of real identification with humanity, His self-consciousness rose to a great height above the common human plane. He makes no account of His Davidic lineage and intimates to the Pharisees that the true thought of the Messiah, in harmony with the commonly accepted significance of a sentence in the Psalms, accounts Him David's Lord.[1] In the parable of the vineyard He represents servants of the owner as being sent to receive the fruits, and last of all the beloved Son,[2] thus placing Himself in a distinctly higher category than the prophetical messengers to Israel. In emphasizing the impossibility of forecasting the day of judgment, He notes that the day is hidden from the knowledge of men, angels, and the Son, indicating by this order of subjects His consciousness that the Son's prerogative stands above that of the whole creaturely universe.[3] He so identifies Himself with the kingdom of heaven which He proclaims as to allow of no antithesis between relation to it and relation to Himself. He pronounces those blessed who are persecuted for His sake.[4] He declares that the giving of a cup of cold water in His name shall have its reward.[5] He claims love and allegiance superior to those demanded by any earthly ties.[6] He represents that confession or denial of Him before men shall earn confession or denial before the Father and the angels.[7]

---

[1] Matt. xxii. 45; Luke xx. 44. [2] Matt. xxi. 33–39; Luke xx. 9–15
[3] Matt. xxiv. 36; Mark xiii. 32. [4] Matt. v. 11.
[5] Matt. x. 42; Mark ix. 41. [6] Matt. x. 37; Luke xiv. 26.
[7] Matt x. 32, 33; Mark viii. 38; Luke xii. 8, 9, ix. 26.

He pictures the awards of the great day of judgment as apportioned according as affection or despite has been shown to Himself.[1] He declares Himself greater than the temple,[2] Lord of the Sabbath,[3] qualified to forgive sins.[4] He characterizes Himself as the stronger than the strong man, the one able to vanquish Satan.[5] He makes Himself the one competent revealer of the mind of God, since no one knoweth the Son save the Father, neither doth any know the Father save the Son.[6] He promises to be in the midst where two or three are gathered in His name,[7] and to supply speech and wisdom to His disciples when they shall be called to answer before adversaries.[8] He utters His message directly, or in His own name, instead of employing the customary prophetical formula, "Thus saith the Lord." He claims to be endowed with all authority in heaven and earth.[9] He describes the angels, whom Jewish thought made the retinue of Jehovah, as sent forth at His behest and serving as His messengers or servants.[10] He represents finally that all nations are to be gathered before Him and to receive at His hands the awards of eternity.[11] To suppose such a line of expressions to come from a simple human consciousness, in one too clear and well-balanced to be subject to measureless illusion, is to suppose what our own experience can never make credible.

---

[1] Matt. xxv. 34–46. [2] Matt. xii. 6.
[3] Matt xii. 8; Mark ii. 28; Luke vi. 5.
[4] Matt. ix. 2–6; Mark ii. 4–10; Luke v. 20–24, vii. 47.
[5] Matt. xii. 28, 29; Mark iii. 27; Luke xi, 21, 22.
[6] Matt. xi. 27; Luke x. 22. [7] Matt. xviii 20.
[8] Luke xxi. 15. [9] Matt. xxviii. 18.
[10] Matt. xxiv. 30, 31; Mark xiii. 27. [11] Matt. xxv. 31–46.

A sane mind in beings conditioned as we are knows itself to be vastly remote from such an order of self-consciousness as is reflected in the Synoptical Gospels.

In respect of trinitarianism the Synoptical Gospels furnish data for inference rather than formal statements. The closest verbal approach to the trinitarian conception is contained in the injunction of baptism as reported by Matthew.[1] The larger basis, however, for trinitarian conviction is given in the total representation of the position and offices of the Son and the Holy Spirit. The heinousness of the sin against the latter argues plainly for His divine rank.[2] As respects the distinct personality of the Holy Spirit the Synoptical Gospels afford no more explicit indication than that contained in the baptismal injunction.

The redemptive work of Christ as related to His death is treated very briefly in the Synoptical Gospels. The scantiness of the reference, however, is no cause for surprise. The disciples were not well prepared for a message on the theme of the redemptive virtue of Christ's death. The notion that the Messiah should go the way of suffering and death was decidedly foreign to their minds. The gospel narratives show that they were stumbled by this thought, and had not become reconciled to it up to the consummation of the tragedy on Calvary. To minds thus inappreciative and resisting the accomplished fact of the death of their Lord and Master must be present before they could be in the proper mood to explore its meaning. It accords therefore with the his-

---

[1] Matt. xxviii. 19.   [2] Matt. xii. 31; Mark iii. 29; Luke xii. 10.

torical conditions that on this theme only a few sentences fell from the lips of Christ. That these assign a high importance to the freely accepted death is indisputable. Sentences like these, " The Son of Man came to give His life a ransom for many,"[1] "This is my blood of the covenant shed for many unto remission of sins,"[2] leave no room to doubt that in the thought of Christ His death was a crowning factor in the establishment of the gracious economy which He represented. The precise ground or reason of the efficacy attached to His death is not stated; neither is it suggested with any such degree of definiteness as to give a basis for a clear-cut exclusive theory. The advocate of the moral influence theory can find support for his contention in the fact that in one of the connections in which Christ forecast His sufferings and death He went on to speak of the necessity and the fruitfulness of self-denial in His disciples generally.[3] This order of association, it may be urged, suggests that Christ's death is to be reckoned as simply the supreme specimen of the power of self-sacrifice to further the interests of righteousness. On the other hand, the one who prefers to find an element of vicarious satisfaction in the death of Christ can point to the fact that in the

---

[1] Matt. xx. 28; Mark x. 45.

[2] Matt. xxvi. 28; Mark xiv. 24; Luke xxii. 20. The fact that only in Matthew's report of the words of Christ is the shedding of the blood expressly associated with the remission of sins, is very inadequate ground for denying that such association was intended. All three Gospels designate the blood as the blood of a covenant shed for others. This is sacrificial language, and under the given conditions is most naturally construed as pointing to a ground or means of remission.

[3] Matt. xvi. 21-25; Mark viii. 31-35; Luke ix. 22-24.

sentence on giving His life as a ransom for many the preposition used is ἀντὶ, the very word which would have been employed if the design was to express the notion of substitution. To neither theory, however, do the words of Christ, taken by themselves, give any distinct and exclusive right of way. To reach a definite outcome on this subject it is necessary to go beyond the Synoptical representation and to take the unfolding apostolic consciousness as presumably reaching the essential points in the meaning of the death upon the cross.

IX. — CHRIST'S TEACHING ON THE PROGRESS AND CONSUMMATION OF THE KINGDOM.

Notice was taken in a preceding section of the fact that many sayings of Christ picture the kingdom as destined to a gradual unfoldment in the world. It was observed also that in some of these sayings the kingdom was viewed preëminently as an interior personal treasure. It remains to be noted here that Christ's conception of divine fatherhood and human brotherhood logically implied a very decided stress upon the social character of the kingdom. In appropriating the word ἐκκλησία, or Church, He made use of a term which gives expression to this social character. The Church is the kingdom viewed particularly in respect of the interrelation of its subjects. It is the society formed under the new covenant. The name Church conveys somewhat more of an impression of organization, definiteness, and visibility than does the comparion term as employed in the Gospels. Only in its ideal character, or in so far as it stands for the actualized reign of God in the world, is the Church identical with the kingdom. The human and accidental elements which are inevitably connected with any organization upon earth, and which began to modify the Christian Church from the start, differenced it in a measure from the ideal which Christ expressed by the phrase kingdom of God or kingdom of heaven.

It is somewhat remarkable that only in the first of the Synoptical Gospels does the word Church occur. Matthew introduces it in two instances.[1] In the view of some critics this exclusive mention is a ground of suspicion, and they are inclined to argue that it is a sign of a catholicizing tendency, or a leaning to a pronounced ecclesiasticism, lying back of the composition of this particular Gospel. But this conclusion is not likely to win very wide acceptance. In the first place, Christ was debarred from speaking of a distinct society, apart from the Jewish communion, until it became appropriate to announce His certain rejection by organized Judaism; discourse respecting the Church that was to be founded upon His person and message was naturally deferred to the closing part of His ministry and rarely had place. Again the contents of the first Gospel do not agree with the supposition that its references to the Church were due outright to a catholicizing tendency. Whatever of churchly import one influenced by later ecclesiastical associations may attach to some of its sentences, it certainly contains statements which breathe the very opposite of a spirit of high ecclesiasticism. Once more, in dialect or verbal peculiarity Matthew's references to

---

[1] Matt. xvi. 18; xviii. 17.

the Church are such that it is difficult to believe that they were the offspring of a doctrinaire temper in the compiler. They sound rather like the unstudied products of the energetic spirit of Christ. Why Matthew alone should have recorded them is doubtless somewhat of a puzzle. But no one of the evangelists undertook to record everything, and in general it is impossible to explain every instance of selection or rejection on the part of a compiler. Matthew's record may indicate a superior interest in church organization; that he went outside of the facts is by no means proved.

While Christ forecast the existence of the Church, there is no evidence that He devised for it a specific constitution or scheme of polity. To take the words wherewith Christ responded to the confession of Peter in the sense of an ecclesiastical constitution does violence to the connection and to the whole spirit of Christ's message. The words square with the confession. In the unwavering intelligent confession of his Master as the Christ, the Son of the living God, Peter stood forth as the first Christian. Accordingly Christ appropriately contemplated him on the spot as the beginning of the foundation of His church, the first stone or rock upon which He might build the spiritual edifice that it was His vocation to establish in the world. It was the spiritual character of Peter revealed in the confession which suggested his serviceableness as a foundation. As this character was plainly not a matter for a legal transfer, so no hint was given of a transfer of Peter's place in the foundation to a line of official successors. The rational inference to be drawn was rather that those, and those only, who might be assimilated to the character of Peter as true confessors of Christ would be fitted to share the honor of a place in the foundation of the Church. To divorce the honorary words addressed to the apostle from their close association with a definite spiritual character in him, and to turn them into a charter for a perpetual official Roman primacy, is to indulge in such violence and wooden insipidity of exegesis that it is almost a wonder that even an intemperate hierarchical ambition could have reconciled itself to this shift.

The foregoing exposition of Peter's place in the foundation is very decidedly sustained by a consideration of the total message of Christ on the subject of binding and loosing. The prerogative which is associated with Peter in this matter is extended in a later reference to the disciples generally. In Matt. xviii. 18-20 we read, "Verily I say unto you, What things soever ye shall bind on earth shall be bound in heaven; and what things soever ye shall loose on earth shall be loosed in heaven. Again I say unto you, that if two of you shall agree on earth as touching anything that they shall ask, it shall be done for them of my Father which is in heaven. For where two or three are gathered together in my name, there am I in the midst of them." The passage taken in its entirety, as it promises the helpful presence of Christ to any company of faithful disciples, favors manifestly the possible execution by any such company of the office of binding and loosing. The foregoing context too is entirely favorable to this interpretation, as it points to duties universally incumbent on Christians and not merely on ecclesiastical rulers. Peter then in the matter of binding and loosing appears only as the first Christian, the typical disciple. No sort of exclusive lordship is assigned to him here. By parity of reasoning we may conclude that in the matter of serving as the foundation he figured simply as the first Christian, the typical disciple, and that it was not in the thought of Christ to affirm for him any exclusive function. How far the mind of Christ was from the notion of concentrated ecclesiastical authority is intimated by these words: "Ye know that the rulers of the Gentiles lord it over them, and their great ones exercise authority over them. Not so shall it be among you: but whosoever would become great among you shall be your minister; and whosoever would be first among you shall be your servant."[1]

It is quite evident that in the strong language about binding and loosing addressed to Peter, and then to Christian disciples generally, Christ contemplated the Church in its ideal character. Only an ideal Church, or one thoroughly dominated by the spirit of Christ, has a guaranty that its binding and loosing on earth will agree with the binding and loosing in heaven. In so far as the Church gives place to an unchristian temper, and departs from the path of spiritual illumination, it must be seriously exposed to faulty procedure in binding and loosing. The notion of an infallibility which is capable of divorce from holy character belongs to a magical and pagan scheme, and is utterly contrary to the ethical standpoint of Christ. As respects the meaning of the

---
[1] Matt. xx. 25, 26.

power to bind and loose, it may be taken either in a legislative or a disciplinary sense. In the former sense it denotes a prerogative of prohibition and permission in matters of conduct, a faculty of judging as to what is compatible with the Christian standing. In the latter sense it signifies a faculty to put on and to take off censures. Either of the two senses naturally implies the other, since rules of conduct are made to be administered, and administration rests back upon rules or maxims. The words of Christ in this relation, therefore, contemplated a spiritual brotherhood in which the collective moral sense, under the guidance of the Holy Spirit, should sustain an essentially correct standard of conduct and effect a corresponding administration of discipline.

The special training which Christ gave a special group of His disciples implies that He designed for this group a sort of leadership. As originally instituted, however, the apostolic office was rather in the prophetical line than in that of the ecclesiastical magistrate. The apostles were first of all preeminent witnesses and teachers as having had the advantage of a preeminent tuition. Doubtless their leadership in these respects caused their judgment to be deferred to, and tended as the years passed to clothe them with a very considerable, though not strictly defined, jurisdiction. But this came about by a natural evolution and the unforced consent of the Christian body. There is not a line of evidence for the notion that Christ made out for the apostles any precise scheme of administrative prerogatives. He sent them forth as missionaries and prophets of the new dispensation, to win such authority as the faithful fulfillment of their missionary and prophetical vocation might bring to them.

It accords with the profoundly ethical character of Christ's teaching that very little prominence was given therein to rites and ceremonies. All that the Synoptical Gospels contain in this line is a few sentences relative to baptism and the eucharist. Respecting the former indeed positive injunction is limited to one sentence recorded by a single evangelist.[1] This one sentence too has not lacked a challenge from the side of criticism. It is alleged that the sentence in which Matthew publishes the command to baptize, with its trinitarian phraseology, is not after the style of speaking characteristic of Christ, and furthermore that it disagrees with the implication of the New Testament that baptism was primarily in the name of Christ simply. In reply, it may be said on the first point that the doctrine of Christ was eminently the doctrine of Father, Son, and Spirit, and that, while ordinarily He did not take pains to collocate these names, there is nothing incredible in the supposition that He may have done so in issuing a final commission to His disciples. As regards the second point, a twofold consideration is properly brought forward. On the one hand the assumption that the so-called formulary in Matthew, supposing it to have been extant in the apostolic era, would necessarily have been taken as a formulary proper, may be questioned. A parallel instance legitimates a doubt on this particular. The New Testament gives no indication of the use of the Lord's prayer as a liturgical form. But, as has been

---

[1] Matt. xxviii. 19.

aptly urged, "this does not prove that the Lord's prayer was not spoken by Jesus. It only proves that the age of the apostles was an age of freedom from forms. When, however, we come to the Didaché (viii. 2, 3), we find Christians enjoined to repeat the Lord's prayer three times a day."[1] On the other hand, there is room to question whether in the references to baptism in Acts and the epistles there was a design to give the precise formula that was used or counted obligatory. The stress was undoubtedly upon the confession of Christ in baptism. In connection with the first converts it was a matter of course that they confessed faith in the Father and in the Holy Spirit. The specifically new element of belief which they were called upon solemnly to profess was faith in Jesus of Nazareth as the Christ, the Son of God, sent to be the Saviour of the world. Naturally, therefore, emphasis was put upon the fact of their being baptized into Christ or in the name of Christ. That this expression could be used in a non-liturgical sense at the very time when the liturgy prescribed baptism in the threefold name is illustrated in the Didaché. While this writing describes the initial Christian rite as "baptism into the name of the Lord" (ix. 5), in its liturgical instruction it enjoins that the rite shall be performed in "the name of the Father, and of the Son, and of the Holy Ghost" (vii. 1). Very likely for a considerable interval there was no distinct sense of obligation to follow a stereotyped phrase. We conclude, then, that an overplus of dogmatism enters into the assertion that Christ could not possibly have spoken the words which

---

[1] Lambert, The Sacraments of the New Testament, pp. 50–52.

Matthew records relative to baptism.[1] At the same time, there is little motive to insist that Matthew repeats here the precise words of the Master. It serves every practical end to suppose that they express essentially His intention. That Christ purposed and sanctioned such a rite as baptism is made probable by the fact that its administration seems to have been treated as a matter of course from the first days of Christianity.

As in connection with baptism, so also in relation to the eucharistic celebration, little in the way of formal injunction can be cited from the lips of Christ. The Gospels represent the Master as taking the eucharistic elements, delivering them to the disciples, and expressing their significance.[2] No plain command is recorded for a repetition of the symbolic acts on future occasions, unless it be in the words of Luke, "This do in remembrance of me"; and it is possible to regard these words as an unauthorized addition to a more authentic text in Matthew or Mark. A suspicion that this is the case finds harborage in the fact that manuscript authority on the text of Luke is divided.[3] But while the special

---

[1] Against such an assertion the following words of a very competent investigator, relative to Matt. xxviii. 19, may appropriately be cited: "I have no trouble in referring back this form of baptism to the Lord Himself, and think that Matthew's Gospel derived the formulary from the practice of the church at Jerusalem." (Kattenbusch, Zeitschrift für Theologie und Kirche, 5te Heft, 1901.)

[2] Matt. xxvi. 26-29; Mark xiv. 22-25; Luke xxii. 15-20.

[3] See Sanday, Hastings' Dictionary of the Bible, II. 636; Lambert, The Sacraments of the New Testament, pp. 245, 246. The former follows Westcott and Hort in excluding the phrase in question. The latter notices that recent criticism tends very largely to retain the phrase. On this side are mentioned Julicher, Schmiedel, Cremer, Schultzen, Schaefer, Clemen, Schweitzer, Bering, and Menzies.

statement in the third Gospel may not be an unequivocal ground of belief in our Lord's intention to found a permanent rite, a basis for such a belief is not wanting. The association which the several Gospels make between the transactions of the last supper and a covenant conveys the impression that these transactions were meant to have an institutional character, since a covenant in Christ's blood is a matter which concerns the disciples of Christ to the end of time, and is intrinsically suitable for a recurring celebration. Very decidedly reinforcing this impression are the traces of a dominant conviction in the early Christian body. Paul writing within about twenty-five years of the death of Christ, expressed the most undoubting conviction that He established the eucharist as a memorial rite to be repeated in His Church till His coming.[1] Now Paul was not so much of a ritualist that he should have had the slightest disposition to invent a rite on his own account. In the essentials of his interpretation he undoubtedly expressed the consensus of apostolic conviction. We hold then that the historic evidence favors the institution of baptism and the eucharist by Christ, that is, His institution or commendation of the emblematic rites bearing those names.

---

[1] The words of Paul, "I received of the Lord that which also I delivered unto you" (1 Cor. xi. 23), must be understood to mean that his instructions to the Corinthians had been based on trustworthy reports as to what transpired at the last supper, these reports being the medium through which the will of the Lord had been transmitted to himself. The supposition that the apostle meant to claim that he received through direct revelation from heaven, at a time when living witnesses of the facts were at hand, a detailed knowledge of Christ's procedure at the supper which preceded His crucifixion, is simply incredible.

Of baptism and the eucharist viewed as parts of a scheme of ecclesiastical magic there is no proper suggestion in the Synoptical Gospels.

In the gospel picture no wide interval is interposed between the beginning and the end of the dispensation. It is more natural for a fervent religious idealism to glance toward the final outcome than to give prolonged attention to intermediate stages. In the case of Christ there was, moreover, a special occasion to paint the scene of glory lying at the end. He was obliged to admit deep shadows into the foreground, to outline a painful and enigmatic scene of suffering, shame, and death. In face of these things it was necessary to hearten the disciples with a glimpse of the triumph lying beyond the shame and the seeming defeat. Therefore Christ passed rapidly over the nearer events in the progress of the Church or kingdom and cheered the disciples with a vision of the grand consummation.

As Christ felt authorized to assume a most intimate connection between the kingdom and His own person, He could consistently identify a triumph of the kingdom with His own triumph, and in pictorial language describe it as a coming of the Son of man, that is, a manifestation of the victorious life and activity of the Christ whom Jewish hatred sought to bind with the fetters of death and the grave. A spiritual outburst like that of Pentecost, or a great judgment like that which sealed the fate of Jerusalem, as it marked a signal era in the progress of the kingdom, showed forth Christ as the living head of the kingdom, and could be accounted in a manner

His coming or self-manifestation. Some sentences in the Synoptical Gospels are perhaps construed with least difficulty when the reference to Christ's coming is taken in this sense.[1] But there are other sentences, such as some of those in the eschatological discourse reported in Matt. xxiv and Mark xiii, which certainly seem to refer to a coming that is coincident with the closing up of the dispensation, a great final coming which is to supplement the office of every preceding visitation and bring the triumph of the kingdom to a perfect fulfillment.

With respect to the time of His coming Christ declined to make a statement. He declared indeed that it was unknown to men, angels, and even to the Son.[2] Some exegetes, it is true, have concluded on the basis of the connected statement, "This generation shall not pass away till all these things be accomplished,"[3] that Christ expected the end of the dispensation to fall within the generation then living. But this involves irreconcilable disagreements. How could Christ confidently affirm that the end was so near and then solemnly disclaim knowledge of the day and hour? It has been said indeed that He thought of the great consummation as close at hand, certain to overtake that generation, but wished to declare Himself uninformed of the precise day and hour. Such an explanation, however, supposes a technicality which is to be declared alien to the speech of Christ. To locate a supreme crisis within the limits

---

[1] Matt. xvi. 28; Mark ix. 1; Luke ix. 27. On the probable displacement of Matt. x. 23 see Stevens, Theology of the New Testament, p. 150.

[2] Matt. xxiv. 36; Mark xiii. 32.   [3] Matt. xxiv. 34; Mark xiii. 30.

of a specific generation was coming to such close quarters that it is immensely improbable that after doing this Christ would have felt called upon solemnly to asserverate that the day and hour of that crisis were unknown to all beings in the universe except the Father. Moreover it contradicts foregoing statements of Christ to suppose that He looked for the end in that generation. For example, shortly before He uttered the eschatological discourse, He had intimated in the parable of the marriage of the king's son [1] that judgment should befall the Jews in the destruction of their city, and that the outside peoples should be brought in to take their place in the kingdom. A representation like this naturally implies a very considerable interval between the overthrow of Jerusalem and the closing up of the dispensation. To conceive that Christ thought that the untutored Gentile nations could be instructed and brought to the status of intelligent and faithful subjects of the kingdom in a few months or years is to conceive of a thing that is contradictory both to the extraordinary insight of Christ and to His explicit teaching on the method of the unfoldment of the kingdom. Our conclusion then is that the evangelists in compiling the sayings of Christ respecting the end, either by omission or imperfect arrangement, have obscured the original connection of some of His words.[2] It involves too much of self-contradiction on the part of Christ to grant that He fixed

---

[1] Matt. xxii. 1-10.

[2] Compare the verdict of Moffatt: "As they stand the Synoptic apocalpyses cannot be brought within the limits of a single personality or situation without self-contradiction "(The Historical New Testa-

the end of the dispensation within the limits of that generation.

It may have been observed that in the above discussion we have declined a means of escaping difficulty which has commended itself to a number of commentators, namely the assumption that the discourse in Matt. xxiv and Mark xiii does not look beyond the catastrophe of Jerusalem's downfall. It belonged, they contend, to the graphic prophetical style to portray any great historical crisis by figures indicative of a general convulsion. It is not necessary therefore to suppose that the strong imagery employed was meant to picture the end of the world. The foresight of the overthrow of the holy city and the nation was a sufficient warrant, before the prophetical standard, for the language used. Now, in response to this plea, we grant that prophetical language is not to be measured by the rules of sober prose. Nevertheless we are not able to persuade ourselves that the evangelists who recorded such words as are contained in Matt. xxiv. 29–31 and Mark xiii. 24–27 believed that anything less was pictured therein than the supreme crisis, the end of the dispensation. The coming described in this connection has every appearance of identity with that which in Matt. xxv. 31 is made the immediate antecedent of universal judgment.

It should be noticed that in the Synoptical representation the final coming of Christ is treated as if identical

---

ment, p 641); also the conclusion of Haupt, that the eschatological discourses in question are a mosaic, composed of many pieces, some of which in the process of combination have not gained an appropriate setting (Die eschatologischen Aussagen Jesu, pp. 21–45).

with His glorious manifestation. No definite local association is given to it. Nothing is said about installation upon an earthly theatre. The coming is placed in immediate conjunction with the act of judging men and portioning out eternal rewards.

Concerning the resurrection which New Testament thought closely associated with the final coming of Christ the Synoptical Gospels offer no very definite specifications. In responding to the Sadducees Christ spoke of the dead as being raised, and He must have understood that His language would naturally be taken by the people in the sense of a bodily resurrection.[1] At the same time, it may be noticed that the argument which He adduces makes rather for the general truth of a vital immortality than for the fact of a reinvestment of the dead with bodies. It is to be observed also that His language is somewhat antagonistic to the idea of a literal reproduction of the present body, since He likens the subjects of the resurrection to the angels in heaven. Whether the wicked are included in the resurrection is not definitely indicated. Some find in the statement that participants in the resurrection are to be as the angels in heaven a token of the exclusion of the wicked. But the inference has a very slender basis, since in the given connection the main intent of Christ was not to define who shall share in the resurrection, but to bring out the fact that family institutions are foreign to the resurrection state. Two phrases of Luke's Gospel may be cited with some plausibility for the limitation of the resurrection to the righteous, mention being made of the "resurrection of

---

[1] Matt. xxii. 23–32; Mark xii. 18–27.

the just,"[1] and the "sons of the resurrection" being characterized as "sons of God."[2] On the other hand, Luke represents Christ as saying that *all* live unto God.[3] Moreover, it may be noticed that the language of Christ, as reported by the Synoptists generally, assumes that all men are subjects of the final judgment, and that it is in line with New Testament thought to reckon those called to judgment as subjects of the resurrection.[4]

The language associated with the theme of the general judgment implies that the awards rendered therein were meant to be understood as expressing final destiny.[5] The word αἰώνιος, it is true, does not necessarily signify endless duration; but that is the only natural sense to give it in a passage which has so distinct an air of finality as belongs to the sentences descriptive of the great day of judgment. As respects the infliction of fire which is foreshadowed, it needs only to be remembered that it belonged to the prophetical dialect to symbolize retribution by the element of fire. There is no more occasion to take the word in a literal sense than there is to so construe the outer darkness which also was used as an emblem of punishment.[6]

---

[1] Luke xiv. 14. [2] Luke xx 36. [3] Luke xx. 38.
[4] John v. 28, 29; Rev. xx. 12, 13; Acts xxiv. 15.
[5] Matt. xxv. 46; Mark ix. 43-48.
[6] Matt viii. 12, xxv. 30.

CHAPTER III

PORTIONS OF THE NEW TESTAMENT MORE OR LESS AKIN TO THE SYNOPTICAL GOSPELS IN THEIR REPRESENTATION OF A PRIMITIVE TYPE OF CHRISTIAN TEACHING

I. — Consideration of the Proper Compass of the Chapter.

THE qualifying clause, "more or less," which is put into the title of the chapter, is by no means superfluous. No subsequent portion of the New Testament reflects precisely the content of the Synoptical Gospels. Either a falling short of the level of the Synoptical teaching is noticeable, or else there is a perceptible advance, in respect of theological construction, beyond the letter of that teaching. Still it is not wholly arbitrary to assign to certain books somewhat of a special association with the type of the first three Gospels. They do not show, at least in a conspicuous degree, the effect of the great currents which came in during the apostolic age to color New Testament speech and thought, whether in the masterful influence of Paul, or the idealistic speculation of Alexandria. They have, moreover, this direct bond of association with the Synoptical Gospels, that they reflect very largely a Jewish environment. However much they may differ from one another, they reveal in common an intimate connection with Judaism.

1. Under this description belongs in the first place the earlier part of the Book of Acts (chaps. i.–xv). In respect of time of composition, it is true, no claim to a specially primitive character can be asserted for this book. While there is no adequate reason for questioning the unanimous verdict of the early Church that the Luke whose name is connected with the third Gospel was its author,[1] it cannot be proved that he wrote it before the closing decades of the first century. It has been argued that the writer of the history must have laid down his pen by the year 64, otherwise he would have recounted events of such marked interest as the Neronian persecution and the martyrdom of the great heroes of his story. But this is a precarious ground for a positive conclusion. A politic regard for the interest of a party that had no certain standing-room in the empire may have led to silence on a Roman persecution; or the author may have been interrupted in his task and had no opportunity to complete it; or it may have answered the purpose of his treatise, as being very largely

---

[1] The principal considerations which may be urged for the Lucan authorship have been rendered as follows: "It is the one assumption which gives a natural and adequate explanation (1) of the fact that at the end of the second century and at the beginning of the third, St. Luke was accounted its author by writers representing the chief churches of Christendom; (2) of internal characteristics of the Book, the traces of medical phraseology in the language and the abrupt transition from the third person of the historian to the first person of the eye-witness. Further (3) it enables us to give a reasonable account of the sources whence the writer derived his knowledge of the events, widely separated in time and place, which he records." (Chase, The Credibility of the Book of the Acts of the Apostles, p. 28. See also Hawkins, Horae Synopticae, pp. 148–154.

a missionary sketch, to have traced the progress of Christianity from Jerusalem to its establishment under apostolic oversight in the imperial capital. It is thus quite gratuitous to identify the point at which the history closes with the time of composition. Two or three decades may have intervened. To grant this, however, does not necessarily collide with the supposition of a relatively primitive cast in the teachings of the first part of Acts. Written memorials probably antedated the time when Luke wrote, and were utilized by him. Many scholars think that they find evidence that this was the case, though the documentary basis does not stand out prominently on account of the free way in which Luke used his materials.[1] But let the method of composition have been what it may, the theology of this portion of the New Testament has unmistakably a simple, unelaborated, archaic cast. Critics like Holtzmann, while very free to challenge the historical character of various features in the opening chapters of Acts, confess that their theology, especially as embodied in the reported speeches of Peter, conveys an impression of a primitive Christian consciousness.[2]

2. The second of the canonical books which may be given a place under the title of the present chapter is

---

[1] Among those who have expressed doubt as to the possibility of distinguishing successfully the sources of Acts are Baur, Schwegler, Hilgenfeld, Weizsacker, Holtzmann, Beyschlag, Pfleiderer, and Riehm. On the other hand, Zeller, Overbeck, Wendt, J. Weiss, and Jungst have favored the possibility of discriminating these sources, at least to a considerable extent.

[2] Neutestamentliche Theologie, I. 374. Compare Schmiedel, article "Acts" in Encyclopaedia Biblica.

the Epistle of James. As in case of Acts, the warrant for including this epistle here has little to do with chronology. In fact, on the point of the date of the Epistle of James critical opinion is widely divided. One theory makes it among the earliest, if not the earliest, book of the New Testament. According to another theory it is a second century writing and one of the very latest in the canon. The advocates of the former allege: (1) One who wished without good warrant to pose as a leader, and to assume the prerogative to address fellow-Christians at large, would naturally have been inclined to borrow a high title. Accordingly the modest title employed, namely, "servant of God and of the Lord Jesus Christ," bespeaks faith in the honesty of the writer, and makes it credible that he was actually a man of essentially apostolic rank, such as James of Jerusalem is known to have been. (2) The absence of any reference to the antithesis between the Mosaic law and the grace of Christ is a token of a time anterior to the controversy in which Paul faced the Judaizers and argued so vehemently for Christian freedom. (3) If it is to be concluded that either of the two took note of the statements of the other, it is more likely that Paul repeated words of James and guarded against a one-sided meaning that might easily be put upon them than that James undertook to criticise statements of Paul. (4) Were the Epistle of James a late writing, we should expect to find in it more traces of the Christian dialect as modified by the influence of Paul's writings.

In behalf of the opposing view it is claimed: (1) There is no certain witness to the existence of the Epistle of

James before the time of Origen. Some portions of First Peter, First Clement, and the Shepherd of Hermas resemble, it is true, statements in the Epistle of James. But the resemblances in most instances are not very specific, and can be explained on the ground of the familiarity of the writers with the same sources. Moreover, if this explanation should be regarded as inadequate for certain items of resemblance, it would still stand in question whether James was not the borrower. So far at least as First Peter is concerned criticism is inclined to affirm that the debt was on the side of James. (2) The epistle in several passages gives a picture of a worldliness and spiritual poverty which cannot be supposed to have been characteristic of an age of primitive zeal and purity, a picture which is first paralleled in the second century writing, the Shepherd of Hermas. (3) The epistle in its references to law never denotes the Mosaic code in its historic sense. It uses the word rather in an abstract and general sense, such as one brought up in Judaism and imbued with its associations would not naturally have appropriated. The usage is a sign of a very considerable journey from the plane of Jewish thought and association. (4) The epistle is shown to be post-Pauline in that it presupposes an abuse of Pauline formulas and takes pains sharply to correct the abuse.

Our purpose does not make it necessary closely to weigh the relative force of these opposing lines of argument. We content ourselves with expressing the conviction that the Epistle of James must be regarded as post-Pauline, at least subsequent to the Epistle to the Romans. Mayor and Zahn, who contend for the early date of the epistle, equally with Harnack, Julicher, and Holtzmann, who argue for a late date, admit that the parallelism between certain expressions in the two epistles shows that one of them took account of the other. The parallelism is certainly very marked. Paul says, "If Abraham was justified by works, he hath whereof to glory" (Rom. iv. 2.) James says, "Was not Abraham our father justified by works, in that he offered up Isaac his son upon the altar?" (ii. 21). Paul says, "We reckon therefore that a man is justified by faith apart from the works of the law" (Rom. iii. 28). James says, "Ye see that by works a man is justified and not only by faith" (ii. 24). It is to be noticed too that in citing Gen. xv. 6, in connection with the verses quoted, both epistles differ in the same way from the Septuagint, reading $\dot{\epsilon}\pi\acute{\iota}\sigma\tau\epsilon\upsilon\sigma\epsilon\nu$ $\delta\grave{\epsilon}$ instead of $\kappa\alpha\grave{\iota}$ $\dot{\epsilon}\pi\acute{\iota}\sigma\tau\epsilon\upsilon\sigma\epsilon\nu$. Now, it is next to impossible that such a list of verbal correspondences should have been simply accidental; and we are only left to ask which epistle took account of the other. Here we cannot agree with Mayor and some others who hold that the reference is on the side of Romans. The language of James gives more the impression of a direct challenge than that of Paul, and the natural conclusion is that the challenged sentiment had already been given unequivocal expression. Moreover, there is nothing known to us in the early history of Christianity which suggests that any occasion for such a strain as that of James could have arisen before Paul's struggle with the Judaizers had led him to proclaim in most emphatic terms the primacy of faith in the matter of justification. The supposition that the occasion came to James from the side of Judaism is not by any means adapted to carry conviction. Sentences emphatically laudatory of faith may indeed have been spoken by some of the rabbis. But there is no assurance that expressions of this order, even if extant at all in the apostolic age, were sufficiently current to be likely to influence those addressed by James. Then, too, it is to be noticed that the use of strong words in praise of the virtue of faith is quite a different matter from openly drawing an antithesis between faith and works to the abridgment of the province of the latter in relation to salvation. We surmise that investigation can never make credible the supposition that a procedure of this sort was sufficiently current in the Judaism of the first century to create a strong demand for rebuttal. Surely not a sentence of the Gospels or of the Pauline epistles conveys the impression that it was characteristic of contemporary Judaism to hold up the notion of salvation by the way of faith as opposed to that of works. The natural inference from these records is the very opposite. Let it be observed that the question here is not whether James was seriously apart from Paul in doctrinal thinking. The question is rather, Did he criticise verbal statements which are actually found with Paul, and which may be presumed to have come to his notice either by the citation of another from an epistle of Paul or by his own perusal of such epistle ? This latter question we are constrained to answer in the affirmative on the grounds just stated.[1] But while granting chronological posteri-

---

[1] Mayor, in his Commentary, endeavors to support his contention for the priority of the epistle of James by citing several statements in the

ority, we may still affirm affiliation with a primitive theological type. Whether later than Romans by a short or a long interval, the Epistle of James is associated with an early stage of doctrinal construction. By general consent it has numerous points of connection with the Synoptical teaching, especially with the sermon on the mount as reported by Matthew.[1] It is essentially a compendium of Jewish-Christian ethics. In so slight a degree does it reflect matured Christian theology that a respectable critic has contended that the epistle, with the exception of two or three brief interpolations, was of pre-Christian origin.[2] But this is an extreme view, and is of course refuted by all evidence of reference to the letter of Paul's teaching, not to speak of the non-Jewish sense in which the term "law" is used.

3. A third writing may be included under the title of the chapter, though perhaps by a right somewhat more subject to dispute than that which can be claimed for the foregoing writings. Some features of the Apoc-

---

Pauline writings which resemble sentences in the former. But the resemblance is quite vague; and when it is observed that the same writer specifies not less than seventy points in which the epistle shows connection with the canonical Hebrew Scriptures, as many points of connection with Philo, more than thirty with Ecclesiasticus, and not less than forty with the Synoptical tradition as reported by Matthew, it must be felt that the approaches in Paul to the words or sentiments of James are in general explained by reference to the common sources, written and oral, which influenced their thought and speech. Furthermore the superior force and originality of Paul suggest that, in so far as there is any evidence of copying, the probability is that James was the copyist.

[1] Compare in order Matt. v. 3, v. 34–37, vi. 19, vi. 24, vii. 1, vii. 16 with James ii. 5, v. 12, v. 2, 3, iv. 4, iv. 11, 12, iii. 10–13.

[2] Such was the theory of Spitta.

alypse associate it in a measure with the Johannine Gospel and Epistles. But, on the other hand, it is rather broadly contrasted in its tone with these books, and it contains distinct points of connection with the primary stage of Christian thought. While purely Christian ideas are not wanting, there is much of a Jewish-Christian cast to the book. Jerusalem is viewed as the religious centre of the world, and is spoken of as the "holy city" and the "beloved city."[1] Heaven is represented as containing a temple in which the ark of God's covenant is revealed.[2] Christ is described as the root of David and the Lion of the tribe of Judah, and in unadulterated Old Testament phrase is set forth as ruling the nations with a rod of iron.[3] The hundred and forty-four thousand servants of God who are sealed upon their foreheads are represented as taken from the tribes of Israel, twelve thousand from each tribe,[4] and the names of these tribes are inscribed upon the twelve gates of the heavenly city.[5] There is also a reminder of the Judaic standpoint in the prominence which is given to the fear of God as an element of piety.[6] Moreover, the intense antipathy to Roman rule which breathes through the Apocalypse is in line with the implacable Jewish hostility which precipitated the desperate struggle with the overmastering power of Rome, and stands in marked contrast with the deferential attitude toward the imperial government which is characteristic of the Pauline Epistles and the Book of Acts. This contrast, it may be

---

[1] xi. 2, xx 9.
[2] xi. 19. Cf. xv. 5, 8.
[3] xii. 5, xix. 15.
[4] vii. 3–8.
[5] xxi. 12.
[6] xi. 18, xiv. 7, xv. 4, xix. 5.

granted, is partly explained, at least so far as relates to the Pauline Epistles, by the extraordinary provocation which was given by the Neronian persecution.

It is this implication of the Apocalypse with Judaism which justifies its being associated with a primitive type of Christian teaching. In respect of date there is no reason to doubt that the Apocalypse is post-Pauline. Though Epiphanius in the early Church used language which suggests that he associated its origin with the reign of Claudius, it has been a well-nigh universal opinion among scholars that the book as a whole was composed at least after the reign of Nero.

If the Apocalypse be taken as a unity and its composition be assigned to a definite limited period, then the competing dates will be the reign of Domitian (81–96) and the years intervening between the death of Nero and the destruction of Jerusalem (68–70). In behalf of the later or Domitian era the following considerations have been urged: (1) Early tradition, as reported by Irenaeus, places the composition of the Apocalypse in this era, and there is no opposing tradition to which equal weight can be attached. (2) The picture of Christian suffering and martyrdom in the book implies a persecution of wider extent than the local onset of Nero at the capital, and reflects conditions which are not known to have prevailed before the time of Domitian. (3) The Apocalypse contains traces of the legend of Nero's destined return after his supposed death. According to the earlier form of this legend, which seems to have had considerable currency, the tyrant did not really die, but was hidden away in the East among the Parthians, and was destined to regain the sovereignty of the empire. According to the later form of the legend he was to reappear as raised from the dead. This form naturally superseded the earlier as time wore on, and there was reason to doubt the fact of Nero's having been preserved alive. In either form the legend might be expected to require an appreciable interval to gain recognition in Christian literature, while an outcropping of the second form in any writing would be an unequivocal token that it was composed two or three decades after the death of Nero. Now the representation that the beast, which may be regarded as a symbol of the tyrant, was and is not and is about to come up out of the abyss (xvii. 8), at least suggests the notion of an invasion from the region of the dead, and so may be taken as a mark of the Domitian era. (4) The inclusion in the list of the Asiatic churches of several not brought to notice in the career of Paul, the rebuke of some of them for a decline in Christian zeal, and the mention of the presence of heretical teachers are items that are best explained on the supposition that the record was made quite late in the century. A like import may be ascribed to several other items, such as the appearance of the phrase "the Lord's day" (i. 10), and the representation that the twelve apostles have their names inscribed on the foundations of the wall of the heavenly city (xxi. 14)—a stretch of honor more likely to have been accorded in the post-apostolic age than in the apostolic.

In this line of evidences those under the first and second specifications may properly be regarded as having most weight. The third specification deals with a problematical topic, while most of the items under the fourth have very little evidential value.[1]

The principal grounds for preferring the earlier date are the following: (1) The most primitive tradition in the main assigned the Apocalypse to the same author to whom it accredited the fourth Gospel, and identified this author with the Apostle John. Now this tradition, so far as it has any weight, speaks for a relatively early date as the probable time of the composition of the Apocalypse. It is next to impossible to believe that it could have been written by the apostle after the composition of the fourth Gospel, and it greatly facilitates the explanation of the contrast between the two to suppose that it was written a couple of decades earlier. Its fiery energy is consonant with the supposition that it belonged to the era when the Boanerges spirit in John had not been fully toned down. Its Hebraic tinge also favors the earlier stage in the author's development, while both the milder tone and purer Greek of the fourth Gospel point to mature years and a prolonged residence in a Greek-speaking community. The tradition respecting identity of authorship on the part of the Apocalypse and the fourth Gospel may indeed be challenged, but if Irenaeus is to be followed in ascribing both writings to John, there are very fair reasons for doubting the correctness of his report as to the date of the former. (2) The interval between 68 and 70, lying between the fearful onslaught of Nero against the Christians and the impending downfall of Jerusalem, was a time well calcu-

---

[1] Compare Terry, Apocalyptics, p. 257; Hirscht, Die Apokalypse und ihre neueste Kritik, pp 25-28, 158, 159.

lated to stir to such an impassioned outburst as is contained in the Apocalypse. (3) There are items in the book which are most easily and naturally interpreted on the ground that its composition fell within the specified interval, not having taken place later than the first months of the year 70. For example, the maximum ordeal represented as visited upon Jerusalem is simply an earthquake which destroys a tenth part of the city and seven thousand of the people (xi. 13). A more emphatic description of harm and desolation would naturally have found place had the writer been able to look back upon the tragic fate of the city at the hands of the Roman spoilers. Again in chapters xiii and xvii a line of seven emperors, corresponding to the seven heads of the beast symbolizing Roman rule, is mentioned. Five, it is said, have fallen, one is, and the seventh is still to come. If we begin the count with Octavian (Augustus), we find the fifth in Nero, and identify the time of writing as the reign of Galba; or, if Galba, Otho and Vitellius be supposed to have been passed by, as not gaining a proper place in the succession, then the first days of Vespasian in 69–70 would be the time of writing.[1] At least this would be the conclusion, unless it be supposed that the apparent standpoint of the author was a mere

---

[1] In virtue of the eminence of his position Julius Cæsar might conceivably be reckoned as the first in the list. But the regular imperial succession began with Octavian. It was first upon him that the title Augustus — $\Sigma\epsilon\beta\alpha\sigma\tau\acute{o}s$ — was bestowed, and there is some reason to think that this name, which was claimed likewise by his successors, is referred to in the mention of "names of blasphemy" as inscribed upon the heads of the beast. Any reason for identifying the wounded head with Nero would also direct to Octavian as the first in the list.

device, and that what is pictured in these chapters as future was not really future; but this is a strained assumption, the motive for choosing the viewpoint after the fifth king being quite decidedly in need of explanation, if that was not the real viewpoint of the writer. Taken in conjunction with the item in chapter xi respecting the limited judgment on Jerusalem, the content of chapters xiii and xvii favors the time proximate to the death of Nero.

The evidence deduced from these two chapters may be regarded as affected by the presence of the legend of Nero's return, if indeed that legend is found here, and especially if it is found in its later form. That the legend is properly discoverable in any form is not the unanimous verdict of criticism. It must be admitted, however, that recent criticism shows a marked tendency to take the affirmative on this point. It must also be granted that what is said in chapters xiii and xvii of one of the seven heads appearing as though smitten unto death, then being healed, and subsequently reappearing and in conjunction with allies taking vengeance on the great city, has rather remarkable points of correspondence with the popular legend about Nero. It is in place, therefore, to inquire, supposing the legend to be actually mirrored in these representations, have we here a decisive note of a date near to the end of the century? To this question it is possible to render a negative answer. The Nero legend in its first form appeared soon after the death of the tyrant, which occurred in June of the year 68. Within a year from that time a pseudo Nero had come forward and been the cause of commotions in Asia Minor and Greece.[1] In the region of the apocalyptic writer there may have been at this time a specially intense excitement over the matter, and hence as tempting an occasion to enrich apocalyptic symbolism from this source as was ever afforded. It is not incredible, then, that the Nero legend in its first form should have been thus early appropriated. In its second form, doubtless, it could not have been appropriated at that juncture, unless the thought of the revelator was quite in advance of popular expectation. The pertinent inquiry concerns, accordingly, the form in which the legend appears. On this point the grounds of judgment are not very decisive. It may be said, however, that there is no compelling evidence for the assumption that the first form of the legend is transcended in the viewpoint of the Apocalypse. Nero robbed of all the glory of imperial rule, driven out as a fugitive, undergoing apparently a fatal wounding by the sword, could be described, without any excess of poetical license, as being the subject of a deadly stroke and as brought to naught, even though it was suspected that he did not actually die. The fact that his reappearing is pictured as an issuing from the abyss may seem indeed to connect him with the region of the dead. But it is to be noticed that the torturing locusts with their prince are also represented as issuing from the abyss. (ix. 2, 3, 11.) A suggestion is thus given that this form of expression was used in connection with Nero rather to emphasize his association with the demoniacal power which rages up from beneath than to depict an actual resurrection.

---
[1] Tacitus, Hist. ii. 8, 9.

It may be affirmed, too, that a writer who was thinking of the resurrection of one who had been dead for a score of years could scarcely have been inclined to describe his being raised up as the healing of a wound. The reference to the beast as one "who hath the stroke of the sword and yet lived" (xiii. 14) conveys rather the idea of a marvellous recovery from a deadly thrust than the notion of a resurrection of one long dead. Thus the evidence adduced from the list of kings in chapters xiii and xvii for the earlier of the competing dates is not necessarily regarded as cancelled by the Nero legend in the form in which it has gained a place in the Apocalypse, if indeed it has gained a place there.

Whatever may be thought of the relative weight of the two lines of evidence bearing on the date of the Apocalypse, it is not easy to nullify altogether the force of one or another evidence in either line. This fact has come very largely to be recognized by scholars, and has led to qualifications of one kind or another being placed upon the unity of the book. The judgment has been gaining currency that if the writing was composed in the age of Domitian it must have incorporated materials belonging to an earlier period, and if it was written no later than the first days of Vespasian it was probably supplemented and published in Domitian's reign. Among those who regard the evidences for a more or less composite structure as conclusive, much variety of opinion has been manifested. Some have supposed that the writer dealt with documents of very appreciable extent, others that his borrowing was confined to matters of limited compass, such as single visions. Some have magnified the tokens of a Jewish basis, others have regarded the sources as predominantly, if not exclusively, Christian.[1] Without looking specifically into these theories or attempting to weigh their merits in detail, we content ourselves with expressing the conviction that a predominantly Christain character pertains to the Apocalypse, and also that it is marked to so large a degree by unity of style that it seems probable that the greater part of it at least was from the hand of a single writer, who used a good degree of freedom to shape his materials according to his own bent. At the same time, we are quite willing to grant with Weizsäcker, Bousset, Porter, and others, that the writer was ambitious to utilize apocalyptic materials at hand, and so gave place to some things that he could not bring into a unified and well-connected scheme.[2] We can readily admit, furthermore, the possibility that the publishing of the book may have been separated by a considerable period from the time of the original composition, and that some items may have been incorporated at the time of publication. The theme is not one that invites to complete confidence.

---

[1] Classifying from this point of view, Rauch distinguishes these groups: (1) Those who hold that the Apocalypse has a purely Christian character — Völter, Weizsacker, Erbes, Pressensé. (2) Those who regard the book as a Jewish work wrought over by a Christian hand — Vischer, Iselin, Rovers, Weyland, P. Schmidt, O. Holtzmann, O. Pfleiderer. (3) Those who regard the Apocalypse as a Christian work with Jewish additions — Schoen, Sabatier, Spitta.

[2] Weizsacker, Apostolic Age, II. 173; Bousset, Die Offenbarung Johannis (Meyer's Series), pp. 143–154; Porter, The Messages of the Apocalyptic Writers, pp. 180, 181. Among the passages which interfere with the continuity of the writing, vii. 1–8, x–xi. 13, and xii are specified.

To assume to know all about the composition of the Apocalypse is a sure way to make conspicuous one's lack of adequate information.

II. — THE TEACHING OF THE FIRST PART OF THE BOOK OF ACTS.

1. This book begins with the thought of the kingdom, and then goes on to give an account of the progress of the Church in the face of Jewish opposition. Primarily both the one and the other term had in the minds of the disciples a close association with Judaism. The form of the question which the assembled disciples asked, namely, "Dost thou at this time restore the kingdom to Israel?" indicates that they still clung to the idea of the Messianic kingdom as a visible realm having its centre in the Old Testament community. The import of Christ's message on the kingdom had not yet been adequately grasped. It took time to spiritualize their thought and bring it up toward the plane of the gospel conception.

Probably in the first instance the Church, or the congregation of believers, was regarded in large part as rather preliminary to the kingdom than as properly identical with the same. The grand distinctive era of the kingdom, it was conceived, would begin when Christ should return. Then His sovereignty would be gloriously displayed. But naturally, as the Christian message went on winning victories, increasing account was made of the actual exercise of Christ's lordship in and through the believing community, and the thought of the Church and that of the kingdom became in a measure blended together.

The history in Acts indicates plainly that in the years immediately following Christ's ascension the disciples esteemed the Church to be not so much a new creation as the consummation of the Old Testament order of things, the assembly of the true spiritual Israel, the elect portion of the Jewish people which had enough of the spirit of faith and obedience to receive the Messiah. Doubtless they expected that the Gentiles would share in the benefits of the gospel message, but not as free from the claims of the Jewish legal system. They had no design to assert independence of that system. The new-born life, however, was mightier than the inherited form. The old wine-skin could not hold the new wine. By the irrepressible impulsion of the spirit and teaching of Christ the company of Christ's disciples was carried forward to an independent position. This was the inner power working toward a transcendence of Judaism. The outward power was a succession of events well adapted to promote the same result. Four or five of these are specially noteworthy. First came the appointment to official position of Hellenists, Jews whose native language was Greek, and who on that account had somewhat of a bond of sympathetic connection with the Gentile world. Some of the men thus appointed appear also to have been of a rather bold and progressive spirit. Commentators have discovered in Stephen a kind of forerunner of the apostle to the Gentiles. It is noticed that he was charged with speaking against the temple and the law. This charge in the form in which it was preferred most likely was false; but it is to be observed that Stephen in his speech before the Sanhedrim took pains to disparage the notion that the divine presence can be confined to any temple which man may build. In saying this he was not indeed going outside of ideas formally acknowledged by the Jews; but the fact that he said it in that particular connection may be construed as a hint of a somewhat free attitude toward the Jewish ceremonial system. Following close upon the martyrdom of Stephen came the persecution which scattered the disciples from Jerusalem and forced them into a broader field. Then came the preaching of Philip in Samaria, and the foundation of a new Christian centre at Antioch. The lesson which Peter received in connection with Cornelius and his household set the door fairly ajar into the Gentile world. Finally the conversion of the most stringent and persecuting Pharisee and the penetration of his soul with the conviction that the way of faith, as opposed to ceremonial bondage, is the way of salvation, prepared for a resolute discarding of Jewish restrictions and for the distinct acknowledgment of the universal character of Christianity. A close approach to this consummation was reached at the Council of Jerusalem, held not later than the year 52, and placed by some recent scholars as early as 47.[1] Even after this date the traditional preference for Judaism asserted itself here and there, but it was a waning factor, and the rapid expansion of the Church in the Gentile world soon condemned it to impotence.

The only church officials who come to view in the first

---

[1] Harnack, Chronologie der altchristlichen Literatur, I. 237.

TEACHING AKIN TO THE SYNOPTICAL 143

five chapters of Acts are the apostles. That they exercised leadership is very evident; that they claimed or possessed a distinct governing supremacy is not apparent. What was urged in connection with the choice of one of the disciples to fill the place of Judas emphasizes more a teaching function than anything else. It was needful, it was said by Peter, to fill up the list of accredited witnesses of the resurrection. In the discharge of their leadership the apostles proceeded rather by way of advice and suggestion than by that of command. Matters of common concern were submitted to the whole assembly, as appears in the choice of Matthias to the apostolate and the selection of the seven to serve in the distribution of charities. Peter's prominence in leadership is explained by the traits of his personality, his readiness in speech and his resoluteness in action. Not a word appears in the Book of Acts which implies that he had a constitutional primacy, or a headship of governing authority.

Next after the apostles the first officers mentioned are the seven whose appointment is recorded in the sixth chapter. In the thought of the Church in subsequent centuries the designation of these men to their special duties was the origin of the diaconate. More properly it may be considered the historical germ of that institution. The diaconate came by a development. The appointment of the Hellenists to serve in the distribution of charities marked an initial stage of the development.

Of bishops there is no mention in the Book of Acts prior to the account of Paul's last missionary journey before his Roman captivity.[1] Elders are first mentioned

---
[1] Acts xx. 28.

in connection with the Church at Jerusalem as being at hand to receive the contribution brought by Barnabas and Paul.[1] Some writers on apostolic history are of opinion that at this stage the term elders denoted rather the senior members of the congregation than officials proper. To our mind there is nothing incredible in the supposition that at an early date the demands of local supervision, which naturally became urgent as congregations were gathered in new and distant places, gave rise to more or less organized boards of elders. It must be granted, however, that the earlier epistles of Paul, dealing as they do with congregations as a whole, give the impression that officialism had not made any great advance by the middle of the century. If then we suppose boards of presbyters to have been constituted at an early date, we are led to conclude that no wide line of cleavage subsisted for some time between them and the congregations which they served.

2. In relation to the person and work of Christ the teaching in the first part of Acts is comparatively undeveloped, and has some special marks of connection with Jewish thinking. These characteristics may have been due in some measure to an accommodation in apostolic discourse to the standpoint of those addressed. Even had Peter's mind been filled with such phrases relative to Christ as are found in Colossians, Hebrews, and the Johannine literature, it would have been poor discretion to dispense them in a speech to unconverted Jews. There was reason for not departing too widely from the Jewish plane of thought on the nature and vocation of

---

[1] Acts xi. 30. See also xiv. 23.

the Messiah. But the motive for accommodated speech is not the whole explanation of the forms of expression that were used in characterizing Christ's person and work. The minds of the disciples were at an initial theological stage on this theme, and they naturally expressed themselves in terms which stand somewhat in contrast with the completed New Testament phraseology. Especially noticeable is the recurring reference to Christ as the Servant of God, παῖς θεοῦ.[1] It gives us the impression of being transferred back to the Old Testament to find this designation. The language of Isaiah evidently governed the choice of words here rather than the customary phraseology of Christ. It is also an Old Testament form of description which is employed when Christ is identified with the prophet like unto Moses who was to be raised up.[2] Such forms of description evidently do not necessitate the predication of any superhuman rank in Christ. They could be placed alongside the words, "Jesus of Nazareth, a man approved of God,"[3] as being agreeable to the theory of the simple humanity of Christ. But on the other hand they cannot be cited as denying superhuman rank. In the point of view of the New Testament writers generally Christ was what these terms imply. That He was also more a

---

[1] Acts, iii 13, 26, iv. 27, 30. While usage on the whole dictates that παῖς should be taken in the sense of "servant," it is to be observed that instances occur both in Jewish and early Christian literature where the word may be regarded as closely affiliated in meaning with the term "child" or "son" See Wisdom of Solomon, ii. 13, 16, 18; Matt. xii. 18; Clement of Rome, Epist., lix. 2–4; Didaché, ix. 2, 3, x. 2, 3; Clement of Alexandria, Strom. vii. 1.

[2] Acts iii. 22. [3] ii. 22.

number of them took pains to teach with sufficient definiteness. These chapters of the Acts, too, are not without intimations of the transcendent rank of Christ. He is represented as having poured forth the divine influences whose working astonished the multitude.[1] The virtue of His name is represented to be the source of miracles at the hands of the apostles.[2] He is characterized as the Holy and Righteous One and the Prince of Life.[3] He is addressed by Stephen as Lord and invoked to receive his departing spirit.[4] It is said of the converted Paul that straightway he proclaimed Jesus that He is the Son of God,[5] and Peter in his address to the household of Cornelius mentioned as a part of the obligatory Christian message the setting forth of Christ as ordained to be judge of the quick and the dead.[6] In the same address he also spoke of Christ as Lord of all, that is, of men universally, of Gentiles as well as of Israel.[7] These expressions taken together may indeed fall short of a complete christology; but it cannot be denied that their tenor is in the direction of assigning to Christ the rank which more dogmatic and constructive portions of the New Testament do assign to Him.

In defining the office of Christ the chapters before us observe complete silence about the function of His death. They indeed witness to an effort to remove the offence attached to the death of the Messiah in the thought of the Jews, by proving from the Old Testament that it was included in the divine purpose.[8] It is also natural to suppose that the disciples who were so sure that God

---

[1] ii 33.   [3] iii. 14, 15.   [5] ix. 20.   [7] x. 36.
[2] iii. 6, 16.   [4] vii. 59, 60.   [6] x. 42.   [8] ii. 23, iii. 18, iv. 27, 28.

TEACHING AKIN TO THE SYNOPTICAL 147

had a purpose in the death of Christ took some pains to form an opinion on the nature or content of that purpose. But no such opinion comes to expression in the first part of Acts. Either because they felt that their views were not sufficiently matured, or because they regarded the minds of their auditors as in no fit state to receive a message on the subject, those who preached Christ in the first days of the Church made, so far as the record shows, no attempt to define the relation of His death to the economy of grace. Their impression that salvation is through Christ was undoubtedly strong and vital. They speak of Christ as "exalted to be a prince and saviour, to give repentance to Israel and remission of sins."[1] They declare, "In none other is there salvation; neither is there any other name under heaven, that is given among men, wherein we must be saved."[2] They announce that "through His name everyone that believeth on Him shall receive remission of sins."[3] By statements like these they clearly manifested their hearty faith in Christ's saving office. But at the same time no recorded word of theirs definitely relates the death of Christ to that office or shows its place therein. On the whole it must be said that in respect of the person and work of Christ this portion of the New Testament falls below the plane of the data contained in the Synoptical Gospels. The declarations of Christ and the revelations of His self-consciousness afford ground for larger inductions than are made here.

3. A prominent feature in this section of the New Testament is the way in which the agency of the Holy

---
[1] v. 31.   [2] iv. 12.   [3] x. 43.

Spirit is brought to the front. The primitive disciples evidently regarded themselves as a theopneustic society. Within the first fifteen chapters of Acts there are nearly two score references to the Holy Spirit. The narratives show an unhesitating conviction on the part of the Church that it was favored with the immediate presence and guidance of the Spirit in all important transactions. Tokens of His energetic working in such signs as the speaking in tongues seem to have been regarded as appropriate accompaniments of the introduction of men into the faith and fellowship of Jesus.[1]

Stress upon the guidance and working of the Spirit naturally gave much scope to the idea of personal charisms, as opposed to officialism and ritual. The man who furnished evidence of being inspired was granted large liberty to exercise his gift. Thus we find that some of the seven went entirely beyond the eleemosynary function to which they were appointed, and freely shared in the ministry of the word which the apostles counted their special function.

As respects rites, no further description is given of the eucharist than a mere reference to the breaking of bread.[2] From a consideration of such data as early Christian history affords it may be concluded that this language refers to a common evening meal, which was concluded with such emblems as Christ employed at the last supper with His disciples.

The central significance attached to baptism is that of

---

[1] Acts viii. 15–17, x. 44–46.
[2] Acts ii. 42, 46. Compare 1 Cor. x. 16, xi. 24. See comment of Knowling on Acts ii. 42 in Expositor's Greek Testament, II 94.

an open profession of faith in Christ and acceptance of Him as the ground of hope for salvation. In one instance, it is true, a verbal connection is made between baptism and the remission of sins.[1] But even here baptism is assumed to have its logical antecedent in repentance, with which faith holds a necessary relation. In all the other references to the remission of sins this is made dependent upon repentance, faith, and calling upon the name of the Lord.[2] It is quite evident, therefore, that the apostle did not think of the bare rite of baptism as bringing remission, but profoundly emphasized all that properly went with the rite in the way of spiritual conditions, including repentance, faith, and sincere confession of Christ. Viewed with a true perspective the first chapters of early Christian history must be seen to assign to baptism a subordinate place in the appropriation of salvation. In several instances water baptism is put in distinct antithesis with baptism by the spirit.[3] It may be said indeed that in these cases the reference is to John's baptism. But it is to be noticed that in relation to Christian baptism the performance of the external rite and the impartation of the Holy Spirit are by no means viewed as necessarily coincident. On the contrary, the two events are assigned to different occasions in relation to those candidates of whose experience we have any considerable account.[4] It was evidently no part of the conviction of the primitive disciples that the working of the Spirit is tied to baptism.

In a single instance, namely in the account of the

---

[1] Acts ii. 38.
[2] ii. 21, iii. 19, x. 43, xiii. 38, 39.
[3] i. 5, xi. 16.
[4] viii. 16, 17, x. 44–48.

Samaritan converts, a special instrumentality seems to be assigned to the laying on of hands in connection with the impartation of the gift of the Holy Spirit. The apostles, it is said, prayed for those who had been recently baptized in the name of Jesus that they might receive the Holy Ghost. "Then laid they their hands upon them, and they received the Holy Ghost."[1] Rationally, of course, it is not to be supposed that the mere laying on of hands brought the Spirit in His regenerating and sanctifying presence to these persons. Moreover, the ethical standpoint of the New Testament forbids such a notion. The question in this instance, it should be observed, is not so much about a regenerating or sanctifying presence as about a charismatic presence — a working attended with some unmistakable manifestation, like the speaking with tongues,[2] which indeed would seem misplaced in an unregenerate person, but yet is not necessarily associated precisely with the effectuation of regeneration. A working of this sort had the virtue of a sign or credential, and served the same purpose as extraordinary or miraculous occurrences in general. The Samaritan incident, therefore, as belonging to an age of special credentials for Christ's servants, is no good warrant for the idea of a permanent tactual arrangement for imparting the grace of the Spirit. Furthermore, nothing prohibits us in this particular case from supposing that the prayers of the apostles had quite as much to do with the result attained as did the imposition of hands.

---

[1] viii. 15-17.
[2] Compare Hort, The Christian Ecclesia, p. 54.

In referring to the speaking with tongues as an extraordinary sign or token of spiritual agency we have expressed the practical import which is assigned to this peculiar gift in the New Testament representation as a whole. While a portion of the vivid account of the Pentecostal scene might convey the impression that the gift of tongues was designed to serve as a means of communicating information in strange languages, the issue of the story shows that even in this instance the gift was rather a sign adapted to arrest attention and to stir feeling than a means of conveying instruction, since the informing message was first imparted in any adequate measure by the speech of Peter. The narrative does not necessarily imply that anything more was included in the extraordinary utterances than brief exclamations in glorification of the marvellous grace of God. It is also to be noted that there is no need to assume that the languages in which these exclamations were embodied were as numerous as the nationalities or countries mentioned; in fact, it is probable that the Jews, gathered from the fifteen districts enumerated, spoke either Greek, Eastern Aramaic, or Western Aramaic, though possibly with some varieties of dialect.[1] What has to be admitted, accordingly, if the Pentecostal narrative is to be approved as based in fact, is simply this: In a state of ecstasy the disciples were empowered to utter snatches from one or another of several languages with which they were not supposed to have the requisite acquaintance. Thus interpreted the Pentecostal narrative will not appear widely contrasted with other accounts of the speaking with

---

[1] Compare A. Robertson, Hastings' Dict. of the Bible, IV. 795.

tongues.¹ The distinguishing item is that the utterances at Pentecost were sufficiently intelligible to convey a distinct meaning to some at least of the hearers, whereas Paul emphasizes the need of special interpretation of any communication in a tongue. In the primary, as in all the later instances, the speaking in tongues was an ecstatic experience, an experience rather of transporting emotion than of reflective thought. Its principal virtue was to serve as a very sensible and impressive token of the presence and agency of the Holy Spirit.

From what has been said on the functions accorded to Christ and the Holy Spirit, it is evident that a practical trinitarianism runs through the first chapters in Acts. In the religious life of the primitive Christian community there was a vital recognition of Father, Son, and Spirit. This recognition, however, so far as discoverable, did not go beyond the practical stage. Of any attempt at formal trinitarian construction not a trace is found.

4. In point of eschatology the chapters under consideration in no wise go beyond the intimations of the Synoptical Gospels. They contain only the simple announcements that Christ is to come again in unmistakable personal manifestation of Himself;[2] that He is appointed to the office of judging the race;[3] and that the heaven must receive Him till the time of restitution of all things.[4] This last statement is best understood in the light of the Old Testament forecast of a glorious consummation of the Messianic kingdom. It points to a time when the message of the Messiah shall have been

---

[1] Acts x. 46, xix 6; I Cor. xiv.
[2] i. 11.
[3] x. 42.
[4] iii. 21.

spread abroad through the world and the nations very largely shall have become obedient to its behests.

III. — THE TEACHING OF THE EPISTLE OF JAMES.

1. Reference has been made to the Jewish tinge of this writing. It has in fact less of a specifically Christian cast than any other epistle in the New Testament of equal length. There is no reference in it to the death or resurrection of Christ and no clear intimation on the relation which faith in Him sustains to salvation. His name occurs but twice. All that is said of Him is comprised in these particulars: He is the Lord Jesus Christ; the Lord of glory; the Lord whose coming is at hand; the judge who standeth before the doors.[1] The predominance of the ethical interest over the theological may account in part for the paucity of reference in the epistle to distinctively Christian tenets, though it may be noticed that in some other New Testament epistles occasion is taken to enforce ethical points by reference to the example of Christ.

2. In relation to the nature of God, James gives prominence to immutability and absolute righteousness. God is He "with whom can be no variation, neither shadow that is cast by turning."[2] He cannot be tempted with evil, and He Himself tempteth no man."[3] In two instances James applies to God the title "Father";[4] but it is to be observed that in the first of these the title has reference only to the divine authorship of nature, to

---

[1] James i. 1, ii. 1, 7, v. 8, 9. [3] ii. 13.
[2] ii. 17. [4] i. 17, iii. 9.

the fact that God is the creator of the heavenly orbs and the ultimate source of their light. In the second instance it is possible that the term may have been employed more after the analogy of its use in the Gospels. An express reference to God's fatherly relation to men, or to man's filial standing before Him, does not occur in the epistle. Indirectly, however, an approach is made to the statement of this evangelical truth, since emphasis is put upon God's readiness to respond to the prayer of faith,[1] and it is said that "the Lord is full of pity, and merciful."[2]

3. Very little is contained in the epistle that can be construed into a declaration of opinion on man's natural condition. James evidently had a vivid impression of man's actual weakness and temptability. He had no thought of encountering a faultless human being. "In many things," he says, "we all stumble."[3] The main ground of this sinful errancy he locates within. He acknowledges indeed the existence of a devil who needs to be resisted;[4] but the characteristic process of sin, he says, is on this wise: "Each man is tempted when he is drawn away by his own lust and enticed. Then the lust, when it hath conceived, beareth sin; and the sin when it is full grown bringeth forth death."[5] The origin of this lust which thus serves as the ground of personal transgression is not stated. That in some sense men retain the likeness of God is implied in the way in which the author reprobates the cursing of men.[6] The language

---

[1] i. 5.
[2] v. 11.
[3] iii. 2.
[4] iv. 7.
[5] i. 14, 15.
[6] iii. 9.

used, however, throws little light on his view of the moral condition in which man begins his earthly life. The epistle falls short of a theory of original sin.

4. The conception of religious life which dominates the epistle is much after the Old Testament order. There is not indeed any reference to the ceremonial requirements of the old dispensation. To that extent the outlook is Christian. But Christianity itself is viewed preeminently as a scheme of law or a code of duty. Stress is placed upon the unity of this law. To violate it in one point is to show lack of respect to it as a whole.[1] In two instances James characterizes the code obligatory on Christians as the law of liberty.[2] The context does not throw any special light upon the sense in which the peculiar phrase is used. The suggestion, however, lies very near that it was designed to signify a law which is adapted to lead its faithful subjects into a true liberty. A principal part of this law no doubt was identified in the thought of the writer with what he calls the "royal law," that is, the law of equal love to the neighbor.[3]

5. Faith is put by James in contrast with wavering and doublemindedness.[4] It is thus made equivalent to a hearty confidence in God and a steadfast repose upon Him. There is no reason to doubt that this was the author's ruling conception of faith. But in discussing the subject of justification he permits the term to be applied to mere intellectual assent, inasmuch as he speaks of it as something which a devil might exercise. Very likely James would not have denied that a faith of this sort is scarcely worthy of the name.

---

[1] ii. 10.   [2] i. 25, ii. 12.   [3] ii. 8.   [4] i. 6, 7.

The fact that in his reference to justification James admitted into the field of vision this empty sort of faith invites the verdict that between his real position and that of Paul there was less difference than might be inferred from their verbal antagonism. If in addition it be concluded that James was thinking rather of the *justificatio justi* than of the *justificatio injusti*, that is, of a seal of divine approbation put upon the career of a servant of God, instead of the primary entrance into a state of reconciliation with God, then the difference will be still further abridged. It becomes us, however, not to overdo the matter of reconciliation by asserting that James gives indubitable evidence of full agreement with Paul. After all just allowances have been made for a special use of terms, the fact remains that the language of James does not safeguard Paul's doctrine of the primacy of faith. While some of the statements of the former suggest that faith is viewed as the life of works, others can be construed as meaning that works contribute to faith quite as much as they receive therefrom. The total discussion leaves the reader free to suppose that works are coordinate with faith in the ground of justification. James guards well against an antinomian abuse of the office of faith; he does not clearly secure to faith, in this relation, its primacy in the attainment of salvation.

In relation to regeneration the noticable feature is the instrumentality in its effectuation which the epistle assigns to truth. The following are its statements relative to this point: "Of His own will He brought us forth by the word of truth." [1] " Receive with meekness the implanted word which is able to save your souls." [2]

---

[1] i. 18. [2] i 21.

Herein the Epistle of James has a bond of association with the first Epistle of Peter and with the fourth Gospel.

6. The epistle gives very little information respecting the Church. It is addressed to the twelve tribes of the Dispersion, and refers to the place of religious meeting as a synagogue. The contents, however, show that it was meant for Christian Jews; or, possibly, for Christians indiscriminately, since "the twelve tribes of the Dispersion" can be understood to be a symbolical designation of the whole Christian body. The epistle contains a single mention of the Church, namely in the injunction that the elders of the Church should be called in to pray for the sick. The fact that this function is devolved upon a plurality of members, taken in conjunction with the direction for a mutual confession of sins, speaks rather for a democratic than for a priestly or hierarchical regime.

7. In the practical teaching of the epistle one of the most striking features is the vehemence with which the author lashes a disposition to do obeisance to the rich and the severity with which he calls the rich to account.[1] Another special feature is the stress placed upon complete abstinence from oaths.[2] With many other portions of the New Testament the epistle is characterized by an energetic inculcation of patience under trial.

In early Christian tradition the James, who has generally been supposed to have been the author, was reputed to have been an unsparing ascetic in his personal habits. The epistle by no means discredits the tradition; but

---

[1] i. 9–11, ii. 1–7, v. 1–6.   [2] v. 12.

on the other hand it affords no certain means of confirmation. Its attitude toward the rich may have been dictated by special manifestations of worldliness and selfishness on their part, and is not necessarily taken as an indication of out and out hostility to the idea of accumulating property. Aside from this, if the epistle contains any manifestation of a predilection for asceticism, it is to be found in this strong language on the necessity of renouncing the world: "Know ye not that the friendship of the world is enmity with God? Whosoever therefore would be a friend of the world maketh himself an enemy of God."[1] Whether this is to be regarded as savoring of asceticism depends upon what is understood by the "world." As the context suggests, James probably meant by the term the province of the unregenerated life, the sphere of intemperate sensuous pleasures. On this supposition his thought would not be unlike that contained in the Johannine injunction against love of the world. In general it may be said that the Epistle of James shows a high degree of ethical intensity. There breathes through it a healthy scorn for a religion of mere creed and profession.

IV.— The Teaching of the Apocalypse.

1. The numerous attempts which have been made to read into the Apocalypse the outlines of all history since the time of its composition suggest that first of all we inquire how far its prophetical outlook reaches, or how much it attempts to teach in a detailed fashion respect-

---

[1] James iv. 4.

TEACHING AKIN TO THE SYNOPTICAL 159

ing future events. An analysis of its contents must show, it strikes us, that it makes no pretence of depicting age-long developments of earthly history, but rather, in harmony with its own definition of its scope, deals almost entirely with "the things which must shortly come to pass."[1] Its horizon is essentially the horizon of the Roman empire. All that is depicted beyond that is depicted in general terms and within the compass of a few verses. The concluding statement respecting the judgment on the beast[2] is separated by only the fraction of a chapter from the description of the final judgment.[3] Now the beast is identified in the foregoing characterizations, beyond all shadow of real ambiguity, with the dominion of pagan Rome. It has its seat upon seven mountains,[4] in Babylon the great,[5] is a world-dominating power,[6] and makes war upon the saints.[7] It is not a monster that is to come on the stage in some future era. Its beginning lies back of the seer's own day. It is a seven-headed beast, and these seven heads " are seven kings; the five are fallen, the one is, the other is not yet come."[8] Such language is obviously incompatible with the notion of any reference to an overgrown ecclesiastical power — a thing not yet on the field at all in the author's day. It is plainly the Roman imperium that the seven-headed beast symbolizes. And the other evil mundane powers that are mentioned (with the exception of Gog and Magog) belong within its sphere. The beast with the two horns[9] most likely represents

---

[1] Rev. i. 1, xxii. 6.
[2] xix. 20.
[3] xx. 11–15.
[4] xvii. 9.
[5] xvii. 5.
[6] xiii. 2–5.
[7] xiii. 7.
[8] xvii. 10.
[9] xiii. 11–13.

the system of pagan superstition and sorcery, full of enmity toward the followers of Christ and in close alliance with the persecuting demigods enthroned over the empire;[1] or else, a fanatical and antichristian power from out the midst of Judaism. The interpretation of the ten kings symbolized by the ten horns[2] is, indeed, in question. Some exegetes have supposed them to denote heads of Roman provinces; others have seen in them the rulers of regions bordering the empire. In any case — and this is the point of emphasis here — they are viewed as contemporary with the empire of pagan Rome. They are the allies of the last in the list of the emperors, that is, of the "eighth who is of the seven." To this impersonation of Roman sovereignty, to this form of the beast, "they give their power and authority."[3] They join with him in the enterprise of establishing his supremacy and are joint cause with him of the burning of the city of Rome. Here ends the detailed prediction with the sketch of this eighth who seems to be regarded as in some sense a reproduction of one of the seven,[4] and who with his allies and worshippers is cast into perdition.

As the seer, according to his own statement, wrote in

---

[1] It is to be noticed that in another connection there is added to the dragon and the beast, as the third member of the evil trio, the *false prophet* (xvi. 13, xix. 20).

[2] xiii. 1, xvii. 7, 12.

[3] xvii. 13.

[4] It has been alleged that the expression, "of the seven," indicates only descent, and that the numeral εἷς would have been expressed if the meaning had been "one of the seven." But this contention is not specially convincing. A precisely parallel instance of the omission of εἷς is found in Acts xxi. 8.

TEACHING AKIN TO THE SYNOPTICAL 161

the time of the sixth king, that is, the sixth Roman emperor, did not expect the imperial line to run beyond the eighth, and has interposed nothing between this closing embodiment of Roman power and the thousand years' reign of Christ, it is quite evident that his forecast did not touch the field of modern history. If the number seven be taken literally, and not as a symbol of the complete succession of emperors, it will need to be concluded that nearly the whole bulk of his predictions contemplated events falling within the limits of the first century. In any event his vision rested on no details of future earthly history beyond the course of the empire then existing. The only mundane power which undeniably emerges beyond the Roman is that described by the names Gog and Magog and pictured as the ally of Satan in his final onslaught[1] As is usual in prophecy, the events near at hand fill up the greater part of the field of vision. The remote is sketched in very general outlines and is closely associated with the closing up of the dispensation.

2. The prominence of the imperial power of Rome in the revelator's contemplation is indicated by the fact that the function of Satan is made to consist very largely in furnishing that power for its ungodly work. The symbol of the one is parallel to that of the other. Satan is the dragon with seven heads and ten horns.[2] He gives to the beast with seven heads and ten horns "his power, and his throne, and great authority."[3] With this striking index of the writer's standpoint other graphic tokens are combined. Indeed, as Ramsay has remarked,

---
[1] xx. 7–9.   [2] xii. 3.   [3] xiii. 2.

"the shadow of the Roman empire broods over the whole of the Apocalypse."[1]

The abhorrence of the Roman imperium which led the revelator to picture it as the preferred agent of Satan was not due merely to the fact that it was looked upon as a centre of persecuting malignity. He regarded it also as the centre of a colossal and corrupting idolatry. The earth, as he represents, was seduced into worshipping the beast.[2] At the time when he wrote, the imperial cult had not been pushed to its full extreme; but already emperor-worship had gone far enough to suggest that the Cæsar was a rival to any god that men might be urged to respect. Already the custom of deifying the dead emperor was in vogue. Already an Augustus and a Tiberius had been honored with religious rites, and a Caligula had "instituted a temple and priests with choicest victims in honor of his own divinity."[3] To the stanch Jewish sentiment of the writer this was of course exceedingly revolting. It is no wonder, when he contemplated this power, at once greedy of the incense of the world and drunk with the blood of saints, that he thought of it as the foremost embodiment of the disposition and energy of Satan. Imperial Rome at the worst was, in truth, a sufficiently genuine specimen of diabolism.

3. Against this colossal embodiment of evil and violence what form does the revelator bring into the field of conflict? Above all the form of a lamb. The beast and its allies make war upon the Lamb, and "the Lamb

---

[1] The Letters to the Seven Churches of Asia, p. 93.
[2] xiii. 4, 5, 12.   [3] Suetonius, "Caligula," xxii.

shall overcome them."[1] It is the peculiarity of the Apocalypse that with images of majesty and resistless authority, with the throne and the iron sceptre, it combines this image of gentleness. Through all its delineation of might and wrath and judgment runs the thoroughly Christian sentiment that the supremacy is with the spirit of gentleness and sacrifice, that the Lamb is the conqueror of the beast. In the greater part of the book the chosen title of the Redeemer is the Lamb. It occurs twenty-nine times, whereas the term Jesus appears less than a dozen times and Christ only about a half-dozen times.

As respects the rank belonging to Christ, the Apocalypse renders a somewhat more explicit testimony than the other writings in the group under consideration. In some of its christological phrases and conceptions it touches upon both Pauline and Johannine representations. Especially does the declaration, " His name is called the 'Word of God',"[2] remind of the prologue of the fourth Gospel. Moreover the total picture given of Christ cannot be said to fall below a Johannine level. While He appears in the form of a son of man in the midst of the golden candlesticks, he bears features which Jewish descriptive art was wont to attach to the Ancient of Days.[3] He characterizes Himself as "the first and the last and the living one," and claims to hold the keys of "death and Hades."[4] He fulfills the function, ascribed in the Old Testament to Jehovah, of searching the reins and hearts.[5] The pneumatic virtue operative

---
[1] xvii. 14.   [3] Compare i. 14 with Dan. vii. 9.   [5] ii. 23.
[2] xix. 13.   [4] i. 17, 18.

in the world is from Him: "He hath the seven spirits of God."[1] The heavenly potentates fall down before Him and hail Him as "worthy to receive power and riches and wisdom and might and honor and glory."[2] He is made joint object of homage with Him that sitteth upon the throne in the ascription which is rendered by the whole creation.[3] He is described as "Lord of lords and King of kings."[4] With the Lord God He constitutes the temple of heaven, and He is the lamp thereof.[5] The river of life issues from the throne of which He is joint occupant with the Father.[6] Such ascriptions in a book which shows a clear sense of the distinction between the divine and the creaturely by reprobating obeisance to angels[7] certainly imply that in the thought of the writer Christ stood above the creaturely sphere. If a few sentences seem to associate Him with that sphere,[8] it is scarcely surprising in consideration of the truth that He was accounted the offspring of David,[9] and brother of men,[10] as well as the Son of God.[11]

The references of the Apocalypse to the Holy Spirit are not sufficiently specific to afford much ground for dogmatic inference. They emphasize a single function, namely that of inspiration or revelation. The Spirit is not mentioned as a source of regeneration or sanctification, unless it be in a general way in the greeting to the seven churches.[12] He appears essentially as the author

---

[1] iii. 1, v. 6. [3] v. 13, 14, vii. 10. [5] xxi. 22, 23.
[2] v. 12. [4] xvii. 14, xix. 16. [6] xxii. 1.
[7] xix. 10.

[8] i. 6, iii. 12. Over against the apparent inclusion in the created sphere in iii. 14 may be cited the apparent exclusion in v. 13.

[9] xxii. 16. [10] xii. 17. [11] ii. 18. [12] i. 4.

or bearer of a message.[1] In one of the forms of description used He is placed in a relation of very intimate union with the Son. The Son is said to have the seven spirits of God [2] — another name probably for the Holy Spirit viewed as inclusive of the complete circle of pneumatic powers and able to penetrate to all parts of the world with His glance.[3]

4. In pronounced contrast with the greater part of the Book of Acts and with the Epistle of James, the Apocalypse distinctly emphasizes the fulfillment of Christ's redemptive work in and through His death. The first doxology to Christ which it records pays tribute to Him as the one who "loosed us from our sins by His blood."[4] Again He is celebrated as the Lamb that was slain and that purchased unto God with His blood every tribe and tongue and people and nation.[5] Once more, the innumerable host of those who celebrate their victory in heaven are represented as owing their perfect cleansing to Him. They have washed their robes and made them white in the blood of the Lamb.[6] These are broad and unequivocal statements of the fact that human redemption depends upon the death of Christ. The manner or ground of this dependence, on the other hand, they do not make manifest. The most that can be said is, that the great stress

---

[1] i. 10, ii. 7, 17, 29, iii. 6, 13, 22, iv. 2, xiv. 13, xvii. 3, xxi. 10, xxii. 17.
[2] iii. 1, v. 6.
[3] Compare Zech. iv. 10. A different interpretation of the seven spirits makes them an exalted rank of angels. The difficulty with this interpretation is the association of them with God and Christ as a source of grace and peace. Such association is accordant neither with the tenor of the Apocalypse nor with that of any other New Testament book.
[4] i. 5.   [5] v. 9.   [6] vii. 9–14.

put upon the slain Lamb, taken in connection with the trend of Old and New Testament thinking on the subject of sacrifice, renders it probable that the apocalyptic writer attached an objective value to Christ's death, considered it to be, from the divine point of view, in some sort a condition of a general economy of grace or a fundamental factor in such an economy.

The pictorial character of the book dictated that it should represent religion more largely on its objective side than in its more interior characteristics. The extent moreover to which it deals with the theme of judgment gave a natural occasion to speak often of the works of men as an index of their deserts and prospects. As a matter of fact works are mentioned much more frequently than faith, and Christ is presented rather in His exterior relations than as a sacred power and presence in the inner life. One statement indeed brings out the thought of intimate companionship with Christ in the present. In the message to the Church in Laodicea He is represented as saying, "Behold I stand at the door and knock; if any man hear my voice and open the door, I will come in to him, and will sup with him, and he with me."[1] This is beautifully significant of close companionship; but generally speaking the Apocalypse stands in contrast with the Pauline and Johannine writings with their warm interest in the thought of an interior life-communion in the present between Christ and His disciples.

The lofty position assigned to Christ and the profound emphasis which is placed upon His blood as a means of

---

[1] iii 20

cleansing imply that a normal religious faith reposes very largely upon Him. It is noticeable, however, that in very rare instances, is there any direct mention of faith in Christ,[1] and that these instances are paralleled by others in which faith seems to be used in a broad way as equivalent to steadfast fidelity.[2] Concerning faith as distinctively the principle of justification before God there is no discourse whatever. With an evangelical valuation of Christ's sacrifice there is conjoined a somewhat legal representation of Christian piety. One statement, if taken literally, reads like a tribute to the ascetic standpoint; but there are reasons for construing the statement in a different sense.[3]

5. The Apocalypse gives a glowing picture of the perfected community of Christ, but says very little respecting the arrangements of the Church upon earth. It speaks rather of churches than of the Church. No nearer description of the church officiary is given than that contained in a bare mention of apostles and prophets. Some have indeed supposed that the angels of the Asiatic churches denote bishops. But there is no proper occasion for such a supposition. It belongs to the pic-

---

[1] ii. 13, xiv. 12.   [2] ii. 19, xiii. 10.

[3] Rev. xiv. 1–5. The exegesis which finds here a commendation of celibacy proper is thus criticised by Titius (Die vulgare Anschauung von der Seligkeit im Urchristenthum, p. 102): "At once the comparison with vii. 4 ff. (also with xx. 12 ff.) makes it improbable that we have to do here with only a troop of ascetics and not with the whole militant host of Christ.... The defilement with women cannot be meant simply of marriage, since that would directly collide with the universally prevalent Christian view; it must refer rather to whoredom. This in fact is an oft-employed image for God-forgetting worldliness (Apoc. xvii. 1–5, etc.; James iv. 4; Hermas, Simil. IX. xiii. 8 f.)." Compare Stevens, The Theology of the New Testament, p. 548.

torial character of the book to bring forward angels at every turn. In all probability the angels of the churches stand for ideal representatives, and the command to deliver a message to the angels of the churches is to be considered as only a more picturesque way of directing that a message be carried to the churches. This view is distinctly favored by the fact that the message in each instance has nothing to do with the standing or history of an individual official, but is wholly occupied with picturing the condition and needs of a Christian community.[1] That the writer's standpoint was not sacerdotal is indicated by his characterization of Christians generally as priests.[2] It is to be noticed further that no sacrament is mentioned, and that in the line of sacrificial service only the offering of incense is specified, which incense in one instance is identified with the prayers of the saints,[3] and in another instance is said to be mingled with the prayers.[4] The highest honor among glorified saints is ascribed to the twelve apostles, in that their names are said to be written upon the foundations of the wall of the New Jerusalem.[5] No reference to the Virgin Mary occurs. The woman pictured as arrayed with the sun, and the moon under her feet, and upon her head a crown of twelve stars, denotes the Jewish theocracy (or the Church as based in the Jewish theocracy), from which the Messiah springs, and the rest of her seed which is subject, with the Messiah, to the persecution of the dragon denotes the true children of the Messianic

---

[1] Compare Holtzmann, Hand-Commentar, IV. 320; Ramsay, The Letters to the Seven Churches of Asia, pp. 69–72.
[2] i. 6, v. 10. [3] v. 8. [4] viii. 3, 4. [5] xxi. 14.

TEACHING AKIN TO THE SYNOPTICAL 169

community who keep the commandments of God and hold the testimony of Jesus.[1] This mention of the seed of the woman is a clear enough intimation that it was not the Virgin Mary that the writer was depicting.

6. In the eschatology of the Apocalypse the most distinctive feature is doubtless the doctrine of the millennial reign of Christ with the martyred saints.[2] Nowhere else in the New Testament is this subject introduced. As near an approach to it as any is contained in Paul's declaration that Christ must reign till He hath put all His enemies under His feet.[3] But there is no distinct assertion here that the fruits of Christ's triumph are to be seen for a prolonged era upon the earth. The statement of Paul, therefore, differs from the apocalyptic representation of the millennial kingdom. The evident sense of the latter is that the cause of Christ, issuing from scenes of mortal struggle, is to enjoy an era of relative ascendency and peaceful triumph in the earth; that a favored company of Christ's servants is to anticipate the general resurrection; and that this company is to share in some special way in the glory and dominion of their Lord during the interval preceding the general resurrection and judgment. That the millennial reign is to be inaugurated by the visible coming of Christ and is to proceed as a visible administration of Christ and the risen saints is not said. It is a fair question whether it was thought by the revelator. Those, therefore, who would make a positive tenet of the idea of a future visible reign of Christ upon earth must build upon a very scanty foundation. They have not so much of a

---
[1] xii. 17.   [2] xx. 4–6.   [3] 1 Cor. xv. 25.

foundation as one definite expression in a single passage of a single biblical writer, but only what may possibly have been the thought of the revelator in penning a single passage.

Aside from the millennial reign the most noticeable feature, perhaps, in the eschatology of the Apocalypse is the fact that the earth comes to view beyond the judgment scene. Heaven does not absorb the whole outlook. Together with the new heaven a new earth appears. The new Jerusalem, too, stands not apart in a heavenly enclosure. It comes down out of heaven from God. In all this representation there was probably little design to make much of locality. The thought is that throughout the regenerated universe a scene of beauty is to be spread and the glory of God made signally manifest. The heavenly model is to be perfectly reflected even in the lower province.

7. In estimating the Apocalypse the thought lies near at hand that its value is not to be measured by the extent of its dogmatic content. There is a healthful tonic in its religious intensity. It supplies a great store of riches to the religious imagination. It dignifies the Christian warfare as part of a great drama that is being led on to a transcendently glorious issue. Well has it been called the epic of Christian hope. Many of its outlooks have perennial charm, and many of its words descend generation after generation like strains of celestial music upon the troubled hearts of men. Let it be granted that some of its delineations were better suited to win appreciation in that age of apocalyptic production than in the present; let it be granted also that it has

some stones of stumbling for the most clear-sighted and unbiased exegete; it is still a book which, through the wealth of its content, fulfills the high function of being profitable unto righteousness.

CHAPTER IV

THE PAULINE THEOLOGY

I. — THE SEVERAL GROUPS OF PAULINE EPISTLES.

1. The two Epistles to the Thessalonians stand by themselves, not only as being probably the earliest in the order of composition, but also as possessing in common a character which distinguishes them from the other epistles of the apostle. This character may be defined negatively as a relative lack of insistence upon doctrinal features which are powerfully inculcated in the central group of epistles. In neither epistle do we discover a line which speaks of justification by faith, or shows up the futility of the legal method of salvation, or paints in strong colors the contrast between the natural and the spiritual man. One line only contains a reference to the death of Christ. Indirectly some of these points may be touched upon in the stress which is placed upon the "grace of Christ" and the "work of faith." It is to be conceded also that a characteristic Pauline conception comes to expression in the view which is taken of the Holy Spirit, as being an abiding resident and principle of sanctification in believing souls, as well as a source of extraordinary gifts. Still there is a noticeable lack of what any one familiar with the sum total of Paul's writings would be disposed to describe as distinctive features

of his teaching. Positively considered, the special character of the Thessalonian Epistles appears in the approximation of their line of thought to the primitive apostolic type, as this is reflected in the early chapters of the Book of Acts. This approximation may be noticed in the prominence which is given to the anticipation of Christ's return, and in a close association of the office of Christ with the great events which belong at the end of the dispensation, as opposed to an explicit emphasis upon His present indwelling. The thought of a mystical union with Christ, which is seen elsewhere to have commanded the intense enthusiasm of the apostle, recedes in these writings behind the objective phases of the Redeemer's work, as these were commonly apprehended in the early days of Christianity.

In explaining the relatively simple and primitive form of teaching which we find here, it is not forbidden to take some account of the consideration that Paul may not have obtained his entire theological outfit all at once. But we are advised against making too much of the notion that he was himself at an elementary stage in his thinking at the time he wrote to the church at Thessalonica, when we consider the moderate interval between these communications and one which represents such a radical and advanced type of Paulinism as does the Epistle to the Galatians. It is altogether probable that in the score of years which had elapsed since his conversion he had pretty well thought through his system. But in dealing with a newly founded community of believers, within which theological speculation and controversy had not yet been fairly started, there was no need of disquisition of the more subtle kind. Accommodation to those addressed is, therefore, the best part of the explanation of the special cast of the Thessalonian Epistles. We may suppose that, in a like use of missionary discretion, the apostle often gave forth a message as little distinguished by subtlety and theological elaboration. His profounder epistles, written to meet great theological issues, are not to be taken as samples of his uniform method as a religious teacher.

Opposition to the Pauline authorship of the First Epistle to the Thessalonians may be said to have been reduced so nearly to the vanishing point as no longer to deserve consideration. In respect of the Second Epistle more doubt is entertained, though the tendency of criticism is clearly toward a favorable judgment. One of the main grounds for suspicion is the passage in the second chapter relative to antichrist or the man of sin. This, it is alleged, agrees ill with the picture of the imminence of Christ's coming in the former epistle, since it projects that coming into the distance, placing it beyond a culminating manifestation of ungodliness. It is also alleged that the apocalyptic passage in question shows dependence upon the Johannine Apocalypse. Neither objection, however, has any great weight. The second epistle corrects indeed an over-feverish expectation respecting the speedy coming of Christ, but it does not dissuade the Thessalonians from the belief that it is relatively near at hand, so as possibly to fall within the existing generation; and the first epistle does not deny that important historical developments are to precede the advent. That great event, it is true, is depicted as likely to overtake the unheeding as a thief in the night; but it is not stated that "the sons of the day" are to be destitute of all faculty to detect signs of the approaching crisis.[1] As regards the assumption of dependence upon the Johannine Apocalypse, it may be replied, that it is quite gratuitous to suppose that the writer drew from that source. If we are to conclude, as exegetes very commonly assume, that by the "one that restraineth" the Roman government is to be understood, then we have in the Thessalonian passage a prominent element to which nothing in the Johannine Apocalypse properly corresponds. As respects the delineation as a whole, we need not suppose any such dearth of sources that Paul could not have written it in advance of the composition of the seer of Patmos. Hints in the eschatological discourses of Christ, Paul's own reflection, and the broad stream of apocalyptic representations in preceding and comtemporary Judaism may reasonably be regarded as affording sufficient materials for the picture of antichrist that is given. In no other connection, it is true, has Paul furnished us an equivalent picture; but, then, it is also true that we are not informed that he had a like occasion again to curb a too exciting expectation of the second advent.

Among remaining objections the reference to a spurious epistle[2] and the marked literary dependence upon First Thessalonians receive the most emphasis. As to the former, it must be granted that we should not naturally expect the appearance of a spurious epistle at so early a date; but it is to be observed that there is no

---

[1] 1 Thess. v. 1–5. [2] 2 Thess. ii. 2, iii. 17.

decisive evidence of the existence of such an epistle. The facts are simply these: Paul found that the enthusiasts were appealing to a letter of his in behalf of their mistaken notions. He was unwilling to admit that a proper basis for these notions could be found in anything which he had written; and so he cast up the question whether a false epistle had not found its way to Thessalonica. His words embody only a surmise of a possible fact. As respects literary dependence, it is doubtless true that Second Thessalonians reproduces to a marked degree the phraseology of First Thessalonians.[1] But it is no unheard-of thing for an author, with or without design, to reproduce from a previous writing. Moreover, it is scarcely more of an enigma that Paul should in a measure repeat himself than that a forger should be at pains to imitate closely the language of Paul through the compass of several chapters, just for the sake of inserting a brief item of apocalyptic representation.

It may be noticed that a couple of time marks, as making for the early origin of the epistle, are favorable to the supposition of Pauline authorship. On the one hand, the reference to the temple (ii. 4) — presumably to that in Jerusalem — points to a date prior to the year 70. On the other hand, the reference to "one that re-restraineth" (ii. 6, 7), in so far as there are grounds for applying this phrase to the Roman government, points to a time anterior to the year 64; since, after the atroci-

---

[1] Wrede makes this the foremost objection to the Pauline authorship of the epistle. He concedes that the content of the apocalyptic passage in the second chapter is not an insuperable obstacle to attributing the epistle to the apostle. (Die Echtheit des zweiten Thessalonicherbriefs.)

ties perpetrated under the hand of Nero, there would be very little incentive in a Christian mind to portray the Roman government as a safeguard against fanatical violence.

2. In the second group of epistles we have a much fuller expression of the intellectual energy, spiritual affluence, and matured theological reflection of Paul than in the one just characterized. The terms which Pfleiderer applies to one of them, in describing it as a "glorious monument of a great religious genius," may with equal right be applied to each one of them. Here belong the epistles to the Galatians, the Corinthians, and the Romans. These writings undoubtedly contain the conceptions which filled and fired the soul of Paul at the zenith of his apostolic ministry. There is no question as to their genuineness, except on the part of a kind of madhouse criticism, such as might disport itself in a pretended proof that Napoleon Bonaparte never had any place in European history. An inquiry can indeed be raised as to whether the list of salutations in the sixteenth chapter of Romans and also some lesser portions of the same chapter belong with this particular writing. There is room likewise for a query as to whether the last four chapters of Second Corinthians did not form originally a distinct communication to the Corinthian congregation. But these are questions of place and time, and involve no objection of any consequence to Pauline authorship. Biblical theology does not need to discuss them.[1]

---

[1] Not a few scholars are of opinion that Ephesus is to be accounted a much more probable destination than Rome for such a list of salutations as is given in xvi. 1-16. On the other hand, it is urged that the

Among these epistles that to the Romans has the least appearance of having been dictated by special local conditions. Very likely there was somewhat in the situation of the Christian community at Rome which made it appropriate for Paul to address to them the special line of thought to which he had recourse. Still there is some reason for the conjecture that the apostle, after a season of spirited controversy, wished to put on record a connected statement of the truths which he counted it his vocation to champion, and was aware that in addressing the congregation at the great capital he was likely to give his apostolic message to the Church at large. In its contents the Epistle to the Romans repeats the cardinal antitheses of the Epistle to the Galatians, namely those between law method and gospel method, between flesh and spirit. It elucidates, however, the antitheses more at length, branches out into related themes, and sketches in fuller outline a theory of history and a philosophy of salvation. The tone of the later writing, though very spirited, is less polemical than that of the earlier; at least, the former gives more indication of a disposition to qualify the radical disparagement of Judaism which

---

proportion of the names which are Roman in form, or which occur in sepulchral inscriptions in the neighborhood of the great capital, makes for the conclusion that this section may properly be reckoned a part of the original epistle to the church of Rome.

Recent criticism has exhibited a tendency to rate the last four chapters of Second Corinthians as an independent epistle. However, in the absence of adequate means of decision, the modest suggestion of Jülicher is quite in place. "There remains for us," he says, "matter for surprise in the change of tone and bearing, but we have a much more imperfect knowledge of the situation of the writer than did the first readers by whom alone Paul wished to be understood." (Einleitung, p. 78.)

the Pauline theory might be thought to imply. Through its varied contents the Epistle to the Romans illustrates, to a special degree, the many-sided ability of Paul.[1] In the Corinthian Epistles we have glimpses of the dogmatic postulates contained in Romans and Galatians. But they are made to share the field of vision with a great variety of practical questions, such as the administration of a restless, inquisitive Greek society, under the pressure of a sensuous civilization, naturally had to confront. More than any other of his writings they give us a full length picture of Paul as man and administrator. At the same time their theological contribution is important. No where else has the apostle given anything like so full an expression of his thought on the subjects of the Lord's supper and the resurrection.

3. A distinct group among the Pauline writings is constituted by the series of prison epistles, or those addressed to the Philippians, to Philemon, to the Colossians, and to a circle of Asiatic churches. This last came to be styled the Epistle to the Ephesians. But historical evidence favors the conclusion that Ephesus was not mentioned in the original letter, and its contents are decidedly adverse to the supposition that it was specially meant for a congregation in which the apostle had labored for a long interval. Recent scholarship to a very large extent regards it as a circular letter, designed for a list of churches some of which at least Paul had not visited in person.

---

[1] "Here the entire Paul," says Julicher, "presents himself to our contemplation: the rabbinical scholastic, the inspired poet, the sober farsighted pastor of souls, and the keen thinker, who with unsparing resolution carries out the lines which make all to proceed from God and to end in Him." (Einleitung, p. 92.)

In this group of epistles there are indications that the mind of the writer was still tenacious of the points of view which had been championed in Galatians and Romans. But these are not thrust to the front as they were in the earlier epistles. The author proceeds as though the crisis of the battle against Judaic legality and exclusiveness had passed, and there was a good prospect for the cause of Christian freedom and universalism. He contents himself therefore with brief statements or intimations of the principles for which he had contended in the controversy with the Judaizers, and gives room, if not to strictly new points of view, at least to a fuller consideration of special features of his faith. This is true in particular of the teaching respecting Christ and the Church contained in Colossians and Ephesians. The substance of this teaching, it is not to be denied, had already been brought to view, since in the preceding group of epistles large views are broached respecting the headship of Christ and respecting the significance of redemption for the creature universe in general.[1] But it is characteristic of these prison epistles that they exhibit a special interest in asserting the universal lordship and unifying function of Christ, and that they make more distinct account of the Church as one great unity than appears in any previous writing of the apostle. We speak here in particular of Colossians and Ephesians, since Philippians is a confidential and affectionate communication to a beloved congregation, and shows only in minor degree a dogmatic purpose.

On the question of the authorship of these epistles a

---

[1] 1 Cor. viii. 6; Rom. viii. 19–22.

relative unanimity has been reached in favor of the composition of Philippians by Paul. A very considerable consensus has also been established for the Pauline authorship of Colossians. Ephesians meets a somewhat larger current of doubt; but is favored nevertheless with a good list of scholarly defenders of its Pauline origin. A principal ground of challenge, as brought forward against both Colossians and Ephesians, is the advance in theological construction shown in these epistles. In reply, three facts are properly noticed. The advance, as was indicated above, was no leap to a new position discordant with that previously advocated; it consisted only in a more emphatic putting of points of view already broached.[1] Again, since writing the last in the foregoing group of Epistles, Paul had passed years in imprisonment, and it is quite conceivable that in his relative retirement

---

[1] This is very clearly illustrated, as respects Ephesians, in the following· "The exalted christology might seem incredible at so early a period but for the simple fact that in every essential feature it is corroborated in undeniably genuine passages. Disregarding the parallels in Colossians, as disputed, we find the same conception of Christ as preexistent in 2 Cor. viii. 9, Phil. ii. 5–11; as the image of God, archetype of redeemed humanity, in Rom. viii. 29, 2 Cor. iii. 18, Phil. iii. 21; as beginning and end of creation in association with God in 1 Cor. viii. 6, xv. 22–28; as lord of all created being in heaven and earth and under the earth, triumphant over angelic and demonic powers in Phil. ii 9–11, 1 Cor. xv. 24 ff.; as agent of a cosmic redemption in Rom. viii. 19–22. And this is but the negative half of the argument; for in 1 Cor. i. 24, 30, ii. 6–10, 16 we have hints that Paul also has a philosophy wherewith he could put to shame the speculations of the Corinthians, had he deemed them prepared for it, — a philosophy which was concerned with Christ as the power of God and the wisdom of God. It consisted of a revelation of the 'hidden mystery of God which he preordained before the worlds unto our glory' (1 Cor. ii. 7; cf. Rom. xvi. 25–27; Eph. i.

from active work he had matured theological construction in one direction or another. Finally, it is not improbable that Paul had a special occasion for the amplification and strong putting of the distinctive themes of these epistles. As many commentators have observed,[1] they seem to contemplate an incipient Judaic type of Gnosticism, a scheme in which ceremonial and ascetic peculiarities were combined with an exaggerated view of the mediation of angels. In combatting this form of error the apostle naturally emphasized strongly the unique headship of Christ and the universality and completeness of his reconciling office; and from this standpoint he could not well do otherwise than give a certain emphasis to the Church as a great spiritual unity affording an exemplification of the unifying work of Christ.

The objection that phrases of second century Gnosticism, such as " pleroma," occur, is by no means formidable. This term was not unknown to Paul's earlier vocabulary, and he was sufficiently in repute with many of the Gnostics to make it entirely credible that they bor-

---

4–12, iii 9–10), and set forth the divine plan in creation and redemption (1 Cor. ii. 9–11). Again, what have we in Romans as a whole but this same theme of the revealed purpose of God in creation and redemption (xi. 31–36)? Here the full extent of what is meant by the cosmic atonement is but darkly hinted in chapter viii, and the union of Jew and Gentile in the new people of God in chapters ix–xi is only a hope. But in Ephesians, with the supplemental parallels of Colossians, Paul opens wide to us, as no imitator could, the doors of that comprehensive cosmic philosophy of his faith " (B. W. Bacon, Introduction to the New Testament, pp. 118, 119).

[1] Among others Von Soden, Haupt, Lightfoot, Moule, and T. K. Abbott.

rowed from his phraseology.[1] In general it may be said of Paul's vocabulary that variation through a wide scale is nothing intrinsically improbable. The creative force of the man, joined with a continuous change of environment, naturally wrought for the use of new terms. As Mahaffy has noticed, the roving Greek writer, Xenophon, presents a parallel in respect of a progressive vocabulary. His later tracts abound in words — many of them used only once — that are not contained in his earlier writings,[2]

In reply to the further objection that one of the epistles under consideration incorporates, in moderately varied phrase, portions of the subject-matter of the other,[3] it may be said that the admission of this fact does not make seriously against the Pauline authorship of either. Indeed, the most satisfactory explanation of the resembling features in the two lies in the supposition that they were composed near the same time, and that much in one was sufficiently in the memory of the writer to be reproduced in the other. Another than the author of Colossians, attempting to blend parts of it with matter of his own, would almost inevitably have given more of

---

[1] Criticism manifestly tends to the conclusion that nothing in the references to heresy in Colossians necessarily points to a time subsequent to the rise of the great Gnostic systems. In the opinion of Julicher the Gnosticism opposed here was even older than Christianity (Einleitung, p. 105). "That there existed," says Harnack, "a Jewish Gnosticism, before there was a Christian or Jewish-Christian, is indubitable" (Geschichte der altchristlichen Litteratur, I. 144).

[2] Cited by Salmon, Historical Introduction to the Study of the Books of the New Testament, p. 470.

[3] A marked relation of this sort is undeniable. It is estimated that out of the one hundred and fifty-five verses contained in Ephesians seventy-eight show a distinct kinship, in point of phraseology, with Colossians (Salmond in Expositor's Greek Testament, III. 215).

the appearance of patchwork to his composition than Ephesians actually presents; and the same may be said of Colossians, should Ephesians be deemed the prior epistle.

As respects the relation of contrast between the two epistles, a satisfactory explanation, it may be admitted, is not quite so readily afforded. And here the burden of objection falls undoubtedly upon Ephesians. For Colossians a weighty attestation is provided in the fact that it reflects the same historical situation which is implied in the letter to Philemon, the genuineness of which is so thoroughly evidenced by its tone and content that the criticism which attempts a challenge inevitably discredits itself.[1] Along with this advantage the Colossian epistle can claim to stand apart from the general body of the Pauline writings by a somewhat narrower margin of peculiarity than that which distinguishes the Ephesian epistle. The latter carries to a greater extreme the feature of complex sentences — sentences formed by the addition of clause to clause in long succession. It gives also a special impression of mysticism, and shows the most points of approximation to the Johannine type of any writing which bears the name of Paul.[2] But while the case is stronger for

---

[1] Well does Renan say of this little epistle: "Few are the pages which show so pronounced a tone of sincerity. Paul alone, so far as it appears, was capable of that short masterpiece." (Saint Paul, p. 13.)

[2] Ephesians shows a likeness to the fourth Gospel in the stress upon both love and knowledge, in the symbolical use of the terms "light" and "darkness," in the reference to the indwelling of Christ, in the description of regeneration as a quickening of the dead, in the representation of sanctification or cleansing as taking place by the medium

Colossians than for Ephesians, it does not follow that the Pauline authorship of Ephesians is made improbable. In a man of such versatility as was Paul variation in mood and in the absorbing point of view may be supposed to have been capable of effecting very appreciable differences in writings adjacent to one another in the chronological order. Then, too, the fact that Ephesians was, at least in a relative sense, a general epistle, written without respect to the local conditions of any specific congregation, may be regarded as favorable to the free movement of reflective thought, and so tending to impart to this product of the mellower years of the great apostle a distinctive tone. But whatever remains to be explained, we find in the deep soul of Paul the probable source of this mighty effusion, as against any man who would venture to impersonate Paul. It carries in itself no mean attestation of genuineness in the vitality of sentiment with which it is pervaded. As Findlay remarks: "For our author the revelation has lost none of its novelty and surprise. He is in the midst of the excitement it has produced, and is himself its chief agent and mouth-piece. This disclosure of God's secret plans for the world overwhelms him by its magnitude, by the splendor with which it invests the divine character, and the sense of his personal unworthiness to be intrusted with it. We utterly disbelieve that any later Christian writer could or would have personated the apostle, and

---

of the word, in making the gift of the Holy Spirit dependent on the ascension of Christ. Compare i. 4 in Eph. with xvii. 24 in John; ii. 2 with xii. 31; ii. 5, 6 with v. 21, 25; iii. 6 with x. 16; iii. 17 with xiv. 20, 23; iv. 7 with iii. 35; iv. 8–10 with iii. 13, xvi. 7; v. 8 with xii. 35; v. 11, 13, with iii. 20, 21; v. 26 with xv, 3, xvii. 19.

mimicked his tone and sentiments in regard to his vocation, in the way the critical hypothesis assumes. The criterion of Erasmus is decisive: Nemo potest Paulinum pectus effingere." [1]

4. The Pastoral Epistles, or those addressed to Timothy and Titus, must be regarded as composed an appreciable interval after all other extant writings associated with Paul. As Zahn states, there is no tenable ground for maintaining their Pauline authorship unless the release of the apostle from the Roman imprisonment described in Acts and his renewed missionary activity are accepted as facts.[2] If from the hand of Paul, the Pastoral Epistles must have been written at a stage in his life quite distinct from that represented by Philippians, Colossians, and Ephesians.

As respects external evidences, the genuineness of the Pastoral Epistles is fairly well supported. The ground for doubt lies mainly in their spirit and contents. On this score the following objections are urged: (1) It is difficult to believe that Paul in writing to his familiar companions in labor could have thought it necessary to speak in such a defensive strain respecting his apostolic vocation as appears in various sentences of these epistles.[3] (2) The tone of the addresses to Timothy and Titus is excessively paternal. We should not expect that the apostle, in communicating with men who had been for years trusted colaborers, would think it necessary to remind them of the most ordinary duties. Then, too, the reference to Timothy's youth cannot be regarded as apt,

---

[1] The Epistle to the Ephesians in Expositor's Bible, p. 6.
[2] Einleitung, I. 435.   [3] 1 Tim. i. 12-17, ii. 7; 2 Tim. i. 3, 11.

when it is considered that he must have been older than was Jesus at the time of His crucifixion and quite as old as was Paul at the beginning of his apostolic ministry. (3) As regards language, these letters afford a very equivocal testimony for Pauline authorship. The list of words that do not occur elsewhere in the writings of the apostle is relatively large; and moreover there is a marked absence of the characteristic Pauline particles.[1] (4) The way in which the writer lumps together heretical teachings, and simply denounces rather than refutes them, is below the plane of Paul's discrimination and intellectual fertility. (5) In respect of force and continuity of thought there is a decided falling short of the Pauline measure. (6) While a certain base of Pauline conceptions is apparent in the epistles, the governing tone is more akin to post-apostolic moralism, or the early Catholic system, than to the tenor of Paul's dogmatics. In place of the Pauline stress on faith, as a means of reconciliation and transforming union with God, and on the life of sonship, we have a recurring mention of the good conscience, of godliness, of sound doctrine, and of faith viewed as one of the virtues or even as a sum of truth to be confessed.[2]

On the other hand, it is urged that there are personal items in the Pastoral Epistles which cannot reasonbly be

---

[1] The following particles and prepositions are mentioned by Bacon (Introduction, p. 139) as being wanting: ἄρα, διό, διότι, ἔπειτα, ἔτι, ἴδε, ἰδού, μήπων, ὅπως, οὐκέτι, οὔπω, οὔτε, πάλιν, ἐν παντί, πότε, ποῦ, ὥσπερ, ἀντί, ἄχρι, ἔμπροσθεν, ἕνεκεν, παρά with the accusative, σύν.

[2] The use of faith in this objective sense occurs in 1 Tim. iv. 1, vi. 10, 21; Titus i. 4.

attributed to any other hand than that of Paul; that they contain genuinely Pauline turns of expression; that they include not a few names of which there is no mention either in the Acts or in the epistles of Paul, whereas one attempting to impersonate the apostle would naturally have borrowed from these sources such names as it might be convenient to use; and that Paul, feeling that he had paid his debt to constructive theology, might very naturally in communications to administrators diverge from the line pursued in his earlier epistles, and put a special stress upon matters pertaining to church order. That there is a very appreciable weight in some of these considerations is intimated by the tendency of recent criticism, even when denying the Pastoral Epistles as a whole to Paul, to admit that they were based upon notes or fragments of genuine epistles. So have decided among others Hesse, Harnack, McGiffert, and Bacon. Among those who accept this conclusion it is the common verdict that of the three epistles Second Timothy bears most of a Pauline impress. As the subject now stands, we consider that we shall be rendering sufficient tribute to critical objections by separating this group of epistles from the rest, and treating of their subject matter in the concluding section of the chapter.

II.— THE SOURCES OF THE PAULINE THEOLOGY.

The question of Paul's relation to Pharisaic Judaism and to the Alexandrian theology, as having already been discussed,[1] does not need to be considered in this con-

---

[1] See Chapter I.

nection. There are other factors, however, which may be supposed to have entered into his equipment. Here belong the evangelical tradition, the familiarity of the apostle with the Old Testament, and special features of his experience and personality.

1. The scanty reference to matters pertaining to the life of Christ which is found in Paul's epistles cannot be taken as any sure token that he did not entertain a lively interest in the facts of that marvellous biography. The epistolary literature of the New Testament in general is relatively silent respecting the works and the words of Christ. In brief productions of this order the writers not unnaturally occupied themselves with cardinal inductions from the whole sum of gospel facts, and left to the teacher, present with the congregation, to give by word of mouth the more concrete picture of the Master. That Paul did not reserve a place for extracts from the gospel story cannot, then, be regarded as by any means significant of an indifferent attitude. No more is a trustworthy evidence of lack of interest to be found in that remark to the Corinthians in which he disparages the notion of knowing Christ after the flesh.[1] To know after the flesh is to know according to mere externals, to judge by things secondary and adventitions, a Jew for example by his lineage, a rich man by the trappings of wealth, a scholar by his use of technical language. From such artificiality and externalism Paul says that he had graduated. Since God had revealed His Son in him he had known Christ in the spiritual wealth belonging to His person and office. This revised point of view does

[1] 2 Cor. v. 16.

not imply that henceforth he took no interest in the facts of Christ's life; it denotes rather that he was disposed to judge them by a better than an external standard, being now in condition to grasp and appreciate their significance as being manifestations of the Lord and Saviour of men, and not merely incidents in the career of a certain Nazarene teacher.

On the side of positive considerations for the conclusion that Paul took pains to acquaint himself, as far as was possible, with the content of the evangelical tradition, we may adduce the natural effect of his enthusiastic love and devotion to Christ. How should not the earthly ministry of Him in whom was centred his hope for himself and the race be an object of earnest and affectionate interest? Then, too, it is in evidence that at an early point in his course he took pains to confer with one of those who were best able to recount the gospel story.[1] No record, it is true, is afforded us respecting the subject of conversation in his fifteen days' interview with Peter; but it is difficult to believe that the converted Pharisee did not utilize the occasion to learn what a foremost eye-witness of the life of Christ was able to impart. It may also be suggested that Paul's companions, Barnabas and Mark, in virtue of their association with the primitive disciples, were able in a measure to supply him with the content of the genuine evangelical tradition. Again, he has indicated quite explicitly that he took pains to acquaint himself with that tradition insofar as it bore on certain important matters.[2] Furthermore, in the language of Paul an occasional echo of the

---

[1] Gal. i. 18.   [2] I Cor. xi. 23, xv. 3-7.

words of Christ may be discovered.[1] Once more, while it is true that the apostle seems to place the maximum stress upon the death of Christ rather than upon his life, yet it is quite manifest that he could not have dissociated the import of the death from the quality of the life by which it was prefaced. Indeed, he has profoundly emphasized the fact that the one who gave himself to death upon the cross was the perfectly obedient Son of God who knew no sin.[2] Occupying this point of view he must be supposed to have been interested in the content of Christ's life as affording ground for confidence in His actual realization of the ideal of sinless obedience.

It results from the foregoing that it does poor justice to Paul's theology to regard it as a speculative system projected from his own mind and swinging clear of a historical basis. It was founded upon historic antecedents. Back of it all was the revelation in and through Christ. According to his own conception the apostle figured, not as a free-handed system-maker, but as an expounder of the import of indubitable facts. In respect of form his exposition is no doubt somewhat remote from Christ's teaching. In place of the calm, overmastering, intuitional method of the latter, we have the struggle of the disputant, earnest argumentation running here and there into a subtlety that taxes the exegetical faculty of the reader. The difference is like that between the appearance of the stars when viewed on the face of the overarching sky and their appearance when

---

[1] Gal. v. 21; 1 Cor. vi. 9, vii. 10, ix. 14, xv. 50; Rom. xii. 19-21; 1 Thess. ii. 15, 16, iv. 15-17, v. 1-6; 2 Thess. ii. 2.

[2] Rom. v. 19; 2 Cor. v. 21; Phil. ii. 8.

they are reflected in the moving and uneven sea.[1] Still, with all its contrasting features, the Pauline exposition has very close affinity with the teaching of Christ. In apprehending the interior and gracious character of the kingdom, as it was conceived by his Master, the apostle to the Gentiles was in advance even of the most free-spirited leaders within the group of the original disciples.

2. In estimating the extent of Paul's dependence upon the Old Testament two things need to be kept in mind. In the first place it must be granted that the spiritual revolution through which he passed and the task to which he was assigned made him in an emphatic sense a man of the new dispensation. He regarded the message of God in Christ as the unrivalled disclosure of divine wisdom and love. His heart was enkindled in the thought of the greatness of the gospel consummation. It seemed to him to outshine all the glory of past religious history. To be conformed to it he regarded as nothing less than becoming a new creature and getting into a new world. From this standpoint he naturally did not hesitate, when the occasion came, to cast a disparaging glance at the legal system of the Old Testament. He described it as a system more properly symbolized by the estate of a handmaid than by that of a free woman, corresponding rather to the earthly Jerusalem under a yoke of servitude than to the free city of God, the Jerusalem that is above. It has been concluded by many exegetes that Paul meant also to disparage the legal system in his representation that it was ordained through the ministry of angels,[2] and was thus entitled to inferior honor as compared with

---

[1] Compare Beyschlag, II. 25.   [2] Gal. iii. 19.

THE PAULINE THEOLOGY 193

the scheme of grace which obtained a primary illustration in God's dealing with Abraham, and came to its full manifestation in the Lord Jesus Christ. This rendering is favored by the antithesis which the author of the Epistle to the Hebrews makes between the Old Testament message voiced through angels and the more glorious message voiced through the Son of God.[1] But on the other hand, it is to be observed that the connection of angels with the giving of the law is mentioned in the speech of Stephen as a means of emphasizing the sanctity and importance of the law.[2] It is to be noticed also that the New Testament picture of the second advent shows that it was in line with the religious custom of the age to dignify a great event by associating the ministry of angels therewith. In the absence, then, of a formal contrast between direct divine agency and angelic agency, there is room for a shade of doubt as to the meaning which the apostle designed to put into his words. He may have brought in the reference to the mediation of the law through angels in deference to the current Jewish description. It may be granted, however, that the reference seems to acquire increased pertinency if taken as designed to mark the secondary place pertaining to the law.

The other consideration which needs to be kept in mind is, that Paul's vital consciousness of the new in the gospel dispensation is not to be regarded as so far displacing the Old Testament content from his mind but that he retained a large residuum from its teaching. In the background of his theological construction there re-

---
[1] Heb. ii. 2, 3. [2] Acts vii. 53.

mained continuously the general conceptions of God's nature and attributes, of divine providence in the world, of man's nature, and of his metaphysical and ethical relations to God, which are set forth in the Hebrew Scriptures. It is to be observed furthermore that Paul's formal attitude toward the law is not to be taken as precisely descriptive of his attitude toward the Old Testament. As his reference to the justification of Abraham indicates, he found upon its pages anticipations of the divine method which he regarded as distinctive of the gospel dispensation.

Putting the two considerations together, we reach the conclusion that the enthusiasm of Paul's soul was centred upon points of view special to Christianity, but that nevertheless, as a natural result of his training, he held fast a considerable framework of Old Testament conceptions. He cherished but little independent interest in the oracles of the older dispensation; yet his interest was not meagre, inasmuch as he regarded that dispensation as fulfilling a great providential office in preparing for the effectual publication of the gospel.

In his formal estimate of the Hebrew revelation the apostle probably did not take time to revise the current view of inspiration. Where he found matter that was not well suited to edify, a favorite exegetical expedient of the age invited him to help out the lessons of holy writ by recourse to typical or allegorical meanings. Still, instances of this style of interpretation do not abound in his epistles. For the most part they are such as might easily be suggested to a mind filled with the vision of Christ and convinced that the real function of the Old Testament was to prepare the way for Christ.[1] To a mind thus conditioned it could seem only an unworthy impoverishment of the significance of the sacred oracles to tie them down continuously to the plain literal sense. And in truth, whatever may be thought of the apostle's manipulation of typical meanings in Old Testament passages, it cannot be denied that in the very nature of the case an earlier stage in a progressive unfoldment evolves types of things pertaining to the later and more perfect stage. Evolutionary science of the most unpoetic description will not shun to acknowledge this truth.

3. The experience of Paul cannot be reckoned a subordinate factor in his theological equipment. In both of its divisions, Jewish and Christian, it served to furnish him with intense convictions. For a man of his earnestness of spirit to attempt to work out salvation by the legal method was naturally fruitful of insight into the difficulties of the method. His attempt to measure up to the law, however successful in outward and superficial respects, he knew to be a failure in respect of the deeper requirements. Renewed struggle brought a renewed sense of his shortcomings. The inward schism seemed past healing. He recognized the goodness of the standard which the law set before him, but mastery was wanting over the impulses which were continually exciting to rebellion. So the commandment which was ordained unto life became like a sentence of death. The ordinary Pharisee would have eliminated much of the bitterness of the situation by dwelling on the grounds of

---

[1] See Gal. iv. 21–31; 1 Cor. x. 4; 2 Cor. iii. 13–17.

self-approval. But Paul was not an ordinary Pharisee any more than Martin Luther at Erfurt was an ordinary monk. So he pushed on in the attempt to work out his justification before the law, and knew full well the smart and pain of conscious failure. Here was the preparation for his transformation into the Christian apostle. It has been conjectured that the reasonings and the demeanor of the Christians whom he pursued in his persecuting zeal had wrought in some measure to undermine his assurance that he was serving the truth in his onslaught upon them. In point of theory this is not incredible. There is, however, no warrant for it in recorded history. The New Testament gives no hint of such an antecedent of Paul's conversion. The only preparation for conversion to which it points us is the negative preparation involved in the painful striving for salvation on a legal basis, which is sketched in the seventh chapter of the Epistle to the Romans. The experienced impotence of the Pharisaic method to bring spiritual life and inward satisfaction disposed him to embrace a method which should approve itself as really successful, and to advocate it with whole-souled ardor.

With the revelation of the risen Christ came the vision of the new and the better method. What he could not achieve by the way of self-subjection to the law he found attainable by faith upon Christ. It was as if a friendly hand had reached down from the sky and lifted him up to a new plane of living. In union with Christ he had peace, sense of emancipation, power for overcoming self and the world. His horizon was at once greatly widened out and greatly illuminated. His sympathies broke over their old bounds, and an end was brought into view, so glorious and so vividly apprehended, that in its pursuit suffering and privation could be regarded as subtracting practically nothing from the sum total of personal well-being.

These contrasted orders of experiences could not fail to act potently upon Paul's theological thinking. They seem to have borne fruit very speedily. The Pharisaism of their subject was inverted, or turned in respect of cardinal features into the opposite. The experience of legal bondage and the experience of emancipation through Christ combined to divert his appreciation from the method of legal performance to the method of faith, of trustful self-committal, of heart union with a gracious Redeemer. In renouncing dependence upon the legal method he relinquished the main support of Jewish exclusiveness, for it was in particular the law which fenced Israel away from the rest of the world. In a scheme of grace no good reason could appear for maintaining dividing lines between Jew and Gentile. Paul advanced, therefore, readily to the standpoint of Christian universalism. The method and the greatness of his own deliverance dictated that he should look to Christ as representing an economy gloriously transcending the old legal economy. By natural sequence he regarded Him as not merely the Jewish Messiah but the world's Saviour. He was true to the lessons of his experience in that he gravitated into a theology Christo-centric and world-embracing in its outlook.

The special manner in which Christ was revealed to Paul before the gates of Damascus had doubtless its effect upon his habitual representation of his Master. The image which remained before his mind was that of a transcendently glorious being, so that spontaneously he confessed His lordship, and through his ministry continued by preference to call Him the Lord Jesus Christ. Still it would be a mistake to suppose that Paul's glance was directed solely to the glory of Christ as the ascended Lord. He has indicated very distinctly that the humiliation of his Master was much in his thought. The one conception wrought with the other to enkindle simultaneously reverence and affection. The result was a devotion, an absorption in Christ marvellously intense and unwavering. Next to Christ's own sense of union with the Father in heaven the most unique expression of the inner life of the spirit in the New Testament is found in Paul's sense of union with Christ.

The characteristics of Paul's personality cannot be regarded as holding an indifferent relation either to the espousal or the propagation of his special theological type. At the foundation was genuine earnestness. Half-hearted allegiance to what he esteemed to be the truth was foreign to his disposition. Depth of feeling and energy of will were quite as much factors in his make-up as strength of thought. He was far from being the passionless logician or hard-headed scholastic. Doubtless he had a certain fondness for argument and a good degree of argumentative force and dexterity.. But the fire of emotion was ever blending with his thinking and inciting his speech to pass over from the plane of logic to that of oratory. This combination gives great vitality to his writings and makes them a perpetual source of spiritual impulse, though of course it involves some liability of mistaken interpretation, especially on the part of those who refuse to recognize the element of fervid oratory and insist on construing the apostle as a mere logician. His nature was too broad to be described by a single category. It was after an ecumenical type. Jewish depth of religious feeling, Hellenic zest for argument and speculation, and Roman energy of will and consequent ability for conquest had each a counterpart in the apostle to the Gentiles.

III.— GENERAL CONCEPTIONS OF GOD, OF THE WORLD, AND OF THE RATIONAL CREATION, WHICH UNDERLIE THE PAULINE EPISTLES.

Paul's conception of God may be defined as the Hebraic modified by the revelation in Christ and by personal experience. On the metaphysical side he manifests no ambition to serve as an expounder of the divine nature. The ideas which he brings forward in this relation are the same as those to which Old Testament prophecy at its zenith gave expression. He abides by its combination of distinct personality with transcendent greatness. So far as can be judged, he attributes the being as well as the particular forms of things to creative efficiency. The creation was a means of bringing to manifestation the invisible power of God.[1] He is the one God of whom are all things.[2] He is able to do exceeding abundantly above all that we ask or

---

[1] Rom. i. 19, 20. [2] 1 Cor. viii. 6; 2 Cor. v. 18; Eph. iii. 9.

think.[1] Instrumentalities which the natural judgment of men condemns as feeble and ineffective He is competent to arm with victorious potency. The foolishness of God is wiser than men, and the weakness of God is stronger than men.[2] All striving is empty of result apart from His cooperation. Neither is he that planteth anything, nor he that watereth, but God giveth the increase.[3] To glory in men is to fail of all sense of perspective. Before God's unsearchable wisdom and omnipotence any creaturely endowment passes utterly out of the field of competition.[4]

In portraying the ethical nature of God the apostle takes account preëminently of love and righteousness. His tribute to the former is limited only by the resources of his vocabulary. To his thought the love of God manifested in Christ is like a luminous abyss whose height and depth and length and breadth surpass all the measurements of the human understanding.[5] It is the primal motive power in the divine heart, a spring overflowing with benefits in advance of all desert. "God commendeth His love toward us, in that while we were yet sinners Christ died for us."[6] It shapes the divine administration throughout its wide domain. To those who are responsive to its claims all things are made to work together for good.[7] It is exceedingly tenacious, holding those whom it has won with bonds which neither life nor death nor angels nor principalities nor powers can sever.[8] It is the pattern to which appeal may be made

---

[1] Eph. iii. 20.   [2] 1 Cor. i. 18–25.   [3] 1 Cor. iii. 7.
[4] 1 Cor. iii. 18–23; Rom. viii. 31, xi 33.   [5] Eph. iii. 18–19.
[6] Rom. v. 8.   [7] Rom. viii. 28.   [8] Rom. viii. 38, 39.

in behalf of all gracious conduct among men. The tenderness of heart which prompts one freely to forgive his fellow has its archetype in God with His generous message of forgiveness.[1] He is the God of love and peace.[2]

The indirect tributes which the apostle renders to the love of God vie with the direct. Among these must be reckoned the incomparable hymn contained in the thirteenth chapter of First Corinthians. It is not indeed specifically the love of God that is celebrated in this lofty strain. But such an eulogy as is here recorded must be regarded as containing an implicit reference to the divine nature. To commend love as the highest possible endowment in those who are born of God and exalted into His likeness is equivalent to declaring that it is supremely characteristic of God Himself. The apostle may also be regarded as celebrating the praise of divine love in all his discourse about the grace of God.[3] For what is grace, on the divine side, but love viewed as operative in the bestowment of unearned benefits? Once more, Paul renders tribute to the same theme in his emphasis upon the divine fatherhood, since this is a name for deep and enduring affection. His exposition of this aspect of divine character and relationship does not, it is true, carry us back fully into the atmosphere of the Gospels. Jesus had a prerogative in the exposition of this theme which has fallen to no other. He spoke as the child of the household who dwelt in unclouded intimacy with the Father. Paul could speak only as the

---

[1] Eph. iv 32.   [2] 2 Cor. xiii. 11.
[3] Rom. iii. 24, iv. 16. v. 15–21; 2 Cor. viii. 9; Eph. 1, 6, 7, ii. 7, 8, iii. 2.

converted man and the theologian. He leaves no room for doubt, however, as to his lively interest in the subject. At the opening of every epistle he makes reference to God as Father. He indicates that a chief part in the ministry of the Holy Spirit consists in producing a sense of love and fellowship which shall call forth the name of Father in the spontaneous utterance of the heart.[1] Furthermore, he characterizes fatherhood in God as reaching to the widest limits. He is the Father from whom every family in heaven and earth is named.[2]

The divine righteousness, of which Paul prefers rather to speak than of the divine holiness, was doubtless fundamental to his thought of God. As used by him it stands for essential rectitude, conformity in feeling and in conduct to the ethical reality of things as it is disclosed to His all-penetrating glance. It is incompatible with any artificial judgment or attitude, and so excludes respect of persons.[3] For the same reason it is a ground of wrath, not as though it shuts out compassion, but because in the fitness of things, in proportion as a man gives himself to sin and cancels in himself the potentiality of goodness, he becomes an object of displeasure to Him who cannot have pleasure in sin. In fact the apostle speaks of an expenditure of goodness, forbearance, and long suffering upon those who at the same time by their impenitence are treasuring up wrath against the day of wrath.[4] Righteousness, as true to the reality of things, dictates wrath against the sinner in the man, while simultaneously it permits, not to say requires, compassion

---

[1] Rom. viii. 15, 16; Gal. iv. 6.
[2] Eph. iiii. 15.
[3] Rom. ii. 11; Gal. ii. 6.
[4] Rom. ii. 4, 5.

toward the man in the sinner.[1] As regards the relation of righteousness to love Paul has not intimated that there is any disharmony between the two. Nothing that he has said stands in the way of the rational consideration that righteousness puts no veto whatever on the benevolent aim of love, and merely conditions, as wisdom may be conceived to do also, its manifestation.

Along with stress upon the love and righteousness of God the apostle urges a very emphatic view of the sovereign control of God over the course of history. Taken by themselves some of his sentences, it must be granted, may seem to carry over the notion of a masterful providence into an affirmation of arbitrary power, and so to collide with the proper conception of both love and righteousness. But it is a well-approved canon of interpretation that fervid oratorical discourse must be taken according to its tenor. Now it is beyond question that Paul teaches the freedom, responsibility, and gracious opportunity of men in general.[2] Expressions in this line have no less claim to notice, in a judgment on his position, than expressions which magnify the overshadowing prerogative and might of God. Holtzmann, it is true, prefers to discern in the latter the philosophy of the apostle, and to take the former as spoken in a homiletical or oratorical vein.[3] We find, however, no warrant for this discrimination. On the contrary, there are no passages in Paul's writings which have more the appear-

---

[1] Augustine, Tract. in Joan, cx. 6; Beyschlag, New Testament Theology, II. 93.
[2] Rom. i. 28, 32, ii. 4–11, 26, 27, vi. 12, 13, x. 12, xi. 19–23.
[3] Lehrbuch der neutest. Theol. II. 169,

ance of fervid oratory than those which push to the utmost the notion of divine sovereignty. This is clearly the fact in relation to the passage which more than any other repudiates limitations upon divine choice and action.[1] The apostle is engaged here in an *ad hominem* argument. He wishes to disarm the man who, in his conviction that a preferred place belongs to Israel, is stumbled over the advancement of the Gentiles. Hence he exalts the will of God to the utmost as against all grounds of precedence recognized by men. He puts forward the most extreme instances that he can find. He disparages utterly man's ability to call God to account, and compares the prerogative which He has over creaturely instruments to that of the potter over the clay. He thus asserts the right of God as against any human challenge. But does he go on to say that God, on His part, is minded to exercise this right with unfeeling arbitrariness? Just the reverse. Having silenced the partisan of Judaism who would limit the divine choice according to his own narrow preference, he proceeds to illustrate that the actual policy of God is in the highest degree benevolent, accordant with the conduct and the needs of men, and directed to the end of bringing as many as possible to the salvation in Christ.[2] Are the Jews cast off for the time being? It is on account of their lack of faith. Are the Gentiles elected? It is because they follow after righteousness by faith, and their admission is not designed to shut out the Jews, but to provoke them to jealousy and to bring about ultimately that all Israel should be saved. Are the Jews brought in? It

---

[1] Rom. ix. 14-24. [2] Rom. x., xi.

is not that the opportunity of the Gentiles should be abridged, but that the receiving of them should be to the world at large life from the dead.[1] God's hand is doubtless conceived as a powerful factor in the historic process which leads to the great end in view. But the historic process itself, with its special expedients and combinations, becomes an inept play except as it is viewed as a necessary means of operating with free agents, who are open to persuasion and whose consent needs to be won. It is out of reason to suppose that the apostle did not regard such a process as having a principal ground in the freedom of its subjects. Thus, in spite of the hard sayings with which he rebuked the Jewish assumption of a special claim upon God, the tenor and outcome of the apostle's argument show his conviction that the divine procedure is at once directed by the largest benevolence and respectful of man's free agency. In no other connection has he used language which certifies to a different conviction. The divine election of which he speaks in several instances[2] is viewed indeed as being before the standard of man's deserts perfectly gratuitous, but there is no declaration that it is irrespective of the consent of the individual to divine overtures, or that it arbitrarily secures to one, and arbitrarily excludes from another, the measureless boon

---

[1] So greatly does Paul modify in the following chapters the picture of overmastering sovereignty given in the ninth, that this remark of Garvie can hardly be counted extravagant: "The arbitrary omnipotent potter is a caricature of controversy, not a portrait of faith; and Paul has himself to abandon his own work." (New Century Bible, Romans, p. 224)

[2] Rom. viii. 29, 30; Eph. i. 5, 6.

of eternal life. The conditions on man's side, which the apostle so distinctly recognizes when he discourses on the appropriation of salvation, he must have supposed, in all consistency, to have been regarded by God in the shaping of His eternal purpose.

In the view of Paul, God is revealed in the natural world, in conscience, in human history at large, in the life of the Jewish nation, and finally in Christ as the image of God's perfection and the complete expression of His gracious will. Upon the revelation in nature he touches but lightly, noticing in general terms that the visible world testifies to the power and divinity of the Creator.[1] Possibly in popular discourse he may have made more ample reference. Were we to judge, however, from his writings, we should conclude that nature was no such book of divinity to him as it was to Jesus. The poetic sensibility toward the objects of the natural world which has left its tinge upon the Gospels is not discoverable in his epistles. Not a passage can be cited which shows that he was penetrated with the charm of natural scenery. He has indicated, nevertheless, that in one point of view he had a sympathetic bearing toward nature. He felt the shadow of transitoriness and decay hovering over her domain. It seemed to him that she had been despoiled of her ideal, in order to keep company with the despoiled children of God. By a figure of speech he represents her as if conscious of the cleft between her state of vanity and the ideal designed for her in the divine mind, and so describes her as groan-

---

[1] Rom. i. 19–20.

ing after the glorious era when, in conjunction with the completed redemption of the sons of God, she shall be redeemed from bondage, and present thenceforth a scene unsullied by corruption and death.[1]

No formal exposition is given by the apostle of his conception of the cosmic system. We gather, however, that he recognized an ascending series of spheres. He makes a passing mention of an under world.[2] Recalling an ecstatic experience of his own, he represents himself as caught up to the third heaven.[3] Again, he pictures the risen Christ as ascending far above all heavens.[4] Probably in all this there was little aim at exactness. We take sufficient account of his language, if we regard it as recording simply a general impression that in the world system there is a gradation of spheres to which belong severally different measures of divine manifestation.[5]

As in relation to the cosmic spheres, so also in relation to the classes or ranks of spiritual being, Paul is not to be regarded as having attempted to define with precision. It is quite evident that he thought of angels, and likewise of evil spirits, as constituting a sort of hierarchy; but as is intimated by variation in the terms used, he did not assume to have an exact knowledge of gradations within the hierarchy, and enumerated them rather for the sake of extending the point of view which he

---

[1] Rom. viii. 19–23.   [2] Phil. ii. 10.   [3] 2 Cor. xii. 2.   [4] Eph. iv. 10.

[5] That Paul does not mention specifically a sphere above the third cannot be regarded as decisive of the scheme which he had in mind. It is known that Jewish thought very generally assumed a series of seven heavens. (Salmond, article "Heaven," in Hastings' Dict. of the Bible.)

happened to be enforcing to the widest possible limit, than for the purpose of giving a lesson in angelology.[1] The angelic powers, as he conceived, share in the benefit of Christ's reconciling work, in the sense that that work removes barriers between different parts of the rational creation, and fulfills its aim in joining all closely together in one spiritual unity.[2] On the functions of angels he says next to nothing. Incidentally he refers to them as witnesses of the extremity of despite and suffering appointed to the apostles.[3] According to one interpretation of the enigmatic passage in 1 Cor. xi. 10, he had in mind the Jewish thought that angels are guardians over the constituted order of the world and interested in keeping each rank to its proper place.[4] If this was actually the thought of the apostle, it implies an eminence and jurisdiction in angels that do not harmonize well with the supposition that he thought of men as qualified to judge angels of the unfallen class. Moreover the general New Testament picture of good angels as trusted agents of the heavenly kingdom, and as rendering an ideal service to that kingdom, is far from suggesting their amenability to human judgment. It is to be esteemed doubtful, therefore, that Paul, when he spoke of Christians as destined to judge angels,[5] distinctly included the obedient order in his thought.

---

[1] See Eph. i. 21; Col. i. 16, ii. 10; Rom. viii. 38; 1 Thess. iv. 16; also 1 Cor. xv. 24; Eph. vi. 12.

[2] Col. i. 20.   [3] 1 Cor. iv. 9.

[4] Heinrici, Sendschreiben an die Korinther. Compare Toy, Judaism and Christianity, p. 153. A competing interpretation makes the reference to be to the respect due to angels viewed as heavenly guests, present at the meeting for worship.

[5] 1 Cor. vi. 3.

In relation to evil spirits, Paul indicates his recognition of a certain headship in Satan by naming him the prince of the power of the air.[1] This expression, joined with the reference to the spiritual hosts of wickedness in the heavenly places,[2] makes it probable that he thought of the lower or atmospheric heaven as the special seat of evil spirits. His language in 1 Cor. x. 20, 21 points to a belief that demons were patrons of heathen idolatries, and the vivid description of spiritual antagonists in Eph. vi. 12 makes it quite evident that he credited the evil host with a considerable agency in the world. Still, we are warned against attributing to him a too emphatic notion of diabolical workings when we observe that in his most sombre picture of the origin and progress of sin among men, as given in the Epistle to the Romans, he makes no reference to Satan or to the evil spirits confederated with him. It is properly observed also that Paul was not at all minded to concede that the natural world is the property of Satan. As was noticed above, he associated its destiny with the ideal consummation awaiting the children of God. Moreover the cosmic significance which he assigned to Christ implies that the world falls under divine ownership, and that Satan has no real title to its rule. Thus a point of view which seriously compromises the divine headship over the world cannot be charged against the apostle.

In his description of man Paul is distinguished among New Testament writers by the extent to which he inclines to the use of trichotomist terminology. To desig-

---
[1] Eph. ii. 2.   [2] Eph. vi. 12.

nate the highest in man he employs the term "spirit" ($\pi\nu\epsilon\hat{v}\mu a$). In referring to this factor his language is not always so definite as to exclude the inquiry as to whether he means the Holy Spirit resident in men, or the human spirit regarded as the proper organ for communication with the divine and as quickened and illuminated thereby. This naturally results from the fact that the aim of the Holy Spirit and of the human spirit ruled by the influence of the former must be identical. That Paul considered a finite spirit to be a constituent of the human individual as such is made abundantly evident by his references.[1] While the apostle, on the whole, assigns a certain preeminence to the spirit, it may be questioned whether he went so far as to distinguish it from the soul ($\psi v \chi \acute{\eta}$) in respect of substance. 1 Thess. v. 23 may indeed be cited in favor of an affirmative conclusion; but the apparent distinction here may be regarded as due to amplification for the sake of emphasis.[2] In various connections the apostle seems to include under the term soul the whole nature of man as a subject of emotional and volitional experience.[3] His total usage, however, implies a certain contrast between soul and spirit. The former may be said to denote the interior man in close relation to the sensuous side of his being, the latter the interior man as holding Godward relations. This contrast is especially conspicuous in the adjective forms $\psi v \chi \iota \kappa \acute{o} s$ and $\pi v \epsilon v \mu a \tau \iota \kappa \acute{o} s$.[4] The

---

[1] Rom i. 9, viii. 16; 1 Cor. ii. 11, v. 4, 5, vii. 34, xiv. 14, xvi. 18; 2 Cor. ii. 13, vii. 1, 13; Gal. vi. 18; 1 Thess. v. 23.

[2] Compare Luke x. 27.

[3] Rom. ii. 9, xiii. 1; 2 Cor. i. 23, xii. 15; Phil. i. 27.

[4] 1 Cor. ii. 14, 15.

apostle's use of the word mind (νοῦς) answers partially to that of spirit, as being put in opposition to the flesh.[1] It denotes in such connection the seat of the reflective intelligence. In 1 Cor. xiv. it is associated with the ordinary sphere of consciousness, while the spirit is viewed as capable of being rapt up into ecstatic fellowship with God.

A further distinction of the Pauline anthropology is an explicit stress upon race connection. No other New Testament writer has made any specific account of the bond with the sinning Adam. Paul distinctly accentuates such a bond. Exegesis has sometimes concluded, on the basis especially of Romans v. 12, that he even thought of the whole race as sinning in Adam and undergoing condemnation with him. Attention has been called to the force of the aorist tense in the clause "all sinned" (πάντες ἥμαρτον), as indicative of a definite past act of sin, and not merely of the fact that all who have lived have fallen at one time or another into sin. And where, it is asked, is this definite act to be found except in the trespass of Adam? But this argument rests on a very unsubstantial ground. The aorist of ἁμαρτάνω is repeatedly used in the New Testament in the sense of the perfect, and has been so rendered by the translators.[2] In short it is quite gratuitous to charge upon Paul the artificial notion that the whole race sinned and incurred guilt in the sin of Adam. What the apostle may reasonably be regarded as designing to teach is, that the Adamic trespass was the fountainhead of the general tendency

---

[1] Rom. vii. 23, 25.
[2] Rom. ii. 12, iii. 23; Luke xv. 18, 21; 1 Cor. vii. 28.

in men to sin, and thus a source of ultimate condemnation, since a pronounced tendency commonly passes on into act. The sin of Adam was the sin of his posterity only in the sense of being a potentiality of sin in them, just as the crucifixion of Christ was a potentiality of the crucifixion of the sinful nature in men.[1] Nothing that the apostle has written requires us to suppose that he thought that the condemnation strikes men before the evil potentiality issues into act. The words in Eph. ii. 3, "by nature children of wrath," are to be compared with the statement in Rom. ii. 14, that "the Gentiles do by nature the things of the law." In neither case is the reference to a birth condition proper. The Gentiles are not so much born doers of the law as born with a nature the unfoldment of which brings them in due time to a sense of the obligations of the moral law. In like manner Jews and Gentiles are not literally born children of wrath, but born with natures which universal experience shows tend to the order of works which invite the divine displeasure.[2]

The darker phases of human condition are doubtless sketched in the Pauline writings with much vigor. But the counterpart is also painted with a powerful hand. The apostle indeed runs into a glowing optimism when he considers the possibilities and certainties of human destiny on the side of connection with the Second Adam.

---

[1] Rom. vi. 6; 2 Cor. v. 14.

[2] On the character and scope of the suggestions which antecedent Judaism may have furnished to Paul respecting the relation of Adam's sin to the race, see F. R. Tennant, The Sources of the Doctrines of the Fall and Original Sin.

If we put together the elements of the Pauline view of the world system, we must acknowledge that it has a somewhat imposing aspect. It is notably a world that is under a law of movement. Things are in procession. The various ranks of being are directed toward a lofty consummation. Not only are all things from God; all things are likewise to Him.[1] For the creation generally the goal lies in a sphere of incorruption and transfigured existence, where God is all in all, not as overbearing distinctions of individuality, but as beatifying and harmonizing all beings through their close relation to Himself.

IV. — THE CHIEF PAULINE ANTITHESES — FLESH AND SPIRIT, LAW AND GRACE.

The reader of the Pauline epistles very soon discovers that the term flesh ($\sigma \acute{a} \rho \xi$) is frequently used in a larger than the plain physical signification. While literally it denotes the pliable substance of a living physical organism, and thus is related to body ($\sigma \hat{\omega} \mu a$) as the specific to the general, in many instances it evidently incorporates an ethico-religious sense.[2] From what point of view did the apostle attach to it this meaning? Did he proceed from the standpoint of Hellenic dualism, and thus regard the flesh in virtue of its material as intrinsically evil, from its very nature antagonistic to the spirit in man with its sense of obligation to a moral ideal? Or, did he, putting a part for the whole, intend to denote by the flesh unrenewed human nature, man viewed as dominated by

---

[1] Rom xi. 36.
[2] For example in Rom. vii. 18. viii. 4–9; Gal. v. 16–24.

the desires and passions which have their sphere of manifestation especially in the bodily members? The latter we believe to be by far the more credible interpretation. The main reasons for preferring it, as against the narrower meaning in the direction of Hellenic dualism, are the following: (1) The apostle includes in his catalogue of the works of the flesh various orders of sins which have no special association with the physical members.[1] The natural inference is that by flesh he meant more than the mere instrument of the sensuous life. (2) The connections in which the phrase, "our old man," is used are such as to show that its meaning is substantially equivalent to that assigned to the flesh.[2] We have accordingly a plain hint that the latter term connotes something beyond the sensuous nature proper. (3) The apostle refers to Christians as those who can appropriately be reckoned as being no longer in the flesh.[3] This is as much as indicating that flesh is not a name for an intrinsically evil substance; for, in that event disengagement from its contamination and thraldom could not well be thought of as realized anterior to its literal destruction or severance from the spirit. (4) Paul dignifies the body by representing it as worthy to be quickened by the Spirit of God, as fit to be offered to God in sacrifice or consecration, as being the temple of the Holy Spirit, as being a subject along with soul and spirit for complete sanctification.[4] It may be alleged, it is true, that body as *form* is to be distinguished from flesh which is a term

---

[1] Gal. v. 19–21.
[2] Rom. vi. 6; Eph. iv. 22; Col. iii. 9   [3] Rom. vii. 5, viii. 9.
[4] Rom. viii. 11, xii. 1; 1 Cor. vi. 19; 1 Thess. v. 23.

THE PAULINE THEOLOGY 215

descriptive of *substance*. But certainly in most of the instances just cited the distinction is impertinent. Who can believe that the apostle meant to give such terms as sacrifice, sanctification, and indwelling an exclusive application to corporeal outlines? He has plainly discountenanced such artificial construction in that, on the one hand, he has represented the flesh itself to be a subject for sanctification,[1] and on the other has pictured the body as the seat of the same disorderly motions which he has ascribed to the flesh.[2] (5) The apostle indicates that he did not regard the flesh, in the character of material substance, to be intrinsically evil, inasmuch as he conceives Christ both to have come in the flesh and to have been sinless. The latter point is unequivocally asserted in 2 Cor. v. 21. The former point is implied in Paul's ascription of real birth and real death to Christ.[3] It is also intimated in the statement that Christ came in the likeness of sinful flesh ($\grave{\epsilon}\nu$ $\dot{o}\mu o\iota\acute{\omega}\mu a\tau\iota$ $\sigma a\rho\kappa\grave{o}s$ $\dot{a}\mu a\rho\tau\acute{\iota}a s$), and was instrumental in condemning sin in the flesh.[4] The interposition of the word "likeness" in this text is to be regarded as a token of the apostle's unwillingness to attribute *sinful* flesh to Christ while yet he attributes flesh to Him. (6) In treating of the origin of sin in the Epistle to the Romans Paul does not make it a necessary offspring of the sensuous nature with which man was originally endowed, but ascribes it to the trespass of Adam.[5] It has been contended indeed that the contrast which, in another connection, he draws between the first Adam and the last Adam[6] implies that the

---

[1] 2 Cor. vii. 1.   [3] Rom. i. 3; Gal. iv. 4; Phil. ii. 8.   [5] Rom. v. 12-19.
[2] 1 Cor. ix. 27.   [4] Rom. viii. 3.   [6] 1 Cor. xv. 45-47.

former from the start, as possessed of flesh, had in himself a positive ground of sin. But there is inadequate reason for supposing that the apostle fell into the self-contradiction implied in this interpretation. In the passage under consideration he takes Adam in general as a type, without pausing to discriminate closely between his state before the fall and that which was characteristic of him afterwards. As he stands out in history he appears, on the whole, weak, earthly, corruptible, and so may be placed in contrast with the thoroughly incorruptible and pneumatic nature of the risen and ascended Christ. As respects man before the fall, it is not at all necessary to suppose that the apostle thought of him as characterized by a positive bent to evil, as well as by immaturity and lack of firm grasp on the higher good. Thus the teaching in Romans, ascribing the origin of sin to an act rather than to a necessity of nature, may stand as truly representative of the apostle's conviction, and serve to confirm the conclusion that by flesh he means, when he gives the term an ethico-religious significance, not the physical substance of the body, but the natural or unrenewed man, whose passions and desires find a special vehicle of manifestation in the bodily members. (7) Had Paul thought of the fleshly substance as intrinsically evil, he would naturally have been driven to show a larger predilection for ascetic theory and practice than he has exhibited. On that basis we should not expect from him such sentences as appear in the Colossian Epistle.[1] No one who was immersed in the postulates of asceticism would naturally have written in that strain.

---

[1] Col. ii. 16, 20–23.

The Pauline antithesis between flesh and spirit denotes that man's being is a battlefield of opposing tendencies, and that there is no chance for him to fulfill his true end save in alliance with a power which is able to reinforce the Godward tendency, and to make it more than a match for the earthward. A similar meaning belongs to the antithesis between law and grace.

By the law, as the term is employed in the more formal discussions of the apostle, is meant the Mosaic law in its entirety. This in its moral part distinctly proclaims the law which is written upon man's conscience, and thus deepens responsibility for obedience. The great office of the law, as described in the epistles to the Galatians and Romans, is so to convict men of their sin, and so to reveal to them their bondage in sin, that they shall be prepared to accept the divine remedy. It provokes to sin, that is to concrete sinful acts (παραβάσεις, παραπτώματα), in the sense that it challenges the natural impulses of men, and thus brings their latent sinfulness (ἁμαρτία) to manifestation. By reaction against it the sinner comes to a knowledge of himself as a sinner condemned and in thraldom. There is no question about its sanctity. It is holy, righteous, and good.[1] The trouble with it is its practical impotence to bring salvation. Here it always fails. Its office is rather to convince of the need of salvation than to save. It is a schoolmaster to bring men to Christ. It educates up to receptivity for the method of grace, the method of self-committal to a Redeemer and of personal heart union with

---

[1] Rom. vii. 12.

Him. At the point of this consummation the law in one sense is abrogated. Christians are not under law but under grace.[1] That is, their standing is not measured by their record of legal obedience but by their present relation to God in Christ. This relation, however, inevitably involves willing compliance with the ethical requirements of the law. The renewed heart in virtue of a spiritual dynamic coming from a personal affiance with the Saviour yields a measure of obedience which it could not render on the plane of mere legal striving. Thus, in another sense, the law is established. While it ceases to be the object toward which the Christian believer looks for justification, it becomes in its ethical content the ideal toward which a power of life, as well as his own continuous endeavor, transports him.

Criticism has been passed upon Paul's exposition of the function of Old Testament law. It has been said that the whole intent of the law was not exhausted in merely bringing the sinfulness of men to manifestation, and so convincing them of the need of a gracious rescue at the hands of God; that the law in fact aimed to develop a positive righteousness, which, if not of an ideal type, had nevertheless a certain worth for human society and the divine kingdom. The criticism would not be wholly unjust, if Paul's silence on this aspect of the subject were to be taken as equivalent to denial. But it is not necessarily so taken. Paul had occasion to checkmate an attempt to thrust the law forward into the place of a rival of the gospel. Naturally therefore he considered the law preëminently, not to say exclusively, in its relation to the gospel, and dwelt upon the fact that its

---

[1] Rom. vi. 14.

office was fulfilled in preparing for a more potent and gracious dispensation by convincing men of their sinfulness and need. Over against the partisans of an ultra legal scheme he considered it important to set forth the incompetency of the law to reach the supreme end— assured, personal salvation. He was passing judgment upon it in relation to this end. That he counted it incompetent to bring to this high goal is no sure token that he would not have been willing to concede to it a useful office in modifying individual and community life.

The exigencies of the time in which he wrote called forth the apostle's exposition of this theme. In its main tenor, however, that exposition is of perennial significance. It remains for ever true, that at the stage of maturity religious living must be on the basis of heart fellowship and spiritual dynamic, and that a scheme of formal rules belongs to a preliminary and inferior stage.

V.—The Person of Christ.

Since Paul did not attempt a minute exposition of christology, it is little cause for surprise that his language falls short of an explicit declaration of Christ's possession of a complete human nature. The tenor of theological discussion in his day did not call for an unequivocal expression on that subject. We have, however, measurably satisfactory hints of his position. In stating that Christ was "born of the seed of David according to the flesh," that He was of the stock of Israel, that He was born of a woman under the law, that He was made in the likeness of men, and that He holds a position which entitles Him to be spoken of as the last Adam,[1] the apostle has given indubitable evidence that he considered the Redeemer to be truly implicated in the race, and has made it credible that he ascribed to Him the full complement of human attributes. Weiss contends that the ascription of flesh ($\sigma\acute{\alpha}\rho\xi$) to Christ is decisive of the fact that a human soul was recognized in Him, since in the Pauline anthropology flesh in the living man is always understood to be ensouled.[2]

That the Pauline christology assigns real preëxistence to Christ is so obvious that it can be denied only in a most unworthy spirit of dogmatic desperation. Critics of the most varied schools admit the assumption by the apostle of a personal preexistence.[3] No other meaning can reasonably be ascribed to his emphatic description of a voluntary transition of Christ from an estate of riches and glory to one of poverty and humiliation.[4] The cosmic function of Christ and the office assigned to Him under the Old Testament economy involve quite obviously the same conclusion.[5]

Another indisputable feature of the Pauline christology is its ascription to Christ of a nature and rank vastly transcending the proper human scale and reaching up-

---

[1] Rom. i. 3, ix. 5; Gal. iv. 4; Rom. viii. 3; Phil. ii. 7; 1 Cor. xv. 45.
[2] Bib. Theol. des. neuen Testaments, § 78.
[3] Orello Cone by no means takes an uncommon position for the liberal critic when he says: "The terms employed by Paul relative to Christ's coming in the flesh can only by the most violent exegesis be regarded as applicable to an ideal being or principle existing in the divine purpose, when we consider how they must have been understood by his readers." (Paul, the Man, the Missionary, and Teacher, p. 305).
[4] 2 Cor. viii. 9; Phil. ii. 6–8.   [5] Col. i. 16, 17; 1 Cor. x. 4.

ward to a divine plane. A glance at the more salient features of that christology will show that the above terms are not too emphatic. (1) Christ is represented as having a distinct headship over all creaturely ranks. No kind of dignitary beneath the divine throne is allowed to come into competition with Him.[1] (2) The names applied to Christ are such as naturally associate Him with a divine sphere. He is in a preeminent and distinctive sense the Son of God, manifested indeed to be such by His resurrection,[2] but in nature and relation the Son before, as well as after, His appearance in the flesh.[3] He bears the name of Lord ($\kappa\acute{\upsilon}\rho\iota\sigma$), and that in the midst of statements analogous to or identical with those which in the Old Testament set off the name of Deity.[4] It is not disproved that in one instance, outside of the Pastoral Epistles, the term $\theta\epsilon\acute{o}\varsigma$ is applied to Christ, namely in Rom. ix. 5. If, on the one hand, exegetes of a conservative tendency are not entirely unanimous in connecting the high ascription of this verse with Christ, some who are quite the reverse of conservative in temper do not deny the propriety of so interpreting. Pfleiderer, for example, decides that to separate the ascription at the end of the verse from the name of Christ in the preceding part is forced, and also unnecessary in consideration of the fact that in Pauline usage $\theta\epsilon\acute{o}\varsigma$ is not always used in a different sense from that of $\kappa\acute{\upsilon}\rho\iota\sigma$.[5] (3) In various instances an office like that of the Holy

---

[1] Col. ii. 10, 15, 19; Eph. i. 21-23.
[2] Rom. i. 4.   [3] Rom. viii. 3; Gal. iv. 4: Col. i. 13-15.
[4] Rom. x. 9-13; 1 Cor. x. 21, 22; 2 Cor. iii. 16; 2 Thess. i. 9.
[5] The Influence of the Apostle Paul, p. 55.

Spirit in respect of spiritual presence and efficacy is assigned to Christ. His inner nature is described as "the spirit of holiness."[1] He is designated as the spiritual rock which followed and refreshed the fathers in the wilderness.[2] He is described as being in the sphere of His ascension a "life-giving spirit."[3] In opposition to the Mosaic letter, He is declared to be the Spirit whose presence brings liberty.[4] Even as the Holy Spirit is resident in believers, so Christ is conceived to dwell in their hearts in answer to their faith.[5] It is needless to add that this coordination of the agency of Christ's pneumatic nature with that of the Holy Spirit is suggestive of a personality quite above the creaturely range. (4) Endowments and functions are assigned to Christ which are appropriate to a divine plane of being. All the treasures of wisdom and knowledge are said to be hidden in Him.[6] In Him dwelleth all the fullness of the Godhead bodily.[7] He is the one Lord through whom and unto whom are all things; and He is before all things, and in Him all things consist.[8] The awards of the judgment day are in His hand, and before the ultimate display of His glory and might all that opposes shall sink into impotence.[9] He is the source of grace, being so designated in every epistle, either by Himself, or in conjunction with the Father. In the presence of the greatness and universality of His saving office earthly

---

[1] Rom i. 4. See Meyer, Lipsius, Godet, Sanday, and Denney.
[2] 1 Cor. x. 4.
[3] 1 Cor. xv. 45.
[4] 2 Cor. iii. 17, 18.
[5] Eph. iii. 17; 2 Cor. xiii. 5.
[6] Col. ii. 3.
[7] Col. ii. 9.
[8] 1 Cor. viii. 6, Col. i. 16, 17.
[9] 2 Cor. v. 10; 2 Thess. i. 7, 8, ii. 8.

distinctions fade away. He is all and in all.[1] The true believer acknowledges Him as his life, and looks toward Him as the goal of His intensest aspiration.[2] In short, it is as clear as the daylight that in Paul's view Christ rose transcendently above the ordinary creaturely plane. In manifold ways he ascribes to Him the practical value of divinity. It cannot fairly be doubted that he esteemed Him to be in an altogether unique way related to the Father, metaphysically the Son of God and as such anterior to the created universe.

On the other hand Paul seems to have recognized a certain subordination of the Son to the Father. This feature in his christology may have been due in part to the measure in which he unfolds the subject from an economic standpoint. One contemplating Christ fulfilling in the servant form His historic office could very naturally apply to Him forms of expression which would never be suggested in considering Him solely as the preexisting Son of God. Since He was actually the Son of Man, it is no cause for surprise that one or another phrase appropriate to that category should be in evidence, as well as a long list of expressions appropriate to the higher category. Even John, after declaring unequivocally the divinity of Christ, could represent Him to have associated Himself so far with the common human standpoint as to designate the Father "my God." An expression of the same order with Paul is no more than with John an index of a simple humanitarian theory. It is to be granted, nevertheless, that in the total representation of Paul a certain primacy of rank, a certain

---

[1] Col. iii. 11.   [2] Col. iii. 4; Phil. iii. 8, 9.

headship over the Son, is ascribed to the Father. Just how this was conceived is not to be determined from the data which the apostle has given. We are confident, however, that it was not conceived in the sense of the more extreme interpretation of 1 Cor. xv. 24, 28. This passage is an emphatic description of the recession of the Son from the theatre of His mediatorial work, and of the all-comprehending unity which at that point is to be revealed. To suppose that the apostle thought of the recession of the Son in all respects from an exalted plane of lordship is to suppose an incredible disjunction in teaching. He represents this same Son as subsisting in the form of God before entering upon His office of mediation, as the being through whom and unto whom all things were created, as the goal of his own highest hopes and deepest aspirations. How then could he think of Him as being really displaced from lordship? A soul so worshipful in its attitude toward Christ as that of Paul, so enkindled with love to Him, so pervaded with a sense of spiritual dependence upon Him, could not picture for Him a place in the heavenly and eternal kingdom inferior to that which is assigned in the lofty imagery of the Johannine Apocalypse.

In two instances Paul describes in emphatic terms the transition of Christ from His antecedent state of riches and glory into the state of humiliation.[1] In recent times speculative christology has built upon these representations a radical doctrine of *kenosis* or self-depotentiation, to the effect that the Son of God, stripping Himself of the divine mode of being, came, in respect of conscious

---

[1] 2 Cor. viii. 9; Phil. ii. 6, 7.

life and activity, wholly into the measure and mode of a human soul at the beginning of its career. The incarnation, it is claimed, meant the immeasurable transformation from a divine to a purely human mode of subsistence, out of which by a process of development the divine mode was at length regained. Some names of considerable theological eminence have been subscribed to the doctrine. But it has little chance of coming into the ascendant. Not only is it rationally indefensible; it is exegetically gratuitous. So far as we are able to judge, the weight of New Testament scholarship is decidedly on the side of the conclusion that Paul did not design to describe a metaphysical *kenosis*, a real self-depotentiation, but only a change as to form of manifestation. His thought was, that the preëxistent Son, instead of being disclosed in His native divine form, resplendent with a glory correspondent with His rank, presented Himself to the human race in the form of a servant. The supposition that in the incarnation He was lost to Himself, temporarily self-eliminated, is not required by the apostle's language.

It is not certain that Paul was ready to answer all sorts of questions about the nature and divine relation of Christ. While he has made statements which serve as a ground of metaphysical inference, he dwelt preëminently in the sphere of practical contemplation. In emphasis on the actual value of Christ to the individual and the race he reached a mark which no later writer, whether an Augustine, a Bernard of Clairvaux, a Luther, or a Wesley, has transcended. The most fervid hymns which the Christian centuries have produced evince no warmer devotion than that which informs his words. It is worth while to read his epistles a score of times, just to get the measure of his love for Christ, and to see into what glorious captivity that love could transport a stalwart man.

VI. — The Holy Spirit.

It was noticed in the preceding section that Paul in some instances ascribes to the pneumatic nature of Christ such offices as in other connections he associates with the Holy Spirit. This may indicate that in respect of spiritual agency he did not set off the province of the one from that of the other by any distinct line of demarcation. It by no means proves that he identified the two. His total representation offers us reasons for thinking that he did not. If he speaks in some instances of the Spirit of Christ as operative in men,[1] he speaks in more numerous instances of the Spirit of God as thus operative.[2] The apostle accordingly gives no ground for merging the Holy Spirit into the person of the Son rather than into the person of the Father. If it should be concluded that he meant to give no distinct standing to the Holy Spirit, the necessary inference would be, that he felt at liberty to apply the name now to the Father and now to the Son, according as he might wish to represent the one or the other as operative in the spiritual domain. As regards the question of his intent to postulate a distinct standing for the Spirit, the data are not very abundant, since he treats the subject

---

[1] Rom. viii. 10, Gal iv. 6
[2] Rom. viii. 9; 1 Cor. iii. 16, vi. 11, xii. 3, 2 Cor. iii. 3; Eph. iv. 30.

from the economic or practical point of view. The facts to be noticed are that in various connections he mentions the Spirit alongside of the Father, or alongside of the Son, or together with both.[1] Thus his language is as suggestive of the trinitarian conception as any discourse could be expected to be which was not governed by a distinct effort at metaphysical construction.

The distinctive feature in Paul's doctrine of the Holy Spirit is its stress upon His agency in the production and sustentation of Christain character as such, His immanence to the believer as a source of sanctification. It is not to be supposed that this point of view was ignored, much less consciously discarded, by any group of Christian teachers. Yet it must be confessed that there are tokens in the first part of Acts of a disposition to emphasize in particular the charismatic working of the Spirit. According to the tenor of the Samaritan incident, recounted in the eighth chapter, the presence of the Spirit seems to have been identified with a special afflatus manifesting itself in such sensible tokens that any bystander, though of the stamp of Simon Magus, could recognize them in their peculiarity. Paul on his part also gives a place to this charismatic working, but he unequivocally assigns to it a subordinate rank. The great office of the Spirit, as he represents it, is to produce in men the ethical and religious values which fill out character to its proper ideal. The fruits of His presence are love, joy, peace, long-suffering, kindness, goodness, faithfulness, meekness, temperance.[2] With

---

[1] Rom. viii. 16, 26, 27; 1 Cor. vi. 11; 2 Cor. vi. 6, 7, xiii. 14; Eph. ii. 18, iv. 4–6.

[2] Gal. v. 22.

these fruits no equipment of mere power can compete. The ability to speak with tongues or to remove mountains is a poor accomplishment, in comparison with the love which enkindles to all well-doing and consumes all inclination to ill-doing.[1] Here the teaching of the apostle comes grandly into line with that of the Synoptical Gospels, with its profound emphasis upon the worthlessness of any and every performance in the name of religion when divorced from an ethical basis.

VII. — The Reconciling Work of Christ.

Eminent exponents of the liberal school of criticism in recent times have concluded that in Paul's exposition of the redemptive work of Christ the "objective-juridical" and the "subjective-ethical" representation run side by side, and that neither is sacrificed or subordinated to the other.[2] Exponents of a more conservative scholarship also quite generally acknowledge that the two forms of representation are closely associated in the Pauline writings. In our opinion this is the view which has the best exegetical right. It is to be confessed, both that Paul gave a place to an objective aspect, and that he joined with this a very decided stress upon a subjective aspect. In other words, it is necessary to credit him with the conviction that Christ's work, especially as consummated in His death, met at once a

---

[1] 1 Cor. xiii. See also Rom. v. 5, viii. 14–16, xiv. 17; 1 Cor. vi. 19; 2 Cor. xiii. 14; 1 Thess. i 6, Eph. i. 13, 14, iv. 30.

[2] Holtzmann, Lehrbuch der neutest. Theol. II. 117; Pfleiderer, Urchristenthum, 223–236.

demand of the divine character and administration, and a need on man's part for a most potent incentive to faith and obedience.

A preliminary ground for the conclusion that Paul's thinking included the objective aspect is found in the fact that it was not foreign to the religious mind in his day. As has been noticed, the Pharisaic school in which he was trained, while not on the whole well affected toward the specific notion of a suffering Messiah, was committed to the idea that, in virtue of the solidarity of Israel, the suffering of one member might have atoning worth in behalf of another. Then too the Hebrew Scriptures were easily suggestive of the possibility of an efficacious offering for sin. The picture in the fifty-third chapter of Isaiah could not well be excluded from the mind of a disciple who was inquiring after the meaning of the crucifixion of his Lord. It was not necessary, therefore, for the apostle to travel afar in order to reach the notion of an atoning or reconciling work that was inclusive of an objective aspect.

A more positive ground for imputing this notion to the apostle is found in his recognition of a wrath element in God.[1] The recoil of the divine nature from sin, though not viewed as excluding compassion toward the sinner, was regarded as most genuine. It is quite conceivable therefore that it should have been accounted a thing to be reckoned with in a general plan for dealing with sinners. The fact that man, rather than God, is represented to be reconciled does not prove that it was considered a matter of indifference to God how He

---

[1] Rom. i. 18, iii. 5, v. 9; Eph. v. 6.

should set to work to bridge over the chasm between Himself and the offending race. This representation naturally followed from the emphasis which, in the mind of the apostle, was placed upon the truth that it is God who takes the initiative in the scheme of reconciliation. There is no denial here of the divine recoil against sin. God is the reconciler as instituting the whole scheme of reconciliation; it may be also that He is viewed as reconciled in the sense that the scheme of reconciliation is so constituted as to express His judgment against sin, and thus to take away the barrier to the fullest expression of His grace toward sinners. In briefer terms, He may be viewed as satisfying the demands of His righteousness through the special method of His grace.

Proceeding a step further, we note that Paul indicates quite clearly his conviction that the work of Christ was actually a tribute to the wrath or righteousness side of the divine nature, and that there was real occasion for such a tribute in connection with a dispensation of measureless grace. In Rom. iii. 25 he speaks of Christ as being in His death a propitiation or means of propitiation; and the context indicates that the motive for the propitiation was the practical necessity of showing forth the righteousness of God, as against an appearance of laxity or indulgence toward sin.[1] Faith is associated

---

[1] This much of meaning inheres in the passage even though the term ἱλαστήριον be rendered "mercy-seat" rather than "propitiation." In the given context a blood-stained mercy-seat must be regarded as symbolically declarative of the idea of atonement or propitiation. As respects choice between the two renderings, reference to the terminology of the Septuagint version of the Old Testament and to patristic interpretation would dictate a preference for the expression "mercy-seat."

with the propitiation as the indispensable instrument for personal realization of the benefit for which it provides. The propitiation itself is contemplated as essentially consummated once for all by the death of the sinless Redeemer. In virtue of it God appears as just, or supremely regardful of the claims of righteousness, while yet He graciously pardons him that hath faith in Jesus.

In various connections the apostle uses language which is substantially equivalent, in its suggestion of an objective aspect of atonement, to the description of Christ's work as a means of propitiation. He gives to Christ's death the value of an offset to the condemnatory sentence of the law, declaring that Christ redeemed us from the curse of the law, having become a curse for us.[1] He says similarly that God made Him who knew no sin to be sin on our behalf.[2] He speaks of reconciliation in the past tense, or as something accomplished by the death of Christ while we were yet enemies of God — a form of expression which suggests that he considered the death of Christ as the basis of reconciliation, the

---

On the other hand, the sudden intrusion of an image which affords no real explanation of the foregoing statement, and which involves the awkward indentification of Christ with the lid of an ark on which sacrificial blood was sprinkled rather than with the sacrifice itself, is something which one may justly hesitate to attribute to the apostle. It is not a matter for surprise, therefore, to find a considerable tendency in recent exegesis to accept "propitiation" or "propitiatory" as the proper translation of $ἱλαστήριον$. While Olshausen, Philippi, Tholuck, Lange, Cremer, Ritschl, Gifford and Terry have advocated the superior claim of the term "mercy-seat," Meyer, Lipsius, Godet, Sanday, Denney, Stevens, Garvie, Cone and others have justified the rendering which appears in our standard English versions.

[1] Gal. iii. 13.   [2] 2 Cor. v. 21.

ground of the gracious economy in which forgiveness of sins is assured.[1] A like implication is contained in the statement that through one act of righteousness the free gift came upon all men to justification of life.[2] This act of righteousness, if not to be identified with Christ's obedience unto death must still be regarded, according to the analogy of Paul's teaching in Rom. iii. 24–26, as based upon the same, and is accordingly indicative of the idea that the general dispensation of grace is founded in Christ's death. A hint in the same order is contained in this collocation of question and answer, "Who is he that condemneth? It is Christ that died."[3] The words perhaps do not necessarily point to the death of Christ as an objective basis of acquittal, but in the light of preceding statements in the same epistle they are very naturally taken in that sense. It is likewise permissible to put in evidence expressions to the effect that Christ died for our sins,[4] or that we are justified by His blood.[5] In the dialect of the age such expressions were associated with sacrificial offerings for the removing of sins.[6] Finally the death of Christ seems to be set forth as the basis of the universal offer and dispensation of pardon in the strong words, "In whom we have our redemption through His blood, the forgiveness of our trespasses."[7]

The marked antithesis which the apostle asserts between Christ, as the sinless Redeemer, and all men as sinners, and the vital sense which he manifests of un-

---

[1] Rom. v. 10.   [2] Rom. v. 18.   [3] Rom. viii. 34.
[4] 1 Cor. xv. 3.   [5] Rom v. 9.
[6] See 1 Cor. v. 7; Eph. v. 2; Heb. v. 1, vii. 27, ix. 7, 12.
[7] Eph. i 7.

qualified obligation to His saving office, are a sufficient guaranty that he did not think of himself, or of any other, as a real partner in Christ's work of atonement. When, therefore, he speaks of filling up that which is lacking of the afflictions of Christ[1], it cannot be his design to intimate that he expects to supplement the propitiatory or atoning work of the Saviour — a work which in fact is not described elsewhere in the New Testament by the term employed here ($\theta\lambda\hat{\iota}\psi\iota\varsigma$). Two interpretations may claim consideration. It is possible that the apostle in this connection spoke in a general way of the afflictions of Christ as endured for the kingdom, without reference to their atoning virtue, and from this point of view considered them as properly followed up in the suffering of Christians for the kingdom. As Lightfoot notes, sufferings may be either *satisfactorial* or *aedificatorial*, having an efficacy to found a gracious economy, or serving to build up the Church, and in sufferings of the latter kind any faithful Christian may share. Again it is possible that Paul spoke from the standpoint of a very vivid conception of mystical union with the Redeemer, and deemed it admissible to designate as Christ's afflictions those which His members are called upon to endure in His name and for His sake. This interpretation has the advantage of superior simplicity, and is withal quite congenial to the Pauline way of thinking.[2]

As was stated, the objective point of view by no means absorbed the whole attention of the apostle. If he regarded Christ, on the one hand, as the atoning Redeemer

---

[1] Col. i. 24.
[2] Compare Peake, Expositor's Greek Testament, III. 514, 515.

upon whose work of holy obedience and self-sacrifice the universal economy of grace rests, he regarded Him on the other hand as an actual power of life in the midst of humanity. By His great deed of love He draws men into a faith and a fellowship which are profoundly efficacious to renovate character. He that truly believes upon Him can be said to be crucified with Him, and with Him to be risen from the dead.[1] The law of the Spirit of Life in Him makes free from the law of sin and death.[2] His cross is the symbol of a virtue which extirpates the old selfish and worldly inclination, and transports a man into a new world of love and service.[3] The believer is in Christ. There is, so to speak, an effective contact, a mystical union, between him and the life-giving personality of his Lord.[4]

It is congruous with this point of view that Paul gives to the resurrection of Christ a close association with His saving office.[5] His resurrection serves to make practically effective the divine lesson contained in His death. It shows that His death was not the death of a sinner but of a Saviour. It presents Him also as victorious over the last enemy. Accordingly it stimulates to faith in Him as an adequate source of life for the present and the future. Only the risen Christ, victorious over death, Himself an heir of incorruption, can invite to faith in His vocation to be a creative and quickening power in men and a bearer to them of eternal life.

---

[1] Rom. vi. 5–9. [2] Rom. viii. 2.
[3] Gal. ii. 20, vi. 14; 2 Cor. v. 15, 17.
[4] Rom. viii. 1; 1 Cor. i. 30; 2 Cor. xiii. 5; Eph. ii. 7, iii. 17, iv. 15, 16; Col. iii. 3, 4.
[5] Rom. iv. 25; 1 Cor. xv. 14; Phil. iii. 10.

Very different degrees of appreciation have been awarded, and are likely still to be awarded, to these two sides of Christ's work. The fact which biblical theology has to recognize is that the two aspects are closely associated together in the Pauline exposition of the office of the Redeemer.

The apostle, it may be noticed, while evidently penetrated most deeply with the sense of the importance of Christ's death in the economy of grace, has not occupied much space in explaining the inestimable value which he attached thereto. He has made it clear, however, that he considered Christ's delivery of Himself to the ordeal of the cross, to have been a great ethical deed, and has given reason for believing that he esteemed the ethical quality of the deed indispensable to its value. This appears in the antithesis which he draws between the disobedient Adam and the obedient Christ.[1] In more succinct terms the same conviction is intimated in the words which picture the humbled Son of God as "becoming obedient even unto death, yea, the death of the cross."[2] Herein a basis is afforded for a close association between the death and the life, since the obedience which came to a culminating expression in the cross ran through the whole career of the incarnated Redeemer.

VIII.—JUSTIFICATION AND REGENERATION.

The juxtaposition of these two terms is not inappropriate. As justice cannot be done to Paul's theory of the reconciling work of Christ without taking account of two

---

[1] Rom. v. 12–21. [2] Phil. ii. 8.

different but closely associated aspects, so is it with respect to his theory of the appropriation of salvation by the individual. It has an objective aspect, and in that view is justification. It has also, distinguishable in thought, but not separable in fact, a subjective aspect, and from that standpoint may be styled regeneration.

The weight of Protestant scholarship is very distinctly on the side of the conclusion that Paul used the term justification in the objective, judicial sense, making it to denote the pardon of its subject, or his induction into an approved standing before God, rather than the fact of his being made just or righteous by an inner transformation.[1] In favor of this consensus of interpretation may be cited in the first place the meaning which antecedent and contemporary Jewish usage assigned to the Greek word (δικαιοῦν) which is rendered to "justify." The word occurs about forty-five times in the Septuagint, and almost invariably, if not quite so, in the objective or judicial sense. It is used in the like sense in the Pseudepigraphic writings, such as the Psalms of Solomon, Fourth Ezra, and the Apocalypse of Baruch.[2] In the second place reference may be made to the statement of Paul respecting the impossibility of justification by the works of the law. This impossibility was evidently affirmed by him on the ground that the law will inevitably condemn a man because of his imperfect fulfillment of its precepts. The failure of the legal method to bring justification is

---

[1] Weiss, Holtzmann, Beyschlag, Pfleiderer, Lipsius, F. Nitzsch, Kaftan, Meyer, Godet, Sanday, Bruce, Stevens, and Cone are a few of the many who so interpret.

[2] Sanday, Comm. on Romans, p. 31.

thus identified with its inability to remove the condemnation or curse of the law.[1] But if lack of justification is made synonymous with condemnation, it is quite obvious that justification is designed to express an approving sentence. A third evidence in favor of the objective signification is found in sentences which place justification in direct contrast with condemnation. The following will serve as examples: "Not as through one that sinned, so also is the free gift; for the judgment came of one unto condemnation, but the free gift came of many trespasses unto justification."[2] "Who shall lay anything to the charge of God's elect? It is God that justifieth; who is he that shall condemn?"[3] Still another very clear indication that Paul attached the objective meaning to justification is contained in his use of the term "reckon" or "impute" ($\lambda o\gamma i \zeta o\mu a\iota$) in connections where justification was the subject under discussion. Here belongs a large part of the fourth chapter of Romans. The case of Abraham is treated by the apostle as a typical case. He sees in it a foreshadowing of the gospel plan of justification. He thus plainly evinces that in his thought the justification to which he is pointing out the way is identified with the approving sentence of God.

The connection suggests a reference to Paul's peculiar use of the phrase "the righteousness of God" ($\delta\iota\kappa a\iota o\sigma \acute{v}\nu\eta\ \theta\epsilon o\hat{v}$). When he speaks of this righteousness as something given to man in response to his faith he seems to treat it as the equivalent of justification.[4]

---

[1] Compare Rom. iii. 20 and Gal. ii. 16 with Gal. iii. 10, 11.
[2] Rom. v. 16.   [3] Rom. viii. 33, 34.
[4] See Rom. i. 17, iii. 21, 22, x. 3; 2 Cor. v 21.

In other words, it denotes that approved standing with God which cannot be gained in the way of legal performance. It is God's righteousness in the sense that He is its gracious author, the source whence comes the sentence which takes a man out from a state of condemnation and consequent spiritual deprivation. It is made man's righteousness in the sense that by his faith he is set in the relation of an approved child of God, and given a title to all the benefits which belong with that relation.

Adoption is a term which is also closely associated with justification in its objective significance. It denotes induction into the relation of sonship.[1] A subjective counterpart belongs undoubtedly with the relation. But the instituting of the relation is as distinctly an objective transaction as is justification. In fact the one transaction differs in conception but slightly from the other. For God to grant an approving sentence to one whose normal and designed place is that of a son in His household, is practically equivalent to a distinct instatement in the relation of sonship. According to the report of Paul's speech at Athens, he acknowledged that in a certain sense men are by nature children of God.[2] But in his epistles he regards the filial relation as practically denied by the alienation of men from God, and treating of them as candidates for a spiritual order of life he naturally contemplates them as subjects for induction into sonship.

While Paul gave to the salvation of the individual this objective aspect, there is not the slightest indication that he thought of it as separable in fact from that inner ex-

---

[1] Gal. iv. 5; Eph. i. 5.   [2] Acts xvii. 28, 29.

perience of grace which initiates and sustains the regenerate character. The antinomian suggestion that divine grace may redound to the justification of a man apart from personal reformation of life he repudiates with the utmost vigor. To believe upon Christ unto justification is equivalent in his view to a decisive renunciation of sin. "We who died to sin," he exclaims, "how shall we any longer live therein? Our old man was crucified with Christ that the body of sin might be done away, that so we should be no longer in bondage to sin."[1] He represents release from condemnation and inward renewal to be synchronous events. The one who attains unto the former is made free from the law of sin and death by the law of the spirit of life in Christ Jesus, and if any man hath not the Spirit of Christ, he is none of His.[2]

The condition of justification, and, by reason of intrinsic connection, of regeneration also, is commonly represented by Paul to be simply faith. The combination of repentance with faith, which appears in the Synoptical Gospels, and also the explicit emphasis of those Gospels upon confession of Christ, are not characteristic of the recorded teachings of the apostle. There is indeed a passing reference both to the one and the other.[3] But in Paul's exposition of the conditions of attaining to salvation a well-nigh exclusive stress is placed upon faith. He declares it distinctive of the gospel that therein is revealed a righteousness of God by faith unto faith.[4] He represents faith to be the means of giving practical effect to the propitiation in the blood of Christ.[5] He

---

[1] Rom. vi. 2, 6.   [2] Rom. viii. 1, 2; Col. iii. 3, 9, 10.
[3] 2 Cor. vii. 10; Rom. x. 10.   [4] Rom. i. 17.   [5] Rom. iii. 25.

makes faith the immediate condition of spiritual sonship. "Ye are all sons of God, through faith, in Jesus Christ."[1] In repeated instances he bases justification upon the sole condition of faith.[2] Moreover, he views faith as being continuously a principle of the religious life.[3]

The apostle who conditioned so much upon faith could not, in all likelihood, have given it a superficial meaning. The term signified to him much more than mere intellectual assent. He has indicated that he thought of faith as issuing from the centre of man's personality and expressing his volitional and affectional nature, in that he says with the heart man believeth unto righteousness.[4] A like implication belongs with the description of the specifically Christian principle as a faith that works by love.[5] To the same effect also is the representation that faith is a means of vital union with Christ, so uniting its subject to Him that it becomes appropriate to speak of a mutual indwelling.[6] In short, it is manifest that the faith which Paul exalts as the condition of salvation signifies nothing less than a thorough self-committal to God in Christ. It stands for this great ethical deed, and so contains implicitly not a little that might be designated by other names. By virtue of necessary connections thorough self-committal to God in Christ involves a penitent forsaking of sin, a loyal confession of Christ, and a sincere espousal of the path of obedience to the known will of God.

---

[1] Gal. iii. 26.
[2] Rom. iii. 22, 26, 28, iv. 22–25, v. 1, 2; Gal. ii. 16, iii. 11, 12. See also Eph. ii. 8; Phil. iii. 9.
[3] Gal. ii. 20; 2 Cor. v. 7.
[4] Rom. x. 10.
[5] Gal. v. 6.
[6] Eph. iii. 17; Gal. ii. 20, iii. 26–28.

Paul did not suppose that faith saves in its own virtue as a work or personal performance. The antithesis which he makes between salvation by works and salvation by the free gift of God in Christ emphatically negatives a supposition of that sort. The method of faith, he distinctly affirms, is the method according to grace.[1] He conceives, therefore, of faith as the graciously appointed condition of salvation rather than its meritorious ground. It is not necessary, however, to imagine that he rated it as a mere indifferent instrument, serving by appointment a useful purpose, but having no ethical worth in itself. Without doubt he considered it to be intrinsically a noble and ennobling activity of the human spirit, and he has indicated as much by placing it alongside of hope and love among the things that have abiding worth.[2]

In express emphasis upon the office of faith Paul went beyond all other New Testament writers. He was not, however, in this matter a fabricator of strange doctrine. In more poetic and popular form Christ taught the great lesson that faith, in the sense of trustful self-committal, is the channel of the divine mercy and of all spiritual bounty. Nor is it evident that true religion can rationally assign any lesser office to faith. Religion in its highest and purest form is a religion of sonship. As such it must put faith, or filial self-committal to God, in the front rank of requirement and privilege.

This remark naturally directs attention to the fact that in Paul's view the faith which justifies normally issues into a filial consciousness. To be a living Christian and to have a filial consciousness were evidently closely re-

---

[1] Rom. iv. 16.   [2] 1 Cor. xiii. 13.

lated, if not identical, ideas in his mind. To the brethren at Rome he writes, "Ye received not the spirit of bondage again unto fear; but ye received the spirit of adoption, whereby we cry, Abba, Father. The Spirit Himself beareth witness with our spirit, that we are the children of God."[1] The witness *with*, as specified here, must evidently be at the same time a witness *to* the human spirit, since no third party is contemplated. The meaning is that the activity of the Divine Spirit and the accordant or responsive movement of the Christian's own spirit result in a lively sense of a filial standing. As to the mode of the former there is no definite specification. The theory of immediate communication has its advocates, but the apostle's language does not exclude the supposition that the Holy Spirit works dynamically and effects assurance mediately, that is, by enkindling and sustaining the filial temper which cannot well refrain from calling unto God as Father.

In a preceding paragraph reasons were stated for the conclusion that certain sentences of Paul, which give emphatic expression to the idea of divine sovereignty, were not designed to teach that men are arbitrarily inducted into the kingdom or excluded therefrom. It is proper to notice here that there are representations in the Pauline epistles which bear strongly against a particularistic theory, and invite to the belief that the high privilege of sonship is truly set before every man. Such is the antithesis which is drawn between Adam and Christ in the fifth chapter of Romans. Who can read this chapter without discovering that the apostle meant

---

[1] Rom. viii. 15, 16. Compare Gal. iv. 6.

to describe the grace of God in Christ as matching, or overmatching, the evil consequences of Adam's fault? In fact the free gift is described as being for as many as are touched by the blight and condemnation. Again, in the tenth and eleventh chapters of the same epistle, as has been noticed already, God is represented to so manipulate the course of history as shall conduce to the ingathering of the greatest possible number of both Jews and Gentiles. Furthermore, it is to be observed that Paul does not hesitate to speak of Christ as having died for all, or to name the world as the object of the scheme of reconciliation.[1] It is not a little significant, too, that in spite of his luminous confidence as to his standing before God he speaks of the necessity of practising self-discipline, lest he himself should be rejected after having preached to others.[2] That does not look as if he conceived of personal destiny as fixed by an unconditional decree.

IX. — THE UNFOLDMENT AND MANIFESTATION OF THE NEW LIFE.

In setting forth the ideal of the Christian life Paul was far from contenting himself with drawing a general outline. He speaks indeed of sanctification, but he speaks far more frequently of the several elements of a rounded character. It is quite plain that he never imagined that any one could properly be labelled as entirely sanctified, or perfected religiously, who might still be lacking in love, meekness, patience, gentleness

---

[1] 2 Cor. v. 14, 19.   [2] 1 Cor. ix. 27.

or any other Christian virtue. His ideal was inclusive of positive spiritual health and fullness, as well as exclusive of perversities and impotences. To reach it was not by any means, in his view, a mere matter of washing away blots and stains. Judging from references to his own struggle and endeavor,[1] we may conclude that he had very slight confidence in the ability of any one to reach the goal by a sudden spring.

A large place in Paul's ideal of Christian character is given to love. He regards it as the flower of faith, the consummation of the spiritual excellence to which faith opens up the way. Faith is its antecedent, inasmuch as faith initiates the fellowship in which love grows. But here the child may be regarded as surpassing the parent. Not only does the apostle distinctly award to love the primacy in the immortal epitome of ethical religion contained in the thirteenth chapter of First Corinthians; he often commends it as the chief spiritual value. He teaches the Romans that love, as incapable of working ill, is the fulfillment of the law.[2] He enforces the obligation of love in his address to the Ephesians by appealing to the divine illustration of its beauty and efficacy given in Christ, and prays that they may be rooted and grounded in love.[3] He exhorts the Colossians to put on, above all things, love which is the bond of perfectness.[4] He asks for the Thessalonians that the Lord would make them to increase and abound in love one toward another, and toward all men; and while he acknowledges their praiseworthy exhibition of brotherly

---

[1] 1 Cor. ix. 27; Phil. iii. 12, 14.
[2] Rom. xiii. 9, 10.
[3] Eph. v. 1, 2, iii. 17.
[4] Col. iii. 14.

THE PAULINE THEOLOGY

affection, he urges them to abound in love more and more.[1]

In the apostle's eulogy of love he contrasts it not only with all gifts of power, but also with knowledge, quite to the disparagement of the relative worth of the latter. Our present knowledge, he conceives, is so partial and fragmentary, that it will pass away before the higher disclosures of the future, much as the child's stock of ideas gives place to the maturer thoughts of manhood.[2] Also in relation to the conditions of present enlightenment he emphasizes the incompetency of worldly wisdom to take the place of a truly religious disposition.[3] Nevertheless, the apostle has no thought of rating knowledge at a low figure. His strictures are aimed against the assignment to it of inappropriate offices. He includes growth in knowledge in the Christian ideal. Thus he prays for the Philippians that their love may abound in knowledge and all discernment.[4] In like manner he prays for the Colossians that they may be filled with the knowledge of God's will in all spiritual wisdom and understanding, and reminds them that they have put on the new man, which is being renewed unto knowledge after the image of Him that created him.[5] For the Ephesians also he makes request of God that He would give unto them the spirit of wisdom and revelation in the knowledge of Him.[6] He invites them, moreover, to a high estimate of the worth of knowledge when he describes the aim of all church instrumentalities to be "the building up of the body of Christ, till we all attain

---
[1] 1 Thess. iii. 12, iv. 9, 10. [2] 1 Cor. xiii. 8–12. [3] 1 Cor. i. 17–25, ii.
[4] Phil. i. 9. [5] Col. i. 9, 10, iii. 9, 10. [6] Eph. i. 17.

unto the unity of the faith, and of the knowledge of the Son of God, unto a full-grown man, unto the measure of the stature of the fulness of Christ: that we may be no longer children, tossed to and fro and carried about with every wind of doctrine, by the sleight of men, in craftiness, after the wiles of error; but speaking the truth in love, may grow up in all things into Him, which is the head even Christ."[1] Doubtless the apostle might have awarded a larger consideration to earthly science as likely in the long run to favor the maintenance of sound religious conceptions. But that is a point of view with which he does not deal. He contemplates knowledge only in its more immediate and evident connection with religious interests. He manifestly rates it highly where it stands in congenial relations with faith and love.

A noticeable feature in Paul's Christian ideal is the combination which it exhibits of the gentler virtues with the more heroic. The commendation of patience, forbearance, sympathy, long-suffering, gentleness, and the spirit of forgiveness occupies no inconsiderable portion of his epistles.[2]

Less space is given to the inculcation of manful energy, courage, and devotion; but enough is said in their behalf to show that the apostle regarded tender considerateness and militant force to be perfectly compatible attributes of the Christian disciple. The same epistle which records the exhortation to be tender-hearted and forgiving, records also the exhortation to be strong in the Lord, and

---

[1] Eph. iv. 12–15.
[2] Rom. xii. 10–21, xiv. 13–20, xv. 1–3; 2 Cor. vi. 6; Gal. v. 22, 23; Eph. iv. 1–3, 31, 32; Phil. iv. 5; Col. i. 11, iii. 12, 13; 1 Thess. v. 14.

to stand against principalities and powers clad in the whole armor of God.[1] Within the limits of a couple of sentences are given these injunctions: "Let all that ye do be done in love"; "stand fast in the faith, quit you like men, be strong."[2] The apostle, in short, reproduces in the form of precepts the ideal which Christ exhibited in the form of a real life among men. Beyond question the image of the historical Christ was often in his mind as he wrote to his converts such instructions as might assist them to attain unto "a full grown man."

The judgment has been expressed in a few instances that the Pauline theology makes no provision for progressive sanctification, inasmuch as it rates the experience in justification and regeneration as all-transforming, a transference into a state of essential perfection. One can only wonder where this eccentric criticism obtained its petty inch rule for measuring the teaching of Paul. Doubtless the apostle, in the transition epoch in which he wrought, had an urgent call to clarify the conditions of entering the Christian life, and devoted a very considerable part of his discourse to this topic. Doubtless also he profoundly accentuated the transformation which results to the believing soul from earnest trustful self committal to God as revealed in Christ, and vigorously set forth the conclusion that such a soul should reckon itself entirely dead unto sin. But what less could he do in justice to the theme? That he painted in glowing terms the ideal is no sort of token that he ignored the discrepancy between the actual and the ideal. Who can read his epistles, and not perceive that he saw with open

---

[1] Eph. iv, 32, vi. 10-17. [2] 1 Cor. xvi. 13, 14.

eyes the shortcomings of contemporary Christians? Who can take even a casual glance at his messages to his disciples, and not discover that his heart was filled with a great and ceaseless anxiety that all who had received the saving word from him might be so transformed by the renewing of their mind as to prove the perfect will of God, might follow after love until they should be rooted and grounded therein, might walk in the Spirit until they should exemplify all His fruits, might attain unto the measure of the stature of the fullness of Christ, might be sanctified wholly? Indeed, one who runs may read the conviction of the apostle that a goal of spiritual attainment lies distinctly ahead of the converted man, so that he has abundant need to press forward. But, it is alleged, Paul lays down no plan for progressively achieving the needed sanctification. Perhaps he does not in an explicit and formal manner. He does not take pains to distinguish between the demands of the first stage of Christian life and those of subsequent stages. But why should he? Vital union with the Father, through the Son, by the bond of faith, is as much the fundamental demand of all later stages as it is of the primary. And closely linked with this demand is the requirement that conduct in all varied spheres should be actively directed toward conformity to the practical dictates of this union. This latter requirement Paul has not failed to urge with great vigor. While he emphasizes the futility of *dependence for salvation* upon a scheme of works, he never in the least disparages good works as a matter of obligation, congruity, and logical necessity on the part of the reborn man. It appears, therefore, that his disciples were not left without very positive suggestions and directions as to the means of perfecting themselves in Christian character.

The conditions of the apostolic era naturally dictated that only a subordinate consideration should be given to the subject of civic virtue and responsibility. The fact that the management of the State was in the hands of the unbelieving wrought with the expectation that the age would be short to incline Christian teachers to treat but briefly of political duties. Paul takes up the theme only to enforce the obligation of Christians to submit conscientiously to the authority of the State. His vision of the kingdom of Christ as overpassing all bounds of particular nations and countries does not seem to have bred in his mind any disposition to ignore the claims of regular governments. At any rate he strongly accentuates the duty of subjection to those in power as being ordained of God for the public weal.[1] The qualifications upon civil allegiance which conscience and the commands of God may logically involve, he leaves his disciples to discover and apply for themselves. His judgment that it is unseemly for Christians to carry their disputes before the secular tribunals may be expressed in terms disparaging to the notion of believers being judged by the unbelieving.[2] But the stress here is not so much upon the fact of the judgment being rendered by the outside tribunal, as upon its being voluntarily sought by quarrelsome Christians, in place of their trying for a settlement at home. Doubtless the apostle did not intend to hint that slight consideration is in general due to the jurisdiction of the

---
[1] Rom. xiii. 1–7.   [2] 1 Cor. vi. 1–8.

secular power. It is one thing to respect and obey the guardian of civil order; it is quite another thing voluntarily to seek his decision in a case of variance between brethren.

As Paul was conservative in his teaching on the allegiance due to the State, so also he was far from the design to precipitate social revolution. In relation to slavery he contented himself with urging humane treatment from the side of the master and willing service from the side of the bondman. His contribution to the cause of emancipation lay in his distinct proclamation of the essential equality of men in Christ. In no other form probably could he have made so effective a contribution.

In Paul's conception of Christian life in relation to the domestic sphere some contrasted points of view may be noticed. On the one hand, though disclaiming all thought of abridging personal liberty, he expresses a certain preference for the unmarried life.[1] On the other hand, he dignifies marriage as a holy union in the bonds of love fit to be compared to the union of Christ with His Church.[2] On the one hand, he teaches the subordination of woman to man.[3] On the other hand, he affirms that in Christ distinctions of male and female have no place any more than distinctions of Jew and Greek.[4] To bring complete unity of view out of these contrasts is not altogether easy. But the outcome seems to be about this: (1) Entrance into the marriage relation is contemplated by Paul as the general rule for Christians. He considers, however, that in individual instances the

---

[1] 1 Cor. vii.
[2] Eph. v. 22–23.
[3] 1 Cor. xi. 3–10.
[4] Gal. iii. 28.

ends of personal piety and religious service may be best attained by abstinence from marriage. In commending this abstinence he appears to have been influenced, to a considerable extent, by the troublous conditions of the time and the expected approach of the day of Christ's coming. (2) Spiritually man and woman, in Paul's view, stand upon the same plane; but to subserve the ends of household and social order the husband has been vested with a certain headship over the wife. This headship, however, is properly fulfilled only as it is patterned after the self-sacrificing and loving headship of Christ. "Husbands ought so to love their own wives as their own bodies. He that loveth his own wife loveth himself: for no man ever hated his own flesh; but nourisheth it, even as Christ also the Church." (3) Possibly, as has been alleged by some critics, Paul did not fully transcend the antique view of the relative position of the two sexes. But if any of his statements need to be modified, he has himself afforded a basis for the necessary modification in his strong declarations respecting the elimination of all artificial distinctions in and through Christ.

The emphatic view which Paul held of the marriage union naturally inclined him to accord a very scanty place to divorce. He mentions, however, one ground as justifiying the nullification of the marriage bond. If the unbelieving partner will not abide with the believing or Christian partner, let the former depart. "A brother or a sister is not under bondage in such cases."[1] Exegetes differ on the question whether in this statement the apostle licenses the remarriage of the deserted part-

---

[1] 1 Cor. vii. 12-15.

ner. In our view, the words "not under bondage" favor an affirmative answer. The apostle could hardly have thought it necessary to make a formal declaration that the husband or wife was not bound to maintain cohabitation with the deserting party — a thing most obviously impossible. This interpretation, it is true, exhibits Paul as at variance with the letter of Christ's teaching, which at most admits divorce only for the cause of adultery.[1] But Paul may have taken that teaching, as he appears to have taken the instruction relative to oaths, as rather setting up a standard for an ideal society than giving an inflexible rule to be rigorously followed under all kinds of conditions. Not a few writers on ethics have been inclined to take Christ's teaching in this sense.

X.— THE CHURCH AND THE SACRAMENTS.

In the earlier Pauline epistles a local association is for the most part given to the word "Church." It is used to designate a particular Christian society; and where a number of such societies are contemplated the plural form of the word is employed.[2] Only in exceptional instances is the term used in these epistles to designate the whole body of Christians in the world.[3] On the other hand, in the later epistles, notably in Ephesians, references to the Church in the collective sense predominate. This naturally resulted from the more theoretic standpoint

---

[1] Matt. v. 32, xix. 9; Mark x. 5-12; Luke xvi. 18.
[2] Rom. xvi. 4, 5; 1 Cor i. 2, iv. 17, vii. 17, xi. 16, xiv. 33, 34, xvi. 1, 19; 2 Cor. viii. 1, 19, 23, xi. 8, 28, xii. 13; 1 Thess. ii. 14; 2 Thess. i. 4.
[3] 1 Cor. xii. 28; Gal. i. 13.

from which the subject was approached in the later writings. The change of usage is not, therefore, any very decisive evidence either of change in conviction or of advance in ecclesiastical organization.

The number of references to the Church is greatly in excess of that to the kingdom of God. The latter expression is used, on the one hand, to designate the sum of spiritual treasure which belongs to the Christian in the present, the rule of the divine in him with all that it brings for the replenishment of the interior life,[1] and, on the other, in an eschatological sense, to designate the perfected community which lies beyond the era of the resurrection. The latter meaning is especially unmistakable in the declaration that flesh and blood cannot inherit the kingdom of God.[2] As related to the Church the kingdom has the more ideal and transcendental significance. The two are not formally identified by the apostle. Yet it is quite evident that when he comes to picture the Church according to its divine purpose, as he does in Ephesians and Colossians, he puts into it nearly everything that is denoted by the kingdom of God in scriptural usage. It stands forth as the body of Christ, the fullness of Him who filleth all in all, the instrument for making known the manifold wisdom of God, in design a perfect society, holy and without blemish, its members bearing the name and the character of saints, being bound together by the bond of love, and fulfilling harmoniously their several functions, like the parts of a well-framed building or of a living organism.

---

[1] Rom. xiv. 17; 1 Cor. iv. 20; Col. i. 12-14.
[2] 1 Cor. xv. 50. Compare 1 Cor. vi. 9, 10; Gal. v. 21.

Aside from the Pastoral Epistles, the writings of Paul contain little mention of church officials. In Galatians there is no reference to any class of administrators. The only official rank of which indication is given is that of teachers;[1] and it would seem probable from the description given in 1 Cor. xiv that these had no exclusive prerogative in the public service. In First Thessalonians and in Romans there is a general reference to those intrusted with a function of supervision.[2] The Epistle to the Philippians opens with a reference to bishops and deacons, and in Ephesians the work of ministering is represented as portioned out to apostles, prophets, evangelists, pastors and teachers.[3] In this latter enumeration the intent of the apostle was evidently to give rather a full list of ministerial functions than to specify distinct and well-defined grades of officials. Between prophets, evangelists, and teachers the lines of division were not so wide but that one person might belong to the several classes. Something more of an association with the local church, however, probably went with the last term than with the other two. The prophets as inspired preachers and the evangelists as missionary assistants of the apostles exercised their gifts somewhat at large in the Church.

It is to be noticed in connection with the Ephesian passage that the form of the Greek — the non-repetition of τοὺς δὲ — implies that pastors and teachers were thought of as designating one and the same class of officials. The former name is naturally suggestive of a local

---

[1] Gal. vi. 6. [2] 1 Thess. v. 12, Rom. xii. 8. See also 1 Cor. xii. 28.
[3] Eph. iv. 11.

office with a function of oversight. In this character it seems to be identical with the office of bishops mentioned in Philippians. Putting together the Philippian and the Ephesian passage, we are brought to the conclusion that within the sphere of Paul's supervision it came to be counted expedient for the local church to have a group of administrators called bishops or pastors, who might also very appropriately exercise a teaching function, and a second group, called deacons (indicated perhaps by the word "helps" in 1 Cor. xii. 28), whose distinctive service consisted in ministry to the poor and the sick. As for elders, they are not mentioned in the epistles under consideration. The question of their identity with bishops is, therefore, properly postponed till the teaching of the Pastoral Epistles comes to be considered.

On the whole, under the Pauline regime officialism seems not to have been prominent. The apostles, as missionary founders of churches, are represented doubtless as having actually a commanding influence. But they are represented also as minded to direct those under their charge rather by the method of instruction and persuasion than by that of law and decree. Of a monarchical constitution of the Church no hint is given. The declarations of Paul in Galatians rebel utterly against the notion of a Petrine headship or primacy of governing authority.

In the line of solemn rites, or sacraments, the Pauline writings recognize baptism and the eucharist. The former is regarded as typical of union with Christ, as well as instrumental to union with the visible society. In this view it is styled baptism into Christ.[1] To be in union

---

[1] Gal. iii. 27.

with Christ involves, according to the apostle, a dying of the old man and a rising into newness of life. Baptism figures this moral renewal, and thus in picturesque language may be described as a burial and a resurrection.[1] How far the apostle accounted baptism instrumental of the great change which it symbolizes is not definitely stated. But surely it may be argued from the tenor of his thinking that he had no notion of placing it on anything like a parity with such a spiritual condition of the new life as is faith. Repeatedly and energetically he proclaimed faith as the condition of justification, and justification and regeneration were not regarded by him as separated in fact. It puts him in incredible contradiction with himself to suppose that, while lauding the saving office of faith and casting Judaic ceremonialism overboard, he proceeded to condition birth into the new life upon an external rite. "Think of the man," says Bruce, "who so peremptorily said circumcision is of no avail, assigning to baptism not merely symbolical, but essential significance in reference to regeneration. Then how weak his position controversially, if this was his view! How easy for Judaistic opponents to retort, what better are you than we? You set aside circumcision, and you put in its place baptism. We fail to see the great advantage of the change. You insist grandly on the antithesis between letter and spirit, or between flesh and spirit. But here is no antithesis. Baptism, not less than circumcision, is simply a rite affecting the body. You charge us with beginning in the spirit and with faith, and ending in the flesh. How do you defend yourself against the same

---

[1] Rom. vi. 4.

charge?"[1] It is indeed possible, since in the first age of the Church the administration of baptism was often nearly synchronous with the exercise and confession of faith in Christ, and moreover was very likely attended in many instances with tokens of the presence of the Holy Spirit, that the apostle gave it a certain association with the experience of regeneration. But it sadly violates perspective in exegesis to make him the advocate of a theory of baptism which exalts its function to the level of the great spiritual and interior conditions of salvation.

The Pauline interpretation of the Lord's supper sets it forth as a symbol of the unity of Christian believers, a memorial of the self-sacrificing death of Christ, and a means of communion with Him.[2] The communion, κοινωνία, is to be understood in a spiritual sense, as opposed to any conjunction with the real body of Christ. The apostle indicates as much in his statement, that they which eat the sacrifices are communicants (κοινωνοί) of the altar,[3] that is, come into a special relation with the altar, or with the divinity represented thereby. As in the latter instance there is no notion of an appropriation of bodily substance from the object of the communion, so it may be inferred that the former instance implies no such notion. What is said of making one's self guilty of the body and blood of Christ by eating and drinking unworthily, or of earning judgment by not discerning the Lord's body, in no wise contradicts this view. As the context shows there was occasion to rebuke an irreverent dealing with the sacred emblems of

---

[1] St. Paul's Conception of Christianity, pp 237, 238.
[2] 1 Cor. x. 16, 17, xi. 23–29.   [3] 1 Cor. x. 18.

Christ's passion. This profanation of divinely ordained symbols and careless lack of discernment for what they stand the apostle condemns as in effect a trespass against the holy things symbolized.[1] His entire exposition gives no real foothold for a materialistic interpretation of the communion to which the rite is instrumental.

XI. — THE SECOND ADVENT AND THE RELATED EVENTS.

The certain elements in the eschatology of Paul are the second coming of Christ, the resurrection of the righteous in the sense of their investment with incorruptible bodies, and a final judgment before the tribunal of Christ. To each of these items the apostle has witnessed his belief in sufficiently unequivocal terms.

In his earlier epistles Paul evinces a conviction of the possibility, if not indeed of the probability, that the advent of Christ would occur before he himself should be overtaken by death.[2] Further on, this conviction seems to have been relinquished, and in its place we find a presentiment of exit from the earth by the ordinary pathway.[3] Respecting the nature of the second

---

[1] "If it is regarded as a deadly insult to a country when its flag is torn down and trampled in the dust, surely it is an insult to Jesus Christ Himself, and to the great sacrifice of His body and blood, if the symbols of that sacrifice are treated as profane or common things, even though it is not imagined that these symbols, somehow or other, have been transformed into that which they symbolize." (Lambert, The Sacraments in the New Testament, p. 377.)

[2] 1 Thess. iv. 17; 1 Cor. xv. 51, 52.

[3] 2 Cor. v. 1, 8; Phil. i. 20-24.

advent, the Pauline exposition is not necessarily regarded as presuming upon anything more than a glorious and unmistakable manifestation of the ascended Christ to men generally. In his most detailed description the apostle represents, not that Christ is to install Himself upon the earth, but that the saints are to be caught up in the clouds to meet Him in the air, and so to be forever with the Lord.[1] No recorded sentence gives a hint that he thought of a visible reign of Christ upon earth. On the contrary, the spiritual character which he ascribes to the bodies of the risen saints and the transformation of living saints, which he makes coincident with the revelation of Christ from heaven, fairly shut out the idea of an earthly millennial kingdom.

It appears from the Thessalonian epistles that Paul wished Christians to cultivate an inspiring expectancy relative to the advent, but at the same time to avoid disquietude and feverish anxiety. To check an overwrought anticipation he mentions an event which must go before the day of the Lord, namely the disclosure of the man of sin, who is held back by one that restraineth, but in time will gain liberty to run his course of lawlessness.[2] The precise meaning of the representation remains in question. Some exegetes think that no theory better meets the case than the one which assumes that the restraining power designates the Roman government, and that the man of sin stands for a culminating expression of Jewish apostasy and false messiahship.[3] The

---

[1] 1 Thess. iv. 13-17. [2] 2 Thess ii. 1-12.
[3] So Weiss, Bousset, Moffatt, Stevens, Bacon, Adeney, Kennedy, and others.

main difficulty with this theory is the assumption of divine honors by the lawless one. For a Jew to push on to that height of blasphemous pretence would indeed be madness. It is not entirely certain, however, that Paul did not think it possible for a Jewish pretender, spurred on by the excited feeling and desperation of the nation, to fall into the madness of practically usurping the honor and authority of God. The description in 1 Thess. ii. 14–16 indicates how intense at this period was the apostle's impression of Jewish rebellion against God and the truth. If the man of sin was not conceived to belong to an anti-Christian Judaism, it is difficult to interpret the reference to the restraining power in any satisfactory manner. It is an unlikely supposition that the Roman government should be thought of as playing both the rôle of restraint and that of a godless usurpation and lawlessness, that is, through different representatives of the imperial sovereignty. No probable ground can be imagined for the association of self-deification with one of the Cæsars to the exclusion of others. Already before Paul wrote, divine honors had been paid to several emperors and had been ostentatiously claimed by Caligula. For another to proceed in the same fashion would not give him a title to be regarded as a highly exceptional impersonation of ungodliness, the veritable man of sin. This difficulty of finding a suitable meaning for the restraining power, if the man of sin is identified with a representative of imperial rule, tends to turn the scale in favor of the conclusion that the apostle thought of Judaism as the source of this portentous figure. The same conclusion is also favored by the reference to the "apostasy," or "falling away" (ii. 3), since an event of this order is naturally connected rather with an elect people than with one which had not been given a special divine association But while claiming a superior probability for this interpretation, we admit the possibility that the form which loomed up before the apostle's mind may not have been so definite as to be positively identified either with a counterfeit Messiah or with a self-deified Cæsar. He may have thought somewhat vaguely of a culminating expression of revolution, lawlessness, and God-defying presumption.

The resurrection which Paul associated immediately with the second advent, evidently was not understood by him to be a literal resurrection of the body as known to us. The account in 1 Cor. xv emphasizes the radical unlikeness of the body that is to be with that of the present, and the mention of it in 2 Cor. v. 1, 2 as a house or habitation from heaven heightens the impression of unlikeness. But, on the other hand, the apostle uses language suggestive of some sort of historical connection and basis of identity as pertaining to the bodies of the two states He speaks of the body as being sown in one condition and raised in another — sown in corruption and raised in incorruption, sown a natural body and raised a spiritual body.[1] He says that the reappearing Saviour shall fashion anew the body of our humiliation, that it may be conformed to the body of his glory.[2]

---

[1] 1 Cor. xv. 42–44. That the "spiritual" body was not conceived to be made of spirit ($\pi\nu\epsilon\hat{u}\mu\alpha$) may be judged from the fact that the "natural" or psychical body was manifestly not conceived to be made of soul ($\psi v\chi\acute{\eta}$) but of flesh.

[2] Phil. iii. 20, 21.

He represents the high destination toward which the sons of God look with desire to be the redemption of their bodies.[1] Thus with all the intimation of newness and unlikeness there is an implicit assumption of a certain sameness. In what the apostle located this element of sameness, or whether he took pains to define it to his own thought, we have no means of ascertaining. It is a little venturesome to suppose that he anticipated modern theorizing and predicated identity in respect of organizing principle.

There is no doubt that the general teaching of Paul implies a special era of resurrection. It has been suspected by some, however, on the basis of the opening verses of the fifth chapter of Second Corinthians, that Paul changed his view, and in his later days believed that each follower of Christ is invested at death with the resurrection body. But this seems to us an unwarranted conclusion. The second epistle to the Corinthians was written only a few months after the first, in which the contrary view is set forth with sufficient definiteness. Paul naturally would not be ambitious to confuse the minds of the Corinthians by placing before them within so short an interval two ways of thinking that he knew to be contradictory. The tone of the later Corinthian passage is largely explained by the fact that Paul had no such measure of the intermediate state as belongs to us. In the expectation that it would be confined to a brief season, he could practically ignore it, and in the vision of faith paint the being clothed upon with the house from heaven as following close upon the dissolu-

---

[1] Rom. viii. 23.

tion of the earthly tabernacle. Moreover, it is to be noticed that he does not express a certitude that there would be no interval of nakedness, but only an earnest longing to be clothed upon, "that what is mortal may be swallowed up of life." It may be observed that Paul in the preceding chapter uses the ordinary resurrection phraseology, representing himself as expecting to be *raised up* even as was Christ (iv. 14). This as much as hints that the poetic reference to a house or habitation from heaven is not to be construed too definitely, or to be taken as implying a distinct and conscious departure from his former teaching. Not less significant are the words of Phil. iii. 19–21. Here it is represented that the resurrection power of Christ is to be exercised at His second coming. A plain indication is thus given that Paul had not surrendered his earlier thought of a special era for the resurrection.

The resurrection which Paul discusses in his epistles contemplates an assimilation to the glorious form of the risen Christ. In this character it is a resurrection of those only who belong to Christ. The question of the resurrection of the wicked is entirely ignored. Not a single sentence of a single epistle touches upon it, at least in any direct or unmistakable manner. The statement in 1 Cor. xv. 22, "as in Adam all die, so also in Christ shall all be made alive," is no exception. For, to say nothing about an implicit limitation in the phrase "in Christ," the next verse confines the application to those that are Christ's. It is true that some commentators understand by the succeeding declaration, "then cometh the end," the completing stage of the resurrection, wherein the wicked are to be included. But it is immensely improbable that the apostle would have referred in so vague a manner to the resurrection of a division of mankind. Moreover, the words, "then cometh the end," are most naturally understood of the close of the dispensation. Silence on the score of the resurrection of the wicked is not, indeed, necessarily equivalent to a denial of the event. The fact that the apostle was addressing believers, and dealt with the subject from the point of view of their interest, may go far toward explaining his silence. But, on the other hand, it is to be observed that the quickening of the mortal body is given in one connection a certain association with the indwelling of the Spirit,[1] and that in another connection the resurrection from the dead is represented as a prize to be won by strenuous endeavor,[2] and still further that eternal destruction is said to await the wicked at Christ's coming.[3] On the whole, the teaching of Paul's epistles taken by itself is scarcely favorable to the supposition of the resurrection of the wicked. It contains nothing which suggests the conviction recorded in Acts xxiv. 15, unless it be the representation that all men are candidates for the judgment; and before this could be given any decisive weight it would be necessary to prove that Paul thought of the investment of a given subject with a

---

[1] Rom. viii. 10, 11. It is not necessary to suppose here a reference to an actual initiation of the bodily resurrection by the indwelling Spirit. The probable thought is that the working of the life-giving Spirit in man's spirit is a pledge that even the body of the believer shall ultimately be redeemed from corruption and death. (Compare Godet, Comm. on Romans.)

[2] Phil. iii. 11.   [3] 2 Thess i. 5–10.

THE PAULINE THEOLOGY 265

resurrection body as a necessary antecedent of his being judged.

Considerable stress has been laid by some critics on the contrast between Paul's doctrine of salvation through grace and his picture of judgment on the basis of conduct, as though he had inadvertently mingled a Christian and a Judaic point of view. But it is the reverse of a magnanimous exegesis which so interprets. It is quite gratuitous to conclude that into the Judaic form of words Paul put a crass Judaic sense. He never forgot, doubtless, his own central teaching, or conceived that any work apart from the genuine faith which brings the soul into fruit-bearing union with Christ could serve a man before the divine tribunal. The total doing of a man is what Paul may reasonably be thought to have regarded as determining future destiny, and the total doing of a man includes his response to the unmerited grace of God in Christ. Only those who suppose the apostle to make absolutely nothing of man's free agency have any serious occasion to criticise his picture of the judgment.

What lies beyond the judgment is considered by Paul only in a very general way. He contents himself with picturing a scene of unity, a kingdom before which all opposition has given way.[1] The wicked are not assigned any place in that ultimate scene. Did Paul regard them as the subjects of an all-embracing restoration? This view is contradicted by the representation that they are appointed to eternal destruction from the face of the Lord.[2] They pass out of the field of vision either as

---

[1] 1 Cor. xv. 24–27.

[2] 2 Thess. i. 9. The term "destruction" (ὄλεθρος) employed here cannot fairly be regarded as a token that Paul was formally committed to

being reduced to practical impotence or as consigned to non-existence. Our reticence on Paul's position may well match in some degree his reticence on the subject.

XII.— THE TEACHING OF THE PASTORAL EPISTLES.

The Pastoral Epistles add so little of theological subject-matter to the content of the other epistles bearing the name of Paul that it will not be necessary to devote to them more than a few sentences. A tribute is paid in them to the transcendence of God, in that He is described as dwelling in light unapproachable.[1] At the same time His fatherly and compassionate character is not overlooked. Christ is styled the one mediator who gave Himself a ransom for all, the saviour who has abolished death, and the judge of the quick and the dead.[2] In one instance the form of statement in the original seems to imply the application of the divine name to Him.[3] The salvation provided in Him is designed for all men.[4] It is not earned by works; its bestowment is a matter of grace.[5] Christian living is to be characterized by sobriety and self-discipline, though ascetic prescriptions against marriage and the use of meats are to be repro-

---

the doctrine of the annihilation of the wicked. From his point of view it was not worth while to distinguish between an impoverished, wretched existence and non-existence. (Compare Kennedy, St. Paul's Conceptions of the Last Things, pp 120–125)

[1] 1 Tim. vi 16.
[2] 1 Tim. ii. 5, 6; 2 Tim. i. 10, iv. 1.
[3] Tit. ii. 13.
[4] 1 Tim. ii. 4, iv. 10.
[5] 2 Tim. i. 9; Tit. iii. 4–7.

THE PAULINE THEOLOGY 267

bated.[1] Among Christian interests to which great heed needs to be given is the preservation of sound doctrine.

In general, it is easy to observe in these epistles a strain of the characteristic Pauline teaching. Still the standpoint of the foregoing epistles is not fully reproduced in them. The representation of a mystical union with Christ is wanting. In place of the life insphered in Christ we have well-ordered conduct, or godliness, set forth and commended. The voice of Paul as the ardent mystic we do not hear.

As compared with the preceding epistles the Pastoral give an impression of a more settled and developed form

---

[1] 1 Tim. iv. 3, 4. On the other hand, a token of ascetic tendency may be found in these epistles, if the conclusion is to be accepted that the requisition for the bishop, and for the deacon as well, to be the husband of one wife, was meant to discountenance second marriages for the clergy (1 Tim. iii. 2, 12). In favor of taking the requisition in this sense it is urged : (1) There is little reason to suppose a formal injunction here against polygamy, since at that time polygamous practice was too rare both among Jews and Gentiles to give occasion to a prohibition; and least of all could such a practice be expected to have any place among Christians who were honored with official responsibilities. (2) That the reference is not to polygamy is indicated by the fact, that the standing of the enrolled widow is made dependent on her having been the wife of one man ; and surely the writer could never have dreamed that it was necessary to mention polygamy as a disqualification for special ecclesiastical recognition. (3) It is improbable that the direction relative to bishops and deacons was aimed against marital infidelity, whether in the form of divorce, of concubinage, or of casual fornication, since the obligation to avoid these practices plainly pertained to all ranks of Christians.

In reply it is contended: (1) In that age laxity in the domestic sphere was a crying abuse. There was very little conscience in heathen society either as respects divorce or concubinage. Consequently in relation to Christians who had recently come out of heathenism there was need to

of ecclesiastical organization. It seems to be taken for granted that the churches severally will have bishops and deacons.[1] Mention is also made of a class of enrolled widows in a way which indicates that they were employed in the service of the Church.[2] Elders who were such in an official sense are mentioned both in First Timothy and in Titus. In the former they are mentioned as ruling; teaching is also specified as an appropriate function for them, and it is declared the duty of the congregation to provide for their support.[3] In the latter the apostolic legate is directed to ordain elders in every city; but when it comes to a mention of their necessary qualifications the name of bishop is substituted. From the standpoint of these epistles it appears, therefore, that a plurality of official elders belonged to each church or Christian community, that no local ecclesiastical authority was superior

---

lay down very elementary rules for the safeguarding of domestic virtue. (2) The rule in question is recorded among points that may well be regarded as included in the code of common decency. If there was occasion to direct that the bishop should not be a "brawler" or a "striker" it may reasonably be supposed that there was occasion to direct that he should avoid a laxity in domestic relations which would involve a virtual polygamy. (3) In the same epistle which is alleged to interpose a bar against second marriages it is advised that the younger widows should marry (1 Tim. v, 14). On the theory that a second marriage was viewed as a disqualification for enrollment in the class of church widows, this would be advice to the younger widows to make themselves ineligible to enrollment should they be again widowed. But why should they pay a forfeit for doing the very thing incumbent upon them? The writer may be supposed to have had a better regard for consistency than appears on the theory that he wished to describe second marriages as a bar to honor and consideration in the church.

[1] 1 Tim. iii. 1–13; Tit. i 5–9. [3] 1 Tim. v. 17–19.
[2] 1 Tim. v. 3–16.

to them, and that they stand for the same class otherwise mentioned as bishops. As Zahn remarks, "It is the same kind of church constitution to which the Book of Acts witnesses for the churches of Asia Minor in the lifetime of Paul, and which had place, according to the Epistle of Clement, in Rome and Corinth at the end of the first century, and still at the beginning of the second century in Philippi, according to the Epistle of Polycarp."[1]

---

[1] Einleitung in das Neue Testament, I. 461, 462.

CHAPTER V

MODIFIED PAULINISM — HEBREWS AND FIRST PETER

I. — Introductory Considerations.

The assignment of the Epistle to the Hebrews and the First Epistle of Peter to a place under the above heading is not meant by any means to indicate that these writings can be described as echoes or copies of the Pauline theology. Due stress must be placed upon the first member of the heading. Both epistles exhibit a good measure of independence in construing the Christian teaching. It is true, nevertheless, that the Pauline theology is to be rated logically and historically as their antecedent.

The Epistle to the Hebrews makes the Christian universalism, for which Paul had contended, an underlying assumption. It asserts also as great a preeminence as did the apostle to the Gentiles for the gospel economy over that of the Old Testament, though it presents that preeminence under a quite different aspect. Moreover its christology, while developed on one side more fully

MODIFIED PAULINISM 271

than the Pauline, takes up most of the content of the latter.[1]

In First Peter there is a less distinct approach to the Pauline antithesis between the two dispensations and also a less complete reproduction of the Pauline Christology, as might perhaps be expected in a brief communication, dominated by a practical purpose. But, on the other hand, there are special turns of thought and expression in the epistle which seem to give it a more direct association with the Pauline writings than can be asserted for the Epistle to the Hebrews. A list of these has been selected as follows: "Having been begotten again, not of corruptible seed, but of incorruptible." "He that suffered in the flesh hath ceased from sin." "As free and not using your freedom for a cloak of wickedness, but as bondservants of God." "Because Christ also suffered for sins once, the righteous for the unrighteous, that He might bring us to God; being put to death in the flesh, but quickened in the spirit." "For unto this end was the gospel preached even to the dead, that they might be judged according to men in the flesh, but live according to God in the spirit." "Who His own self bore our sins in His body upon the tree, that

[1] "In spite of its divergences from the standard of Pauline authorship, the book has manifest Pauline affinities, and can hardly have originated beyond the Pauline circle, to which it is referred, not only by the author's friendship with Timothy (xiii. 23), but also by many unquestionable echoes of the Pauline theology, and even by distinct allusions to passages in Paul's epistles" (W. Robertson Smith and H. von Soden, art. Hebrews in Encyc. Biblica). The points of affinity with Ephesians are specially numerous. (For the list see Von Soden, Hand-Kommentar.) A very distinct reminder of Paul appears in Heb. v. 12–14 as compared with 1 Cor. iii. 2.

we having died unto sins might live unto righteousness." [1] The points of correspondence with the Pauline type are regarded by many as decisive for the conclusion that First Peter shows acquaintance with Romans,[2] and as establishing a probability that its composition was also influenced by Ephesians.[3]

The authorship of the Epistle to the Hebrews remains a matter of simple conjecture. No happier guess is likely to be made than that which Luther expressed when he referred it to Apollos. The traditional view that Paul was the author has no satisfactory basis in history, and is unmistakably excluded by the tone and content of the writing. As was noticed in another connection, the epistle shows the hand of a man who was well versed in the Jewish Alexandrian theology.[4] To call him a disciple of Philo might imply too much, since he stood in important respects upon a different platform of religious conceptions. Still he shows the effect of his acquaintance with the teaching of the famous Alexandrian idealist.

Almost as far from definite solution as the problem of authorship is that of the destination of the Epistle to the Hebrews. A considerable proportion of recent

---

[1] McGiffert, History of Christianity in the Apostolic Age, pp. 485, 486.

[2] Compare ii. 10 in 1 Pet. with ix. 25 in Romans; ii. 5 with xii. 1; i. 14 with xii. 2; iv. 7–11 with xii. 3, 6; i. 22 with xii. 9, 10; iii. 8, 9 with xiii. 16–18; ii. 13–17 with xiii. 1, 3, 4, 7.

[3] Compare i. 3–5 in 1 Pet. with i. 3–14 in Eph.; i. 12 with iii. 5, 10; ii. 4–6 with ii. 18–22; ii. 18 with vi. 5; iii. 1–7 with v. 22–33; iii. 22 with i. 20–22.

[4] See chap. I, sect. 3.

critics incline to the judgment that it was addressed to a limited circle of readers, to a single community of believers, or to a single congregation in a community. Several favor Rome as the locality of the congregation addressed. To this judgment there is little reason to take exception. The epistle gives less distinct data for locating its readers than for pronouncing on their character. Quite evidently they were largely of Jewish lineage, or at least strongly exposed to Jewish influence. Whatever special items may be cited in favor of their Gentile character and relation are much more than counterbalanced by the general tone and content of the epistle, with its elaborate comparison of Christianity with Judaism and earnest contention for the lofty superiority of the former.[1]

On the side of external evidence there is no special occasion to challenge the Petrine authorship of First Peter. In respect of internal evidence two things in particular have been alleged against its composition by the apostle. In the first place, it is said that the picture that is given of the persecution to which those addressed were exposed, and especially the representation of their liability to suffer *as Christians*, is indicative of a scheme of judicial procedure against the confessed followers of Christ, and so points to a later date than the lifetime of the apostle. In the second place, it is claimed that it is contrary to the probabilities of the case that a leader among the original apostles should give such clear evidence as this epistle contains of being influenced by Paul, and so little token of a vital reminiscence of the

---

[1] Compare Ménégoz, Westcott, Bruce, and Peake.

words and deeds of Christ. In response to the former objection it is maintained that the language of the epistle does not necessarily imply a regular scheme of judicial procedure against the Christians as such. The terms of the description are sufficiently met if we suppose that the Christians addressed were subject because of their faith to ill-will and slander, and consequently were exposed in many instances to a wrongful infliction of pains and penalties. Suspicion, ill-will, and slanderous accusation were quite competent to make them suffer "as Christians," apart from a regular scheme of judicial procedure against them on the score of their religion. Harnack admits that the references to persecution, while they make it probable that the epistle was not composed before the years 83–93, do not exclude the possibility of its having been written one or two decades earlier.[1] In reply to the other objection it is claimed that there is no antecedent assurance that an apostle, addressing a brief communication to a body of disciples who had already been instructed in the rudiments of Christianity, would occupy himself with reproducing details of the gospel history rather than with inductions from that history as a whole. It is claimed also that the epistle which bears the name of Peter is not destitute of tokens of a reminiscence of Christ's words.[2] Furthermore, it is contended that there is nothing incredible in the supposition that Peter may have recognized the eminence of Paul in

---

[1] Die Chronologie der altchristlichen Literatur, I. 454.
[2] Compare i. 4 with Matt. xxv. 34; i. 10 ff. with Luke x. 24; i. 13 with Luke xii. 35; ii. 7 with Matt. xxi. 42; iii. 9 with Luke vi. 28; iii. 14 with Matt. v. 10; v. 3 with Matt. xx. 25, 26; v. 6 with Matt. xxiii. 12.

theological construction, and may have so far familiarized himself with some of his epistles as to have carried over into his own composition somewhat of a Pauline coloring. It is noticeable that as far back as the first stages of the controversy over the relation of Christianity to Judaism Peter held a mediating position between the school of Paul and that of James. The advance of Christianity in the Gentile world and the broadening of his own experience would tend naturally to narrow rather than to widen the interval between him and the Pauline platform. It is to be observed, too, that the epistle in question is no specimen of out and out Paulinism. As opposed to the speculative boldness of Paul it is nearer to the dogmatic reserve of the first part of the Book of Acts, though doubtless making a considerable advance upon the teaching of that portion of the New Testament.

A subordinate objection has been based on the linguistic characteristics of the epistle, the allegation being that it is improbable that a man of Peter's antecedents should have been able to handle the Greek language with the measure of skill exhibited in this writing. This consideration, however, is not very formidable. If it be supposed that the apostle in the course of a long ministry failed to reach any considerable proficiency in the use of the Greek language, there is nothing in the way of the conclusion that he was well served in this matter by his secretary Silvanus.

The assumption of a relation of literary dependence between First Peter and the Epistle of James cannot properly be regarded as prejudicing the claim of the former to a Petrine origin. This is true even if the

Epistle of James be accounted a post-apostolic writing, since critical authority cannot be said to be committed to the conclusion that the literary dependence was on the side of First Peter.[1]

Whether written by an apostle or not, First Peter must be regarded as in content worthy of apostolic authorship. A judgment to this effect is given by Harnack. Though interpreting the internal evidence against the supposition of Petrine authorship, he pronounces the hypothesis of falsification by the writer incongruous with the character of the epistle as a whole. The attachment of Peter's name to it must be imputed to a different hand from that of its author. Should the contrary conclusion be adopted, it would be best, in spite of the difficulties which stand in the way of assigning it to the apostle, to confess him as the author.[2]

A motive for not coupling the second epistle bearing the name of Peter with the first, as a subject for special examination, is found in its diverse content and also in the serious grounds which exist for doubting its right to be reckoned in any proper sense as an apostolic writing. A large proportion of New Testament critics unhesitatingly pronounce it a pseudonymous, post-apostolic composition. It is true that a scholar of the eminence of Zahn considers it possible to defend its Petrine authorship. But he helps himself out with so many hypotheses

---

[1] Points of resemblance between the two epistles may be seen by comparing in particular 1 Pet. i. 1 with James i 1; i. 6, 7 with i. 2–4, 12; i. 23 with i. 18; ii. 1 with i. 21; ii. 11 with iv. 1; v. 6 with iv. 7, 10; v. 9 with iv. 7.

[2] Chronologie, I. 464.

that his argument affords but a paltry ground of confidence. To explain the wide difference between the style and tone of the two epistles ascribed to Peter he supposes that, in the composition of First Peter, Silvanus did much more than serve as a mere scribe, that in fact his aid was so far utilized as to give the writing which he penned a special coloring, whereas in writing Second Peter the apostle may have depended upon his own resources. He supposes further, since Second Peter refers to a former epistle, and this on the basis of the description given cannot be identified with First Peter, that the apostle wrote to the particular circle of readers addressed in Second Peter an epistle which has not been transmitted. Once more he supposes, inasmuch as Second Peter refers to a communication from Paul, that this apostle wrote to the same circle of readers an epistle of which nothing is known aside from this incidental mention [1] Now, a conclusion that calls for so many hypotheses that swing in the air is evidently not very well secured, especially as it has to face the fact that Second Peter is essentially unsupported by external evidence and contains marks of a relatively late origin. One of these marks is the manner in which the writer responds to an occasion for explaining the delay of Christ's coming. What we know of the attitude of vivid expectancy in the apostolic age would not lead us to presume that a representative of that era would remind his readers that a thousand years with the Lord are as one day. Another mark of the same order is the classification which is made of Paul's writings with "the other Scriptures." Even if the term "Scriptures" in

---

[1] Einleitung in das Neue Testament, Vol. II.

this connection is made exclusive of the canonical books of the Old Testament and regarded as signifying a collection of apostolic writings, the statement is a token of a relatively late date, since it indicates a consciousness that a considerable body of apostolic literature was open to the perusal of Christians. Still another mark of a comparatively late date will need to be admitted if it be concluded that Second Peter shows dependence upon the Epistle of Jude. The latter quite distinctly adopts a post-apostolic standpoint in the exhortation: "Remember ye the words which have been spoken before by the apostles of our Lord Jesus Christ; how they said to you, In the last times there shall be mockers, walking after their own ungodly lusts." Scholars are not indeed unanimous in holding that the priority belongs to Jude; but not a few are very decidedly committed to that alternative.[1]

Adding a word in respect of contents, we note that the doctrine of the fall and punishment of a portion of the angelic host is characteristic of both Jude and Second Peter; that the leading motive of the former is to excoriate a species of Gnostic libertinism; that the latter devotes one of its chapters to the accomplishment of the same purpose; that peculiar to Second Peter is the doctrine of the destruction of the world by fire.

II. — THE CONCEPTION OF GOD IN HEBREWS AND FIRST PETER.

The description of God in Hebrews is very much after

---

[1] So Harnack, Julicher, Von Soden, Holtzmann, Beyschlag, Weiss, Moffatt, Bacon, Chase, and Plumptre. Zahn and Spitta assume the priority of Second Peter.

the Old Testament order as placing great stress upon His transcendence and intensity. He is represented as the Majesty enthroned on high.[1] The High Priest who comes before Him to serve as the advocate of men must pass through the heavens and be made higher than the heavens.[2] While thus immeasurably uplifted, God has no touch of indifference in His disposition. He is thoroughly the living God. There is no creature that is not manifest in His sight. All things are naked and open before His eyes. His word is living and active and sharper than a two-edged sword.[3] There is no escape for the one that treats lightly the salvation which He proffers.[4] His vengeance shadows him who profanes holy things, and it is a fearful thing to fall into His hands.[5] He is a consuming fire.[6] Without sanctification no man shall see Him.[7] Judgment is wholly with Him.[8] At least, the epistle names Him the judge of all, and gives no hint that the Son, in addition to the office of mediation, fulfills also that of judging men.

On the other hand, the gracious and amiable side of God's character is brought into view. It is by the grace of God that the Mediator tastes death for every man, and the design of His sacrifice is the bringing of many sons unto glory. In virtue of the great redemptive transaction the throne of majesty becomes a throne of grace to which men are invited to draw near even with boldness.[9] The one who accepts the new covenant comes not to the mount that burned with fire, and was

---

[1] Heb. i. 3, viii. 1.
[2] iv. 14, vii. 26.
[3] iv. 12, 13.
[4] iii. 2–3.
[5] x. 30, 31.
[6] xii. 29.
[7] xii. 14.
[8] xii. 23.
[9] iv. 16.

compassed about with blackness and darkness and tempest, but to mount Zion, and unto the city of the living God, the heavenly Jerusalem.[1] God is to him a Father, who it may be chastens, but in love and for the purpose of amendment and profit.[2] Tribute is thus rendered in strong terms to the divine fatherhood. Yet it must be confessed that the balance of emphasis is on the side of majesty and ethical intensity. It is with the great High Priest that the qualities of gentleness and compassion are more directly and fully associated.

The epistle of Peter recurs less distinctly than Hebrews to the Old Testament conceptions of God's loftiness and energy of righteous will. It intimates indeed that the holiness of God makes very high demands, insomuch that the righteous is scarcely saved.[3] But in general it presents the friendly and compassionate side of divine character and relationship. God is represented as the Father of our Lord Jesus Christ, who according to His great mercy inspires to a living hope through the resurrection of Christ; as the Father who judges without respect of persons; as the gracious Lord; as the faithful Creator; and as the God of all grace.[4]

III. — Hints on the Nature and Rank of Men and Angels.

The language of Heb. iv. 12 is somewhat favorable to the supposition that the author entertained the trichotomist theory, and conceived of the soul as truly distinct

---

[1] Heb. xii. 18–25.
[2] xii. 7–11.
[3] 1 Pet. iv. 18
[4] 1 Pet. i. 3, 17, ii. 3, iv. 19, v. 10

from the spirit. The fact also that he speaks of the spirit as though he considered it to be the part of man relating him to a divine and eternal sphere may be cited for the same supposition.[1] But, on the other hand, there are grounds for inferring that he did not distinguish fundamentally between soul and spirit, and conjoined them in the instance referred to above for a rhetorical purpose, namely, the more strikingly to enforce the truth that the searching and discriminating function of the word of God extends to every part of man's interior being. Several times he mentions the soul in connections which suggest that the term was designed to be inclusive of the highest in man.[2] In First Peter the use of "soul" in the higher and more comprehensive sense is quite apparent. While there is in the epistle something of the Pauline antithesis between flesh and spirit, it departs from Pauline phraseology in speaking of fleshly lusts as antagonizing, not the spirit, but the soul.[3]

There is more of an association of human sinfulness with the flesh in First Peter[4] than in Hebrews; but neither exhibits the Pauline stress upon this point of view. Both are without any distinct doctrine of inherent or inherited depravity, while both reveal a lively sense of human weakness and temptability. Some passages in Hebrews convey the impression that the author was disposed to regard infirmities rather than downright perversity as generally characteristic of men.[5] Yet it

---

[1] Heb. xii. 9, 23
[2] Heb. vi. 19, x. 39, xiii. 17.
[3] 1 Pet. ii. 11. See also i. 9, 22, ii. 25, iv. 19.
[4] 1 Pet. iv. 1–6.
[5] Heb. iv. 15, xii. 1.

would be hasty to draw a positive conclusion from this line of representation, since the writer makes no attempt to paint the state of the world beyond the circle of the Jewish and Christian revelations.

A double measuring scale of man's worth and rank is supplied by the Epistle to the Hebrews. On the one hand we have such a means of estimate as is contained in the picture of the divine relationship of men — their sonship toward God, their oneness with Christ and acknowledgment by Him as brethren, their inclusion under the terms of a covenant instituted through the self-oblation of the Son of God and made effectual through His perpetual priesthood. On the other hand, we have the comparison of man's position with that of angels. In one aspect he is a little lower than the angels.[1] Whether this is because of his subjection to vanity in a state of mortality, or because of a more substantial difference, is not stated. In another aspect he seems to be awarded the superior consideration. Angels are all ministering spirits sent forth to do service for the sake of them that shall inherit salvation.[2] Ministering is not indeed from the New Testament point of view a sure token of subordinate rank, since Christ Himself is said to have come to minister, and in our epistle the entertainment of a minister of the angelic order is depicted as a special honor and piece of good fortune.[3] But if we unite with the ministerial position of angels the two other considerations, that man was constituted only a little lower than the angelic rank, and is destined after the pattern of Christ, far transcending his earthly condition, to be exalted to glory and

---

[1] Heb. ii. 7.   [2] i. 14.   [3] xiii. 2.

honor, the conclusion lies very near at hand that he has no reason to envy angels, even if he has no calling to boast of superiority over them. In the Petrine epistle an identical means of measuring man's rank is given on the side of his divine association; and, while the relation of angels to men is not directly commented upon, they are described as interested students of the gospel dispensation.[1]

It cannot properly be doubted that the writer of Hebrews regarded angels as personal beings. The words, " Who maketh His angels winds and His ministers a flame of fire,"[2] cannot be put in evidence for a contrary conclusion. The author could not have thought it worth while to compare Christ to mere natural forces and to emphasize His superiority to them. The words in question picture the changeful forms of manifestation which were represented in Jewish thought to be characteristic of angels. In all further reference to them there is a sufficiently clear assumption of their personality. They are described as agents of the old covenant as well as ministers under the new,[3] and are said to constitute innumerable hosts alongside the general assembly and church of the firstborn.[4] Of evil angels there is no mention either in Hebrews or First Peter, except that in a single instance each epistle makes reference to the devil.[5] The designation of the devil as the one having the power of death was probably dictated by the thought that sin at once stands in causative relation to death and gives to it

---

[1] I Pet. i. 12.
[2] Heb. i. 7.
[3] Heb. ii. 2.
[4] Heb. xii. 22, 23.
[5] Heb. ii. 14 ; I Pet. v. 8.

its aspect of terror. The evil personality is credited with the office of the sin which he fosters.

IV. — THE PERSON OF CHRIST.

In describing the transcendence and glory of the pre-incarnate Son the Epistle to the Hebrews vies with the later Epistles of Paul and reaches essentially to the level of the prologue to John's Gospel. Its characterization of Him as the effulgence of the Father's glory and the express image of His substance constitutes as distinct an affirmation of metaphysical sonship as can be found in the New Testament. In harmony with this conception of substantial likeness the epistle does not hesitate to apply to the Son the divine name — not only that of Lord, but that of God as well.[1] It also assigns to Him cosmic relations that are thoroughly of a divine order. In the beginning He laid the foundations of the earth, and the heavens are the works of His hands. He upholds all things by the word of His power. He is an object of worship to the highest ranks of created intelligences. As He is before all things, so He is above the plane of the mutation and transitoriness to which they are exposed. They shall wax old as doth a garment, but His years change not. "Jesus Christ is the same yesterday, and to-day, yea, and for ever."[2]

With the divine transcendence of Christ the epistle conjoins a thoroughly human character. Indeed the distinctive feature of its christology is the unstinted recog-

---

[1] Heb. i. 8. [2] Heb. xiii. 8.

nition which it accords to the complete humanity of Christ, in spite of the lofty predicates with which it clothes Him. It goes here quite beyond all parallel in the New Testament. The Gospels indeed afford in superior measure the materials for a picture of the human Christ, but it is the Epistle to the Hebrews which directly discourses upon and emphasizes His community in nature and experience with men. According to its representation in one respect only does He stand apart from men. While they are sinners, He is holy, guileless, undefiled, perfectly without sin.[1] Like the rest of the children He partakes of flesh and blood, and so comes under the power of death. In all things He is made like unto His brethren. He is tempted in all points like as we are, and suffers in being tempted. He feels buffeted and pierced by the gainsaying of sinners. In the days of His flesh He offers up prayers and supplications with strong crying and tears. To Him, as to others, His trials and burdens are a means of development and of equipment for His vocation. He learns obedience — brings to an ideal stage the spirit of obedience — by the things which He suffers. He is perfected also by His sufferings in respect of sympathy, and becomes thus a high priest that can be touched with the feeling of our infirmities. And all this treasure of human sympathy and brotherly feeling He carries into the perpetual office of intercession which He fulfills for men in the heavenly sanctuary.[2]

How did the author of Hebrews reconcile the tran-

---
[1] Heb. iv. 15, vii. 26.
[2] See Heb. ii. 10, 14–18, iv. 15, v. 7, 8, vii. 25, xii. 2–4.

scendence of Christ with this complete implication in human experience? He does not attempt to reconcile the two, any more than the evangelists attempt to construe the unity of Christ's consciousness with its human and its superhuman content. The religious mind as such does not regard a reconciliation as of the first consequence. It finds its needs gloriously met in one whom it can contemplate as both brother and Lord, near by kinship of nature and yet mighty to save. It rests in the assurance that such a Saviour has been made known, and treats as a quite secondary matter the theoretic exposition of His personality.

The christological data furnished by First Peter are much less ample than those contained in Hebrews. There is, however, a probable reference to the preexistence of Christ in the statement that His spirit was operative in the prophets, and also in the reference to His being manifested at the end of the times.[1] A hint of the transcendent rank of the ascended Christ is given in the declaration that angels, authorities, and powers are made subject to Him.[2] Furthermore, the title "Lord" is ascribed to Him.[3] According to the text approved by the revisers, Christians are exhorted to sanctify Him in their hearts as Lord.[4]

V.—The High-Priestly Work of Christ.

Quite beyond the example of any other New Testament writing, the Epistle to the Hebrews illustrates the work of Christ by reference to the Old Testament ritual.

---

[1] 1 Pet. i. 11. 20.   [2] iii. 22.   [3] ii. 3.   [4] iv. 15.

After the manner of the Alexandrian typology it contemplates the ancient tabernacle and its ministry and rites as copies of things in the heavens. They are shadows belonging to a preliminary dispensation. The realities for which they stand are disclosed through the new dispensation. Here faith is directed to the holy place made without hands, to the enduring High Priest, to the sacrifice which is truly effective to put away sin.

The author's consciousness of the superiority of the Christian over the Judaic system was evidently as pronounced as was that of Paul. But his way of illustrating the superiority is quite different. The two writers view Old Testament law from a different angle. Paul considers it as a body of commandments which collide with the natural impulses of men, bring their inherent sinfulness to manifestation, work in them a sense of their bondage and incapacity to accomplish self-salvation, and thus prepare them in the exercise of self-surrendering faith to avail themselves of the grace and power of a Divine Deliverer. As the apostle puts it, the law is a schoolmaster to bring men to Christ. To the writer of Hebrews, on the other hand, the law is preeminently a code of ritual, a scheme of provisions for expiating or covering sins and for opening up an approach for sin-stained men to the holy God. Its aim is the same as that which belongs to the agencies of the gospel dispensation. The ground for disparaging it is its comparative inefficacy. As having but the shadow of good things to come it can never make perfect them that draw nigh.

Along with this contrast there is a somewhat remarkable item of parallelism between Paul and the author of our epistle in dealing with Old Testament precedent. As the former, going back of the Mosaic legislation, finds in Abraham an example of the gospel method, inasmuch as the faith of the patriarch was reckoned unto him for righteousness, so the latter, going back of the Levitical system, finds in Melchizedek a type of the extraordinary priesthood exemplified in Christ. Either representation was evidently fitted to do good service in an *ad hominem* argument with those disposed to contend for the perpetuity and exclusive right of the Mosaic institutions.

In construing the work of Christ the writer of Hebrews does not overlook or lightly value His sacrificial death. It is very noticeable, however, that he regards the priestly office of Christ as rather being initiated by His death than finding therein its conclusion. As in the old economy the slaying of the victim did not so much complete the rite of atonement as provide its necessary basis, so is it in the great transaction which the ancient rite foreshadowed. By His death, wherein He is at once offerer and victim, Christ makes the necessary preparation for fulfilling in the heavenly sanctuary His high-priestly vocation. According to a figurative description which greatly taxes interpretation, He cleanses the belongings of that sanctuary by His blood.[1] A more

---

[1] Heb. ix. 22, 23. Perhaps the best justice is done to this statement if it be understood to denote that, inasmuch as the heavenly sanctuary through the presence of Christ exhibits the tokens of an accomplished propitiation, it is made fitting on God's part to tolerate the approach thereto of the sin-stained, as well as appropriate on their part to assume to draw near. The guilt of the sinner, it may be said, does not proclaim exclusion from heaven, since here the memorials of a propitiatory offer-

intelligible description of His priestly office in the heavenly sphere is contained in the declaration, He is able to save unto the uttermost them that draw near unto God through Him, seeing He ever liveth to make intercession for them.[1] It is not necessary, doubtless, to understand this intercession in the most literal way. The presence of Christ at the throne of God in the nature in which He suffered is a perpetual memorial of His sacrifice, and has thus the virtue of a perpetual request for grace toward those for whom the sacrifice was made.

The imaginative and figurative style of the epistle renders it somewhat difficult to determine just how the author conceived of the relation of Christ's work to human salvation. But the evidence is, in our view, sufficient to warrant the conclusion that, like Paul, he joined

---

ing testify that his guilt is covered. It is made thus a place cleansed from obstacles to cordial communion between God and any believing soul that has a will to seek the divine presence. An interpretation very nearly identical with this is contained in the following comment of Peake: "What is meant by the cleansing of the heavenly sanctuary must be determined by its meaning as applied to the earthly. The ritual of the Day of Atonement was designed not merely to atone for the sins of the people, but to make atonement for the sanctuary itself. The sense of this would seem to be that the constant sin of Israel had communicated a certain uncleanness to the sanctuary. Similarly the sin of mankind might be supposed to have cast its shadow even into heaven. It hung like a thick curtain between God and man, preventing free fellowship, and that not only because it defiled the conscience, so that man was ill at ease with God, but because it intruded a disturbing element into the life of God Himself. Looking at it from a somewhat different point of view, we might take the cleansing to be identical with the removal of the veil in the heavenly sanctuary, since cleansing is for the sake of access." (New Century Bible, Hebrews, p. 191.)

[1] Heb. vii. 25.

an objective with a subjective aspect, making the sacrifice of the great High Priest in some sense a condition of the remission of sins as well as a practical expedient for imparting moral and religious incentive. This conclusion is favored by the general office which he attaches to sacrifice. Possibly, as Ménégoz contends, his thought on this theme approached less closely than that of Paul to the idea of substitutionary suffering.[1] Still he evidently conceived of sacrifice as having distinct connection with the remission of sins, so that when it has laid a basis for remission it is no longer needed, and where remission is excluded because of the wilfulness and enormity of the sin it has no place.[2] The same conclusion is approved by the direct association which is made between the sacrifice of Christ and the remission or putting away of sins. It is mentioned in several instances as though in a summary way and once for all it had taken the ban off from sinners and provided for their access to God. Christ, it is said, sat down at the right hand of the Majesty on high when He had made purification of sins.[3] Through His own blood He entered once for all into the holy place, having obtained eternal redemption.[4] Once at the end of the ages He was manifested to put away sin by the sacrifice of Himself.[5] He was once offered to bear the sins of many.[6] When He had offered one sacrifice for sins for ever He sat down on the right hand of God.[7] What

---

[1] La Théologie de l'Épître aux Hébreux, pp. 183, 184.
[2] Heb. v. 1, 3, ix. 22, x. 17, 18, 26.
[3] Heb. i. 3.
[4] ix. 12.
[5] ix. 26.
[6] ix. 28.
[7] x. 12

less could the author have meant by statements like these than that the gracious economy in which sins are remitted and access to God enjoyed is founded upon the sacrifice of Christ. Furthermore, he seems to attach an objective value of this kind to Christ's work when he includes in His high-priestly vocation the making of a propitiation for the sins of the people.[1]

In its portrayal of the subjective bearing of Christ's work the Epistle to the Hebrews falls in some respects below the Pauline representation. It does not bring out the notion of mystical union with the crucified One and of spiritual transformation through His indwelling as it was brought out by the apostle. The nearest approach that the epistle reveals to this order of Pauline thinking is contained in the description of Christians as "partakers of Christ.[2] In its own way, however, it emphasizes the saving influence which emanates from the manifested Son of God. The sacrifice of Christ, according to its conception, seals the new covenant,[3] and thus is calculated to inspire to a quickening confidence in the great promises connected with that covenant. As a spiritual sacrifice, armed with a spiritual motive-power, it is adapted to free the conscience from the burden of mere legal works, and to lead into a true service of God.[4] Furthermore God is made to appear specially approachable in the thought that at His right hand is the Mediator who came through temptation and suffering to a full measure of sympathy. The disclosure of such a High Priest demonstrates that there is a throne of grace, and

---

[1] Heb. ii. 17. [3] ix. 15.
[2] iii. 14. [4] ix. 14.

invites men in spite of their consciousness of unworthiness to draw near with confidence.[1] Indeed contemplation of His person and work is in such a sense faith-inspiring, that He may fitly be named the author and the perfecter of our faith.[2]

In First Peter there is also a coupling together of the objective and subjective aspects of Christ's work. In accordance with the practical character of the epistle the superior stress falls upon the latter. The sacrifice of Christ is, in fact, in every mention of the same, brought into association with some spiritual effect that ought to follow from its contemplation.[3] But while the writer, in his homiletical use of truth, places the chief stress upon the holy persuasion emanating from the death of Christ, there is no good reason to suppose that he ignored the objective aspect. In his choice of words he pays a probable tribute to it when he speaks of Christ as bearing our sins in His body upon the tree, or when he refers to Him as having suffered for sins once, the righteous for the unrighteous.

An essentially Pauline view of the resurrection of Christ, as an important factor in the total scheme for rescuing and renewing men, appears in First Peter.[4] The Epistle to the Hebrews, on the other hand, takes no pains to specify the value of Christ's resurrection for Christian faith, and contains only a bare reference to the fact.[5] With the death of Christ it conjoins immediately His ascension or entrance into the heavenly sanctu-

---

[1] Heb. iv. 14–16, x. 19, 22.
[2] xii. 2.
[3] 1 Pet. i. 18–21, ii. 24, iii. 18, iv. 1.
[4] 1 Pet. i. 3.
[5] Heb. xiii. 20.

ary. The slight attention paid to the great intervening event may be explained very largely by the writer's engrossment in the description of the high-priestly doing of Christ.

VI. — CHRISTIAN LIFE, INDIVIDUAL AND COLLECTIVE.

The connection which is made in the Epistle to the Hebrews between the remission of sins and the work of Christ suggests that its point of view is not remote from the Pauline doctrine of justification. This term, however, is wanting to its vocabulary, and in its place there is a recurring reference to a work of sanctification or cleansing ($\dot{a}\gamma\iota\acute{a}\zeta\epsilon\iota\nu$, $\kappa a\theta a\rho\acute{\iota}\zeta\epsilon\iota\nu$).[1] A formal mention of justification is also wanting in First Peter. Both epistles direct attention more largely to the progress and perfecting of Christian life than to its initial stage. A special feature of First Peter is its stress upon divine truth as an agent of renewal.[2] A distinguishing characteristic of Hebrews is the prominence which it gives to the view that Christian life is a practical realization of a covenant.

---

[1] Heb. i. 3, ii, 11, ix. 13, 14, x. 10, 14, 29, xiii 12. Denney contends that under his contrasted terminology the author of the Epistle to the Hebrews makes a very close approach to a Pauline meaning. "The people," he says, "were sanctified, not when they were raised to moral perfection, but when, through the annuling of their sin by sacrifice, they had been constituted into a people of God, and in the person of their representative had access to His presence The word $\dot{a}\gamma\iota\acute{a}\zeta\epsilon\iota\nu$, in short, in the Epistle to the Hebrews corresponds as nearly as possible to the Pauline $\delta\iota\kappa a\iota o\hat{v}\nu$; the sanctification of the one writer is the justification of the other." (The Death of Christ, its Place and Interpretation in the New Testament, p. 221.)

[2] 1 Pet. i. 23–25.

It is the counterpart of the better covenant inaugurated through Christ, the fulfillment of the ideal which the ancient prophet sketched when he wrote: "This is the covenant that I will make with the house of Israel after those days, saith the Lord; I will put my laws into their mind, and on their heart also will I write them."[1] In accordance with the perfection of the new covenant its subjects stand in the light of great promises, but are also placed under very grave responsibilities. Infidelity to a covenant sealed with the blood of Christ is a sin for which pardon can hardly be anticipated. Were we to make no allowance for the rhetorical fervor of the writer's discourse, we should say that he counted such a sin to be wholly unpardonable.[2] What he probably meant to assert, however, was the truth that the apostasy in question was so grievous as scarcely to admit of remedy.

A magnifying of the office of hope is characteristic of both Hebrews and First Peter.[3] Both epistles make use of the term in connections where Paul would have been disposed to speak of faith. This is very noticeable in the designation of hope as an anchor of the soul, in the characterization of it as the medium through which we draw nigh to God, and in the description of piety as a hoping in God. In the one formal definition of faith, as contained in the Epistle to the Hebrews, it is given a sense closely allied to hope, being identified with the grasp of the soul on a future and promised good.[4] The ethical potency of faith, however, as a source of present

---

[1] Heb. viii. 6-13, x. 16. [2] Heb. vi. 4-8, x. 26-31.
[3] Heb. iii. 6, vi. 11, 18, 19, vii. 19, x. 23; 1 Pet. i. 3, 13, 21, iii. 5, 15.
[4] Heb. xi. 1.

obedience and righteous achievement is not overlooked. Naturally the relative lack of emphasis on the Pauline notion of mystical union with Christ has an effect on the representation of faith. It is set forth in the epistle rather as a principle of fidelity, steadfastness, and courageous activity than as a means of inner affiance with the Redeemer.[1]

The virtue which is most commended in Hebrews might be defined as Christian hardihood. The exhortations of this eloquent writing breathe a martial spirit, and summon like the notes of a trumpet to a resolute conflict against all the opposing forces which rise up between one and the great recompense of reward. In First Peter along with manful endurance the gentler virtues are emphasized — tenderness of heart, humbleness of mind, and the love that covers a multitude of sins. In the standard of civic and domestic virtue which it sets forth this epistle bears a close resemblance to the writings of Paul.[2]

On the subject of church constitution the two epistles do not afford precise data. Hebrews contains no more explicit reference to ecclesiastical officials than is found in an exhortation to those addressed to remember and to obey those having the rule over them.[3] First Peter refers to elders as being charged with oversight of the flock, and as under obligation to fulfill the charge rather through the persuasion of a good example than through assumption of lordship.[4] In neither epistle is there any

---

[1] Heb. iii. 12–19, iv. 1–3, x. 39, xi.
[2] 1 Pet. ii. 13–18, iii. 1-7.
[3] Heb. xiii. 7, 17, 24.
[4] 1 Pet. v. 1–3.

indication of the sacerdotal theory which makes the Christian body at large dependent on the mediation of a priestly rank. Hebrews contemplates no possessor of priestly functions under the new covenant apart from Christ. It also emphasizes the privilege of believers generally to enter into the holy place, a form of expression which denotes that one man, in the exercise of faith and submission, has as good a right of direct approach unto God as any other.[1] The same thought appears in the Petrine epistle in the designation of Christians generally as a holy priesthood.[2]

Neither epistle contains any reference to the eucharist. Neither countenances the notion that Christianity provides for any proper sacrificial rite. The sacrifice of Christ is the one offering acknowledged by Hebrews,[3] and First Peter mentions besides only those spiritual sacrifices which all Christians offer when they lift up their hearts in faith and devotion.[4] The former epistle has no explicit teaching on the efficacy of baptism. It mentions the term only in a single instance, and then in a way which admits of including under it more than the Christian rite proper, since the plural form is used.[5] The words relative to bodily washing in x. 22 may inclose a second reference. If that be their import, they serve as a token that the writer regarded baptism, after the pattern of the Levitical rites, as a means of ceremonial cleansing. In First Peter an association is made between baptism and being saved, but the context takes

---

[1] Heb. x. 19-22.
[2] 1 Pet. ii. 5.
[3] Heb. ix. 27, 28, x. 10, 12.
[4] 1 Pet. ii. 5.
[5] Heb. vi. 2.

pains to indicate that it is not the mere rite that is thus efficacious, but the rite in connection with a religious attitude. This is described somewhat enigmatically as "the interrogation of a good conscience toward God."[1] Probably the word conscience ($\sigma\upsilon\nu\epsilon\iota\delta\acute{\eta}\sigma\epsilon\omega\varsigma$) is here to be construed as an objective genitive, and the phrase is to be regarded as indicative of an attitude of request for a conscience cleansed from guilt and sin.

VII. — Eschatology.

The trend of the epistle to the Hebrews is emphatically eschatological. The better and the abiding possession, the city which hath foundations, and the kingdom which cannot be shaken are represented to be above and beyond the present life, and are pictured as the proper objects of hope and aspiration.[2] In this sense an eschatological tone dominates the epistle. At the same time it gives very few details of eschatology. There is in it an intimation in line with the early apostolic expectation of the speedy close of the dispensation.[3] The doctrine of an eternal judgment, or one perpetually fixing destiny, is reckoned among elementary teachings.[4] So also is the doctrine of the resurrection of the dead. From the reference to the worthies, who did not accept deliverance that "they might obtain a better resurrection,"[5] some have argued that the author thought of participation in the resurrection as something to be won, and

---

[1] 1 Pet. iii. 21.
[2] Heb. x. 34, xi. 10, xii. 28.
[3] Heb. x. 25.
[4] Heb. vi. 2.
[5] Heb. xi. 35.

consequently did not impute it to the wicked.[1] The ground for the conclusion, however, is not very decisive. A resurrection to honor and blessedness might be counted a prize to be won, as opposed to a resurrection simply to judgment.

The First Epistle of Peter agrees with Hebrews in its stress upon the incorruptible inheritance held in reserve.[2] It also intimates the nearness of the end of the dispensation.[3] Peculiar to the epistle is the statement which it makes respecting the proclamation of the gospel message in the region of the dead.[4] A proper parallel is not to be found in any other New Testament writing. A reference to the descent of Christ into Hades may perhaps, as Meyer contends, be contained in Eph. iv. 9. But it is only in First Peter that there is any reference to the preaching of Christ to the dead. Not all interpreters, it is true, discover that much here. The natural sense, however, of the singular Petrine sentences is that which the early Church imputed to them. The collocation of the clauses in chapter iii points distinctly to the preaching of the crucified Christ and to His preaching among the dead. He was put to death in the flesh. He was quickened in the spirit. In the spirit, that is, His pneumatic nature, still living and active, He went and preached. He preached not to men in the flesh but to spirits, disembodied souls in Hades. He preached, not to those still in the course of their sins upon earth, but to those who had transgressed aforetime. Moreover, according to the intima-

---

[1] So Weiss and Beyschlag.
[2] 1 Pet. i. 4.
[3] 1 Pet. iv. 7.
[4] 1 Pet. iii. 18-20.

tion of iv. 6, He preached to them not an Old Testament message, but the message introduced by His own ministry upon earth, the gospel message. Thus, there are too many items, coherent and pointing in one direction, to admit of any other conclusion than that the writer meant to teach that Christ preached to men in the region of the dead. As the description of this transaction falls between a reference to the death of Christ and the mention of His resurrection, it seems probable that the mission to the dead was located by the writer between the crucifixion and the resurrection.

CHAPTER VI

THE JOHANNINE THEOLOGY

I.—The Question of Authorship.

The fourth Gospel and the first of the Epistles bearing the name of John are so largely akin in style and contents that the reasonable and commonly admitted conclusion is that they must have had the same author. Some points of contrast between them may doubtless be specified. The Epistle is without reference to Old Testament types and precedents, and inculcates more distinctly than the Gospel the idea of propitiation. It contains also some peculiarities in the choice of words and phrases.[1] But these points of difference are much more than counterbalanced by the full list of resemblances. In both the Gospel and the Epistle the same habit of developing a proposition by repeating it in slightly varied form is observable. In both there are the same fundamental representations on the coming of the Son of God in the flesh, on the exhibition of the love of God in the sending of the Son, on the Son being the source of life, on the obligation of brotherly love, on

---

[1] For instance we have in the Epistle παρουσία, ἀνομία, ἔχειν τὸν πατέρα, ἔχειν τὸν υἱόν, ποιεῖν τὴν δικαιοσύνην, ἀρνεῖσθαι τὸν υἱόν.

walking in the light, and on being born of God. In both also there is manifested the same predilection for sharp antitheses, for the coupling together of such opposites as life and death, light and darkness, love and hatred, truth and falsehood, the Father and the world, God and the devil, sonship toward God and sonship toward the devil. In short the reasons are compelling for a close association of the first Epistle with the fourth Gospel.

Early Christian thought, if not with entire unanimity, yet with moderate exception before the last half of the third century, assigned the Apocalypse to the same author who wrote the fourth Gospel and the Epistle. The modern judgment, too, has not gone entirely counter to this assignment. The Apocalypse, however, as has been noticed, differs so far from the other two writings, that it is appropriate to treat of it in connection with a different theological type. The writings accordingly which represent the specific theological type denominated the Johannine are the fourth Gospel and the first Epistle. The style and contents of the second and third Epistles afford indeed no real motive to separate them from the proper Johannine group; but they contain so little theological matter that there is very slight occasion to bring them into consideration.

The author of the Gospel and the Epistle withholds his name. He furnishes nevertheless quite distinct intimations of his identity, or at least of the judgment which he would have his readers form respecting his identity. In the first place, he gives himself out as an eyewitness of the events narrated. Leaving aside the question whether xxi. 24 is to be reckoned as belonging to an appendix from a later hand, we have in xix. 35 this unequivocal testimony: "He that hath seen hath borne witness, and his witness is true: and he knoweth that he saith true that ye also may believe." The use here by the writer of the third person is most naturally construed, not as a reference to an outside party, but as a literary device for naming himself.[1] The declaration, "He knoweth that he saith true," presents the witness as still present over against the recorded testimony on the one hand and the contemplated readers on the other. In line with this interpretation stands i. 14 in the Gospel and i. 1-4 in the Epistle. Only one who had been an eyewitness, or meant to figure as such, would naturally have used the language of either passage. In the second place, while the author goes beyond the example of any other evangelist in the number of instances in which he mentions the names of individual disciples, he practices a continuous reserve respecting the name of a disciple who evidently must have held a conspicuous place in the apostolic group. Jesus upon the cross commends His mother to this disciple. The same disciple leaned upon the breast of Jesus at the last supper and asked of Him a question in response to Peter's beckoning. The same in all probability was one of the two unnamed disciples of the Baptist who were among the first to follow Jesus. Why this withholding of the name of one disciple in the Gospel which shows most freedom in the mention of names? The only plausible answer is that

---

[1] In ix. 37 Christ is represented as referring to Himself by the same third personal pronoun ($\dot{\epsilon}\kappa\epsilon\hat{\iota}\nu o\varsigma$), and Paul in 2 Cor. xii. 3-5 uses ὁ τοιοῦτος in an analogous manner. It is perfectly credible, therefore, that the writer should have used ἐκεῖνος in referring to himself.

the writer identified himself, or wished his readers to identify him, with the unnamed disciple—a disciple belonging apparently to the inner circle of the twelve, and therefore presumably John, since he is discriminated from Peter, and no one in face of the early martyrdom of James would think of him as the writer. That the narrator should prefer to indicate himself in an indirect way is intelligible; that he should have any motive to designate another continuously in that fashion is not intelligible. We are thus held by distinct peculiarities of the writings to the conclusion that the author certainly meant his readers to understand that he was an eyewitness, and have besides a probable indication that this eyewitness was meant to be identified with the Apostle John, the son of Zebedee.

It may properly count somewhat in favor of conformity between the fact of authorship and the clue contained in the writings that early tradition assigned them to the Apostle John, and that history knows of no rival candidate to put in his place. The tradition is as clear and controlling as the analogy of other apostolic writings would lead us to expect. As Meyer says of the fourth Gospel, " The continuity of the attestations to it, and their growing extent in connection with the literature of the Church, are as evident as we ever can and do require for the external confirmation of any New Testament writing." [1] It is true that a party of the second century, the so-called Alogi, challenged the fact of Johannine authorship. But they were an obscure party, had a motive for their challenge in their antipathy to the

---

[1] Comm. on John, p. 14.

Johannine doctrine of the Logos, and were to that degree lacking in critical competency, that they ascribed the fourth Gospel as well as the Apocalypse to Cerinthus. It is hardly worth while, therefore, to bring them onto the witness stand. Their testimony is in truth a little equivocal for the negative side. As Ezra Abbot remarks, "The fact that they ascribed the fourth Gospel to Cerinthus, a heretic of the first century, contemporary with the Apostle John, shows that they could not pretend that this Gospel was a recent work."[1] No respectable critic of the present day would follow the Alogi in putting the Judaizing Gnostic Cerinthus in place of the apostle.

Aside from the weak and self-refuted challenge by the Alogi, there is no positive item in the line of external evidences which can be cited against the traditional theory of Johannine authorship. It has been supposed, it is true, that the position assumed by the Quartodecimans of the Asiatic churches in the Easter controversy, near the end of the second century, involves an adverse comment on that theory. But the supposition is not well taken. If a proper distinction is made between the motive which originally determined the celebration of Easter on the fourteenth of Nisan and the arguments which were employed by individuals two or three generations later under stress of controversy, no real occasion will be found in this whole matter for denying the authorship of the fourth Gospel to the Apostle John. Primarily, it may be presumed, the general thought that Jesus was the true Paschal Lamb, by whose shed blood came

---

[1] The Authorship of the Fourth Gospel: External Evidences, p. 18.

THE JOHANNINE THEOLOGY 305

deliverance to mankind, was regarded as a sufficient ground for memorializing the day on which the Passover feast was celebrated. John and his more immediate followers in the Asiatic churches, apart from all question as to the precise day on which the last supper, or the crucifixion, had place, could have assented, on the specified ground alone, to the custom of celebrating the proper Passover day, the fourteenth of Nisan. Accordingly the fact that some of the Quartodecimans, at a later date, may have given a more specific ground for electing the fourteenth of Nisan — namely, the occurrence of the last supper on that day — a ground not in full harmony with the Johannine chronology of the passion, is of very little consequence. By no means does it import that John could not have lived and labored and written within the domain of the Asiatic churches. He could have done all that, and yet not have been consistently followed by every controversialist as respects chronological data which he had never attempted to turn into a prominent issue. At the time that John's Gospel came into circulation the Synoptical Gospels were an acknowledged authority, and Christians in the Asiatic churches, however little they were inclined to challenge the former, very naturally in one connection or another took account of the chronological data of the latter.[1]

Again, it has been supposed that evidence destructive of the theory of Johannine authorship is discoverable in

---

[1] Compare Drummond, An Inquiry into the Character and Authorship of the Fourth Gospel, pp. 441 513; Stanton, The Gospels as Historical Documents, I. 173-197.

ancient testimony to the martyrdom of the apostle John. The testimony is found in a reputed saying of Papias and in certain forms of statement in the church calendar. Now, for the former no sort of a voucher can be found within at least three centuries from the close of the apostolic age, and besides it is given in too confused and bungling a fashion to command any confidence as against the line of opposing witnesses. As respects the church calendar, it is very questionable whether its forms of statement primarily had any reference to the celebration of the martyrdom of John or any design of specifying the date of his death. So J. H. Bernard argues, and Harnack approves his contention.[1]

A principal negative item urged against the Johannine authorship is the silence of Polycarp in his epistle to the Philippians and of Ignatius in his epistle to the Ephesians. This silence is taken as evidence that John could not have presided over the Asiatic churches and published a Gospel in their territory. But the evidence is far from decisive. Polycarp, in addressing a society with which John is not known to have had any personal relations, had small occasion to refer to the apostle. Ignatius might appropriately have made some allusion to him in writing to the Ephesians. It is to be noticed, however, that he was very sparing of references to the apostles. In five out of seven of his epistles he gives them no specific mention. Even in writing to the Romans he introduces not a single counsel on the authority of Peter and Paul, and only incidentally mentions their

[1] The Irish Quarterly, Jan., 1908; Theologische Literaturzeitung, Jan. 2, 1909.

names. Manifestly the silence of either of these writers affords no weighty ground of objection for one who does not assert, as a canon of criticism, that an epistle must necessarily contain every item that is pertinent to the historical situation existing at the time of its composition.

Over against these meagre grounds of challenge, on the score of external evidences, we may cite the testimony of men able to claim acquaintance with those who could scarcely have been ignorant of the real facts as to the Ephesian residence of John and the original association of his name with the fourth Gospel. Here belong in particular Irenæus and Polycrates. Both were natives of Asia Minor, and the latter was a lifelong resident. Both enjoyed fellowship with distinguished men of an earlier generation. Irenæus in his youth had listened to Polycarp, and Polycrates belonged to a family which had furnished many bishops. Both indicate their undoubting conviction that the Apostle John had labored, as the tradition reports him to have done, in the western section of Asia Minor; and Irenæus besides states explicitly that John wrote the fourth Gospel.[1] It has been alleged indeed that Irenæus very likely misinterpreted the words of Polycarp which he heard in his early years, understanding him to speak of the Apostle John when perchance he spoke of some other John. But it is not at all probable that Irenæus depended in his judgment of John's career simply upon a youthful reminiscence. He was no recluse shut out from the world of his time. He was, on the contrary, a man of affairs, and may be

---

[1] Cont. Haer., iii. 1. 1. See also iii. 3. 4 and the epistles to Florinus and Victor as cited by Eusebius, Hist. Eccl., v. 20, 24.

presumed, in his communication with his elders, such as the venerable Pothinus, to have found means of confirming or correcting the impressions derived from the experiences of his youth. As for Polycrates, a man who spent his life on the site of the reputed activity of the Apostle John, it is quite incredible that he should not have represented a long-standing and thoroughly dominant tradition. Polycrates, it is true, in the scanty extracts from his writings which are extant, does not directly pronounce on the authorship of the fourth Gospel; but indirectly he does refer that Gospel to the Apostle John, inasmuch as he identifies the John whom he mentions with the beloved disciple who is set forth in the Gospel itself as the responsible witness for the facts recorded.[1]

Supplementing the testimony of these eminent witnesses we have traces of the influence of the fourth Gospel upon Christian literature from an early point in the second century. While these traces are not a complete proof of Johannine authorship, they are favorable to the theory of such authorship as making credible the existence of the Gospel at the date to which tradition assigns John's death. In the epistles of Ignatius there are very distinct reminders of Johannine thought and phraseology,[2] and the epistle of Polycarp is not wholly destitute of such reminders. There is fair ground for concluding that the Gnostic Basilides, who was conspicuous in the reign of Hadrian (A. D. 117–138), used the fourth Gospel as one of a collection of Gospels. A growing tendency has

---
[1] Eusebius, Hist. Eccl., v. 24.
[2] Philadelphians, vii, ix; Magnesians, vii, x; Romans, vii.

been manifested by recent criticism to admit the certainty that Justin Martyr made use of the fourth Gospel and it is perfectly clear from Tatian's employment of it in his Diatessaron, that it had in his day a recognized standing among the biographies of Jesus.[1]

It was stated above that history knows of no rival candidate, in relation to the composition of the fourth Gospel, who can legitimately be put in the place of the Apostle John. A rival has indeed been brought forward in the person of a certain Presbyter John; but the credentials which are presented in his behalf are of the most ghostly description. Early tradition offers no plea for the presbyter. When Caius, at the end of the second century, wanted to strip the Apocalypse of apostolic sanction, he shelved off the production onto Cerinthus. There was apparently no Presbyter John in sight at that time to whom responsibility might plausibly be charged.[2] No real authority vouches for the fact that this presbyter ever wrote a line. No trustworthy testimony assures us that he was seen in Ephesus or its neighborhood. The conjecture of Dionysius of Alexandria, more than a century and a half after the Johannine era, that the presbyter may have been commemorated by one of two monuments in Ephesus, is a long way off from the domain of history. The whole sum of evidence which we possess for the bare existence of the John in question is a single line from Papias as cited by Eusebius.[3] The passage in which the line is found runs as follows: "I will not

---

[1] See, on the evidence contained in the writings of this entire list of authors, Drummond, Fourth Gospel; Stanton, The Gospels.

[2] Compare Zahn, Einleitung, II. 449.   [3] Hist. Eccl., iii. 39.

hesitate to put down for thee along with the interpretations as many things also as I once learned well from the elders, and remembered well, strongly confirming the truth about them. For I used not to take pleasure in those who say a great deal, as most men do, but in those who teach the truth; and not in those who mention foreign commandments, but in those [who mention] the [commandments] given from the Lord to the faith, and coming from the truth itself. And also if anyone came on any occasion who had been a follower of the elders, I used to inquire into the discourses of the elders, what Andrew or what Peter said, or what Philip, or what Thomas, or what John or Matthew, or any other of the disciples of the Lord [said], and what Aristion and the Presbyter [or Elder] John, disciples of the Lord, say." Now, it has not always been judged that the John who is numbered among elders and disciples in the second instance is different from the John who is numbered among elders and disciples in the former instance. But suppose we grant, with the majority of recent critics, that it was the intention of Papias to distinguish between the two, what historical conclusion have we established? Simply this, that there was among the early Christians a man by the name of John, who in the thought of Papias was associated with Aristion. The warrant for connecting this John with any extant writing is totally wanting. To put him in the place which the tradition assigns to the son of Zebedee is anything but a historical procedure.

But could the Apostle John have written a book of such extraordinary character as the fourth Gospel or the related Epistle? To this question it may be replied that we have no such precise measure of the mental abilities and peculiarities of the apostle as to be qualified to assert a negative. It is alleged, indeed, that it is inconceivable that a Galilean fisherman should have been competent to write treatises so tinged with mystic idealism. But we have nothing to do here with what a Galilean fisherman could or could not accomplish. John has left no daily report of his intellectual life which assures us that he remained in a perfectly static condition from the year 30 to the year 90. More than one person has taken rank among scholars who had scarcely reached the alphabet at the stage of early manhood. Endowed with a good original soil John's soul might, for aught we know, being enriched during a period of fifty or sixty years by reflection, reading, and experience, have produced writings of the type of the Gospel and Epistle associated with his name.

A grain more of consideration may be awarded to a second allegation, namely, that it is next to inconceivable that a man who lived familiarly with one bearing like Christ the common human form should have entertained and expressed such a transcendent view of His personality. The worshipful attitude toward the Master who had also been the earthly companion is indeed remarkable. But who shall say that it was impossible for a disciple whose deeply enthusiastic soul had been taken captive? The example of Paul refutes the alleged impossibility. It may be said, indeed, that Paul did not company with Christ, and besides got His impression of Him through the medium of a heavenly vision. But

Paul in fact was not remote from realistic ground. He trod the site of Christ's ministry while yet the recollection of it was fresh in the minds of multitudes. He was in close contact with those who criticised and condemned His Lord as well as with those who loved and honored Him. While his thought of the essential glory of Christ may have been helped by the disclosure before the gates of Damascus, it is not certain that the vision made known a brighter form than that which was apprehended by the ardent faith and imagination of the disciple who had been present at the transfiguration scene, and who confidently expected that Christ would be revealed at no distant day in exceeding glory. Furthermore, there is a shade of presumption in assuming that the actual personality of Christ was not such that an appreciative companion might derive from close communion with Him a basis for a most exalted view of His moral beauty and unique connection with the divine. On the whole, there is no more warrant for concluding that the transcendent view in the fourth Gospel was impossible for John than there is for affirming that a converted Pharisee could never have come within a few years of Christ's death to entertain and promulgate the transcendent view contained in the Pauline epistles.

The principal difficulty in the way of assuming the Johannine authorship of the fourth Gospel is the broad contrast between it and the Synoptical Gospels. This contrast is not indeed in its whole extent a ground for rational doubt. On the contrary, some points of deviation are much better explained on the supposition of Johannine authorship than on the opposite supposition.

THE JOHANNINE THEOLOGY   313

Why should a writer who was conscious of reporting at second hand depart from the lines of a history already put in circulation? Would he not have reason to apprehend that his departures from the earlier record would discredit his own composition? On the other hand, one who was conscious that in his possession of facts he was the peer of any possible narrator might, out of the fulness of his confidence, be somewhat indifferent to the exact correspondence of his narrative to the reports of certain other writers. This point of view may be applied to various portions of the subject-matter of the fourth Gospel, such as its account of a plurality of visits on the part of Christ to Judæa, and its apparent location of the last supper on the evening preceding the proper commencement of the passover feast. For aught that anybody knows there was a fair occasion to supplement the Galilean document, on which the Synoptical Gospels may be supposed to have been based, and to revise one or another of their statements. Indeed it is the opinion of eminent exegetes that the Synoptical Gospels themselves point to the fact of an early Judæan ministry of which they give no description.[1] In any case deviations of this kind from the earlier sketches of Christ's life would make quite as much of an enigma on the supposition that the author needed to borrow his facts, as they do on the supposition that he wrote with the assurance of one who felt that he himself had all the requisites of a competent witness.

---

[1] See Matt. iv. 12; Mark, i. 14. Tokens of visits to Judæa not described in the Synoptical Gospels have also been recognized by some in the following texts: Matt. xvi. 1, xxiii. 37–39, xxvii. 57; Mark iii. 22, vii. 1, xi. 2, 3, xiv. 14, xv. 43; Luke x. 25–37, 38–42, xiii. 34, 35.

But though some of the contrasts with the Synoptical narratives constitute no real ground of objection, it must be conceded that the peculiar tone of Christ's discourses in the fourth Gospel and the freedom with which He is represented to have put forth His high claims even at the opening of His ministry constitute a real difficulty. From the other evangelists we should gather that Christ's speech was more terse and aphoristic, and less subtle and mystical, than it appears in the report of the fourth evangelist. We should also conclude that in the earlier stages of His ministry He practised more reserve on the subject of His personal and official rank than appears in the latest biography.

In response to these sources of objection it may be said, that the strong individuality of John naturally made its impression upon his sketch of the life of Christ; that the distance of the time of writing from the events narrated dulled the edge of verbal recollection and facilitated the reproduction of Christ's discourses in a Johannine dialect; that it was appropriate in the concluding biography of Christ to give relatively a large amount of attention to matters supplementary to those reported in the biographies already current, among which matters were included some of the more private and confidential addresses of the Master to His special disciples; and that the appearance of certain aberrant tendencies in christological thinking dictated that an earnest effort should be made to set forth what was deemed the true exposition of Christ's person. These considerations may not fully overcome the difficulties in question. In fact it must be granted that an enigmatic element remains at the end of all attempts to explain this Gospel. The best that can be done is to reduce this element by making large account of the idiosyncracies of the author. He must be rated as an idealist, a mystic, so given to viewing things according to their absolute type as to be habitually occupied with that type, to a relative neglect of primary and intermediate forms and stages. There may be some difficulty in ascribing this peculiar bent to the Apostle John. Still, as has been suggested, our knowledge of the apostle affords no compelling ground for assuming that the marked peculiarity could not have been characteristic of him. It is to be remembered, furthermore, that difficulty is not escaped by placing a negative on the Johannine authorship of the fourth Gospel. If this writing is to be referred to any eyewitness, it might as well be assigned to the Apostle John as to any other. The writing, as has been shown, does make claim to have issued from an eyewitness. Now a denial of the legitimacy of this claim cannot be entered without bringing in very considerable enigmas. In the first place it will need to be asked in the face of such denial, How is the lofty spiritual level of this Gospel consonant with the supposition that it issued from the mind of a counterfeiter? There are manifold sentences in it which age after age speak like a divine music to the hearts of men. How came it about that an insincere mind should have been the fount whence issued these heavenly sayings? Again, it will need to be asked, How explain the measure of circumstantial details which distinguishes this Gospel? Minute specifications on persons, times, and places were not necessary to one who had no other reason for appealing to history than his desire to get a framework upon which he might hang his theological ideas. Neither could he indulge in them, unless personally conversant with the subjects touched upon, without naturally incurring more occasion for correction than has been proved against the author of the fourth Gospel. "Whether we turn," says Lightfoot, "to the Messianic hopes of the chosen people, with all the attendant circumstances with which imagination had invested this expected event, or to the mutual relations of Samaritans, Jews, Galilæans, Romans, and the respective feelings, prejudices, beliefs, customs of each, or to the topography as well of the city and the temple as of the rural districts — the Lake of Gennesaret, and the cornfields and mountain ridges of Shechem — or to the contemporary history of the Jewish hierarchy and the Herodian sovereignty, we are alike struck at every turn with subtle and unsuspicious traces, betokening the familiarity with which the writer moves amidst the ever-shifting scenes of this wonderful narrative."[1] Make this record of circumstantial items the offspring of the well-stored memory of an eyewitness, and we have an explanation both of their multiplicity and of their ability in general to endure such tests of accuracy as are available. Refer them to the invention of one who neither knew nor cared for the facts of real history and they are placed beyond the range of probable explanation both as to quantity and quality.[2] We conclude then, notwithstand-

---

[1] Essays on the Johannine Authorship of the fourth Gospel, by Abbot, Peabody, and Lightfoot, p. 150.

[2] For specifications on persons see i. 35–51, ii 13–20, iii. 1, vi. 5, 8, 68, vii. 3, 5, xi. 1, 16, 49, xii. 2–4, xiii. 6, 23, 26, 36, xiv. 5. 8, 22, xviii. 10–

ing the extraordinary character of the fourth Gospel, that we choose the path of least difficulty when we attribute it, as well as the closely related epistle, to the Apostle John.

The above discussion proceeds on the assumption that the choice lies between assigning the fourth Gospel as a whole to the Apostle John and excluding him from all direct participation in its composition. Theoretically a third alternative is admissible. As the Apostle Matthew is supposed to have written out discourses of Jesus which were incorporated with the first Gospel, so John may be regarded as having contributed a collection of discourses which by a later hand was combined with narratives of the life of Jesus. A theory of this kind is not unknown to New Testament criticism.[1] Evidently it is fitted to

---

15, 18, xix. 25, 38, 39, xx. 24, xxi, on places, i. 28, 44, 46, ii. 1, iii. 23, iv. 5, v. 2, vi. 19, viii. 20, ix, 7, x. 23, 40, xi. 18, 54, xviii. 1, xix. 13, 17, xx. 18, xxi. 2; on times, i. 29, 35, 39, 43, ii. 1, 13, 20, 23, iv. 6, 40, 52, v. 35, vi. 4, vii 2, x. 22, xi. 6, 39, xii. 1, xix. 14. Over against so much evidence of acquaintanceship with Judæa there is no sort of probability that the writer, in saying that Caiaphas was high priest that year, meant to intimate that the office of high priest was a yearly one. The expression does not necessarily have such an import. To one who esteemed the year of Christ's death the year of all years it was not unnatural to term it *that* year in writing to those distant in time and place from the scene of the crucifixion. Doubtless some indications of a relative lack of discrimination may be pointed out in the fourth Gospel. As will be noticed presently, there is apparent somewhat less of care than is observable in the Synoptical Gospels to indicate definitely the components of the Jewish community. Specific references to the scribes or lawyers are wanting, and the broad national term, *the Jews*, is used where some portion of the people might have been named. This characteristic, however, is measurably explained by the relatively remote standpoint occupied in common by the writer and those addressed.

[1] See H. H. Wendt, Das Johannesevangelium, 1900.

render a certain service in explaining peculiarities of the fourth Gospel. But we find no sufficient motive to make use of it either in the evidence that is cited in its behalf or in the extent to which it has commanded scholarly conviction.

II.— SOURCES AND PECULIARITIES.

Various statements in the Johannine writings convey an impression of aloofness from Judaism. It seems to be contemplated not infrequently as a thing external and remote. Were we to take two or three sentences attributed to Christ according to their sound, we might conclude that even He is represented as quite willing to disclaim association with Judaism. He is reported as saying: "All that came before me are thieves and robbers."[1] Again He is said, in addressing the Jews, to have mentioned the ancestral code as "your" law,[2] and to have referred to it in conversation with His disciples about the hatred of the Jews, as "their" law.[3] The meaning of these expressions is not, however, to be overpressed. The first does not denote an intention on the part of Christ to disclaim Jewish antecedents in general, but rather a wish to put Himself in contrast with such misleading guides as false Messiahs and the unspiritual representatives of the hierarchy. As for the other expressions, too large a meaning is put into them when they are made to imply that the speaker acknowledged no part in the law. It may be supposed either that Christ used them to emphasize the truth that the atti-

---

[1] John x. 8.   [2] John x. 34.   [3] John xv. 25.

tude of the Jews was reproved by the very authority which they themselves specially exalted, or that the evangelist, in accommodation to the Gentile surroundings in the midst of which he was placed, substituted "your" and "their" for "the" in citing Christ's references to the law. The latter interpretation may be regarded as commended by virtual parallels in the writer's usage. Repeatedly he refers to the Jews as an entirely outside party, and sets them over against Christ as opponents, using a national term in such connections as the Synoptists apply the party name of Pharisees.[1] By this peculiarity of his vocabulary, standing as it does unrelieved by any expression of hope for the refractory people, he gives a token of separation from Judaism scarcely equalled by any other New Testament writer. Paul indeed uttered grave censures against the Jews; but he also gave evidence of an affectionate clinging to his nation, and was not ready to count its mission in the world as wholly a thing of the past. The author of the Johannine Gospel and Epistles, on the other hand, shows no interest in forecasting a future for the Jewish people. In all likelihood this unique transcendence of the old national horizon was effectively promoted in John by his contemplation of the downfall of Jerusalem, as also by a consideration of the stubborn persistence of the Jews in their rejection of Christ, at the same time that the Gentile world was giving a broad welcome to His message.

While the evangelist assumes this distant attitude toward contemporary Judaism, he does not question the fulfillment of a divine vocation by the Judaism of a past

---

[1] John v. 1, 10, 16, 18, vi. 52, vii. 1, 13, x. 31, xi. 8, xviii. 20.

age. He evinces very clearly his conviction that the Old Testament provided foundations for the gospel dispensation. Christ is represented as claiming before the Samaritan woman that salvation is from the Jews,[1] as coming to His own proper possession in His advent to the Jews,[2] as calling the temple His Father's house,[3] and as referring to the witness of the ancient Scriptures respecting Himself.[4] Events in the life of Christ are exhibited, with much the same freedom that characterizes Matthew's Gospel, as fulfilling Old Testament texts.[5] But while thus the authority and divine function of the Old Testament are unequivocally recognized, it cannot be said that the evangelist shows very much of an independent interest in its contents. He scarcely reverts to it for any other purpose than to elicit types and prophecies of Christ's work and experience. In his epistles there is not so much as one citation from the Hebrew Scriptures and only one reference to facts recorded therein. He appears, in conformity with his view of the cosmic relation of Christ, to have been interested chiefly in what might be called ecumenical truths. Though in the narrative portion of his writings he shows plentifully the results of his recollection of a Jewish environment, it is yet plain that his horizon has become world-wide and that his heart is upon the truths which concern men, not as members of a particular nation, but of the race.

Reference was made in another connection to the

---

[1] John iv. 22
[2] John i. 11.
[3] John ii. 16.
[4] John v. 39, 46.
[5] John xii. 14, 15, xvii. 12, xix. 24, 28, 36, 37, xx. 9.

possible indebtedness of the Johannine theology to the speculative teaching of Alexandria. We may repeat here the conclusion that, while it would be going beyond warrant to affirm categorically that John was directly conversant with the writings of Philo, it seems on the whole probable that he came by some means into contact with his way of thinking. It must be maintained, however, that the evangelist used the Philonic teaching not as a copyist, but as a man of strong original bent uses material from any source. He received from it only what was congenial to his point of view, what, so to speak, he could take into his own blood.

This last remark may be extended to the relation of John's teaching to that of Paul. Doubtless in a general way the Pauline theology was an antecedent to the Johannine. The latter takes up several of the characteristic points of the former. It contains a contrast between the law system of Moses and the grace of Christ. It brings out also the supereminence of faith as a condition of salvation. It has likewise its counterpart to the thirteenth chapter of First Corinthians in the extraordinary emphasis which it places upon love as the test and glory of religious character. It contains furthermore a doctrine of election sufficiently pronounced to remind of Pauline sentences on this subject, and shows in the mysticism with which it is informed a distinct kinship with the Pauline conception of a mutual indwelling on the part of Christ and believers. But yet in reading the Johannine writings we scarcely ever meet a phrase which seems to us at first glance to bear marks of borrowing from Paul. Whatever of Pauline presuppositions are incorporated in them appear to have taken on new form and color by being passed through a mind as strong and confident in its way as was that of the great apostle to the Gentiles. For example, in the reference of the Johannine writer to the Mosaic law there is no trace of Paul's polemical vehemence. He views it calmly, not as a threatened yoke, but simply as a conspicuous factor in a bygone and preliminary dispensation. So too in regard to faith: however highly he may exalt its function, he does not set it forth, after the Pauline fashion, in sharp antithesis to works; he even characterizes it as a foremost work required of those who would aspire to God's favor. Distinctive features also belong to his way of broaching the subject of election and to his mysticism. While then we may affirm a certain obligation of John to Paul, and may question whether he could have written just as he has but for his powerful predecessor, we are still obliged to conclude that he gave forth his own and not another man's treasure. Whatever he appropriated was compelled to receive a Johannine stamp before it was sent forth into the world. Aside from contact with the person and teaching of Christ the Johannine theology had no more influential source than the marked individuality of its author. He wrote as he did because it was in him thus to write. In essential character he was the mystic, the man of contemplation, distinguished more by intensity and depth of feeling than by breadth and versatility of intellect. Getting at truth by intuition, or through the movement and satisfaction of his emotional life, he imparts it by a corresponding method. Of discursive reasoning he makes little or no use; he contents himself with simply presenting to the contemplation of others what had so deep a hold upon his own consciousness. Here he belongs to a different province from that which was often represented by Paul with his argumentative struggle and tension.

It accords with the interior and contemplative character of the Johannine theology that it is centred upon a few supreme truths, and the more immediate deductions from these. The starting point is the highest object of contemplation, the divine nature. This is described under a few comprehensive categories. The same categories for the most part enter into the description of the Son of God as belonging to the divine sphere. Revelation takes its cast from the nature in the Father and the Son. The true recipients of the revelation which is made in and through the Son, are so conformed to the divine nature, that the terms by which it is described belong also to them in a finite sense, and their conduct is in line with the significance of these terms. As for those who are unresponsive to the revelation, their character and deeds are described by an opposite set of terms. Thus the divine nature, viewed with respect to a few distinctive aspects, is made the norm or pattern which governs the whole outlook upon the sphere of moral and spiritual reality. A relatively limited number of phrases suffices for the presentation of the whole subject-matter. So largely does the stress gravitate toward certain central truths that the repetition of propositions in slightly varied form may be said to be more characteristic of the Johannine writings than of any other New Testament books.

Another way of describing the peculiarity of the Johannine theology would be to compare its point of view with that of Scholastic realism. In this assumption of a ground of comparison it is not implied that John was conscious of subscribing to the technical theory of the mediæval realists on the nature of universals. What is meant is, that in his habit of mind the stress fell upon the universal, the comprehensive type, and that the individual was rated as a manifestation of the type. He regarded the concrete visible reality on the field of history as expressive of a more general invisible reality. In pursuance of this way of thinking he took no pains to discriminate intermediate grades of character. In his portrayal of men they fall into broadly contrasted classes. Either they conform to the type which is given in the divine nature, and being begotten of God do not sin, or else they have their prototype in the devil and are given over to transgression. Some mitigation of the sharp antithesis may be provided for; but it is plainly characteristic of the Johannine writings to describe individuals under general terms and to ignore the manifold gradations which fall between extremes.

The limitation of province which results from the concentration of the Johannine teaching upon central truths will readily appear to any one who asks for its conclusion upon various lines of Christian thought. That teaching contains next to nothing respecting the sacraments, and next to nothing respecting the government of the Church. It has no compendium of civil or domestic duty. Of ethical detail in any direction it incorporates but little. The emphasis in it goes to principles or cardinal phases

THE JOHANNINE THEOLOGY 325

of religious disposition, rather than to items of conduct. Its theme is not so much the law of righteousness in its manifold demands as the inner life in its relation to a divine source. As respects the outward demonstration of the life in the Christian, it enforces only the general attitude toward the brotherhood which is dictated by the nature and conditions of that life.

In respect of linguistic peculiarities the Johannine writings are distinguished by a remarkable simplicity. The vocabulary is limited. Period-making is avoided. The subject-matter of a theme is developed by a series of short declarations which are connected by a certain kinship of meaning, but are not structurally articulated. "The constructions," says Westcott, "are habitually reduced to the simplest elements. To speak of St. John's Gospel as written in very pure Greek is altogether misleading. It is free from solecisms because it avoids all idiomatic expressions. The grammar is that which is common to almost all language."[1] The writer's style may be regarded as one among the evidences of his antecedents. Though he wears his Greek dress with a fair degree of ease, he does not conceal his Hebrew training. In the parallelism and symmetry of his clauses it comes quite distinctly into evidence.

III.— JOHANNINE ANTITHESES.

One of the most frequently recurring of these is that between Christ and Christians on the one hand and the world on the other. In this antithesis "the world" de-

---
[1] The Gospel according to St. John, introduction, p. 50.

notes the human race viewed as estranged from the divine life and made incapable of appreciating the divine point of view through the dominance of sensuous and unspiritual impulses and desires. Instances are not indeed lacking in the Johannine writings in which the term is employed in the ordinary sense to denote the sum of created beings.[1] There are also instances in which it refers to the human race without distinctly accentuating its sinful estate.[2] But in a majority of cases the term has an ethical reference, and names a humanity which in its controlling temper is averted from God and His kingdom. The world is described as hating the Christ because He testifies that its works are evil; as ignorant of the Holy Spirit and incapable of receiving Him; as lying in its entirety in the evil one; as being under diabolical headship; as hating the disciples of Christ because they do not belong to itself; as a transient scene of empty display and fleshly lust, to which those who are born of God cannot be supposed to give their love.[3]

The picture which is given of the world seems to promise to the followers of Christ upon earth a continuous encounter with hatred and opposition. The stern prospect, however, is not left without a great mitigation. The disciples of Christ have a pledge of successful resistance to the assaults of the unfriendly power in the fact that He has demonstrated His mastery over the world.[4] It found nothing in Him on which to build its

---

[1] John xvii. 5, 24. [2] John i. 10, xvi. 28.
[3] John vii. 7, viii. 23, xii. 31, xiv. 17, 30, xv. 19, xvii. 14; 1 John ii. 15–17, iii. 13, v. 19.
[4] John xvi. 33.

dominion.¹ In putting Him to death it does not so much judge Him as have judgment visited upon itself.² Thereby is made manifest not only its enmity but its impotence as well. For, the death of the Son of God proves to be the most potent means to draw men out of the bonds of the world, and likewise the direct antecedent of His demonstrated superiority to any death-working power which the world can use against Him.³ Moreover, Christians may take courage in view of their inward furnishing. Greater is He that is in them than he that is in the world.⁴ In the simple fact of their spiritual birth they have a pledge of victory. "For whatsoever is begotten of God overcometh the world."⁵

It is hardly necessary to add that the antithesis under consideration is not to be taken in the sense of a metaphysical dualism. The world does not stand for an intrinsically evil entity, an irreformable, refractory substance. It stands for men who are actually under the dominion of evil, but to whom nevertheless the love of God went out in the sending of His Son. A world that is viewed as being in any sense the object of God's love is evidently not meant to be regarded as intrinsically and hopelessly evil. It may be in one point of view the devil's domain, but it is still a proper subject for a divine message and an attempted rescue.

A second favorite antithesis with John is that between light and darkness. The two terms may be regarded as having an implicit reference to truth. Light is a symbol

---

¹ John xiv. 30.
² John xii. 31, 32.
³ John x. 18.
⁴ 1 John iv. 4.
⁵ 1 John v. 4.

for truth unmixed with error. A nature uncorrupted by falsity in disposition is in affinity with light, capable of receiving and appropriating truth. Darkness, on the other hand, is a symbol of destitution of truth through falsity of disposition. Lacking the right moral purpose and the right moral appreciation men do not and cannot see. Thus the fallen race is described as darkness and as failing to apprehend the light shining into it through the agency of the Word.[1] Furthermore, men are described as being in their alienation from the truth postively averse to the light. The falsity of their disposition makes them practically enemies of the truth. They dread the self-discovery and rebuke which must come from having its light thrown upon them.[2] Here the ethical nature of the contrast expressed by the terms light and darkness is clearly apparent. That the contrast must be understood in this sense is also shown by the association which is made between the two terms and love and hatred respectively. "He that loveth his brother abideth in the light and there is none occasion of stumbling in him. But he that hateth his brother is in the darkness and walketh in the darkness, and knoweth not whither he goeth, because the darkness hath blinded his eyes."[3] The true disposition is illuminating; the false or perverted disposition tends to obscurity and confusion.

In a third Johannine antithesis the opposing terms are life and death. Much the same contrast is expressed by these terms as by light and darkness. Indeed we find the former set used in the same relation in which the latter is employed. Thus in the Epistle it is said, "We

---

[1] John i. 5. [2] John iii. 19-21. [3] 1 John, ii. 10, 11.

THE JOHANNINE THEOLOGY

know that we have passed out of death into life, because we love the brethren. He that loveth not abideth in death."[1] The statement suggests that life belongs with fullness and vitality of the right ethical disposition, while death denotes a deficit of such a disposition. In the Gospel also the two contrasted states are given a close association with moral dispositions, only faith rather than love is here made the determining principle. He that believeth hath passed out of death into life. He that believeth not shall not see life.[2] So far does the stress in the Johannine representation fall upon the moral or spiritual side of the subject that the physical is well-nigh ignored. The declaration which is cited from the lips of Christ, "If a man keep my word, he shall never see death,"[3] is certainly fitted to convey the impression that physical death is of no account.

In addition to these characteristic antitheses there appears in the Johannine writings the contrast between flesh and spirit. It is not made, however, nearly so prominent as in the Pauline epistles. Moreover, it is to be observed that John brings forward a much less vigorous impeachment of the flesh than is rendered by Paul. His words in one connection imply that it serves as a seat of illicit desires.[4] It is not said, however, that it is necessarily or by virtue of its nature given over to this evil office, any more than this is said of the eyes which in the same connection are described as instruments of worldly lusts. In the broader statement,

---

[1] 1 John, iii. 14. Compare 1 John ii. 9–11. [3] John viii. 51.
[2] John v. 24, iii. 36. [4] 1 John ii. 16.

"That which is born of the flesh is flesh, and that which is born of the Spirit is spirit,"[1] the inferior term in the comparison may be interpreted as denoting the natural in opposition to the distinctively spiritual, man considered in the sense relations which are so apt to dominate him in contrast with the same subject made conformable to his higher relations. We should need larger means of definition than we actually possess in order to be certain that in this proposition it was designed to predicate of the flesh positive hostility to the spiritual ideal and not simply lack of appreciation or of true affinity therefor, though the known preference of John for sharp contrasts might warrant the suspicion that he wrote the proposition in the sense of the former alternative. That the proper dualistic notion of the flesh is not imbedded in the Johannine theology is quite manifest. A writer who could emphasize so strongly the reality of the flesh of the sinless Christ, or speak even in figure of eating His flesh, cannot be regarded as harboring any antipathy toward the flesh, as though in the character of physical substance it were evil.

While it trespasses against good exegesis to interpret the Johannine antitheses in the sense of a strict or metaphysical dualism, it must be granted that in the Johannine representation the dark hemisphere is made quite decidedly dark. An extra shade of blackness is given to it by the association of all sin with diabolism. The devil is represented as back of the whole stream of moral evil. He was a murderer from the beginning.

---

[1] John iii. 6.

The first homicidal stroke, whether ministered through the hand of Cain or through the solicitation to the death-working trespass of Adam, was due to him. He sinned from the beginning, from the opening act in the tragedy of moral evil. The world, so far as it is alienated from God, is his kingdom. He is a liar and the father of lies, the father of all evil-doers. Every one that sinneth is of him.[1] In all this, it is observable, nothing is said of the origin of the devil. The assumption is simply that he stands back of all human sinning, not as relieving the sinner of his responsibility, but as coagent with him and as the head with which in sinning he becomes confederated. The emphasis falls quite as much upon the type as upon the causal ground. The effort is to exhibit sin and the sinner as being of the devil-type. As was noticed above, to represent things according to an unqualified type is characteristic of the Johannine writings.

Along with a relative fullness of reference to the prince of the evil kingdom the Johannine teaching combines a relative silence on the subject of angels. It contains no positive statements respecting evil angels or demons, and its references to good angels are very scanty.[2]

IV.—THE DOCTRINE OF THE FATHER AND THE SON.

The superior terms in most of the Johannine antitheses enter naturally into the description of God, since He is the absolute contrast to all that is dark, impoverished, or

---
[1] John viii. 44, xii. 31, xiv. 30; 1 John iii. 8, 10, v. 19.
[2] John ii. 51, xx. 12.

evil. Among the statements bearing on the divine nature three have the form of definitions, namely: "God is spirit," "God is light," "God is love."[1] It would not have done violence doubtless to John's way of thinking had he added, God is life, and God is truth. He has presented us with the meaning which belongs to statements of this kind in speaking of the Father as having life in Himself,[2] and styling Him the true God and ultimate source of all saving truth.[3]

With the definition of God as spirit is to be placed the declaration that no man hath seen Him at any time.[4] As the absolute Spirit He is beyond all cognizance by corporeal means, as He is beyond all limitations of place. One locality can no more possess Him than another. The means of approach to him are and must be spiritual. There is no nearness to Him except in ethical likeness, and no distance except in ethical unlikeness. "Everyone that loveth knoweth God. He that loveth not knoweth not God."[5] The invisibility, therefore, which is predicated of God has no affiliation with the idea of isolation. Whatever note of transcendence may belong to the Johannine conception of God, it makes Him thoroughly accessible to the one having the proper organ of association. Emphatic recognition is given in it to the truth of the divine immanence. Not only is there a reference to an indwelling Christ or Holy Spirit, but it is said of the Father Himself that He is pleased to take up His abode with the

---

[1] John iv. 24; 1 John i. 5, iv. 16.   [2] John v. 26.
[3] John v. 19, 20, xiv. 10, xvii. 3; 1 John v. 20.
[4] John i. 18.   [5] 1 John, iv. 7, 8.

THE JOHANNINE THEOLOGY 333

obedient disciple.[1] Here the Johannine mysticism advances a step beyond the Pauline. No New Testament books, in short, are more emphatic than the Johannine on the divine indwelling.

The affirmation that God is light may be made with the stress upon the inner nature, and thus imply that God is self-luminous, having in the perfect harmony of his intellectual and ethical being no ground of confusion or darkness in Himself. It may be made also with the stress upon causal efficiency, and hence convey the meaning that the universe has in God an unfailing source of illumination. We may suppose the two points of view, as they are perfectly concordant, to have been united in John's thought, and that he meant to describe God as being at once perfectly unshadowed in the sphere of His own consciousness and as infinitely light-giving. There may also be contained in the figure a reference to the nature of benevolence as universally diffusive of benefits.

In the declaration that God is love John brings to a climax the theological statement of the import of the New Testament revelation. The declaration means two things. It means in the first place that God is in fact infinitely benevolent, having the good-will to bring blessing to every creature that in the fitness of things can be blessed. In the second place it means that this unstinted benevolence or good-will is not the result of an arbitrary election, but deeply based in the ethical nature of God. Theologians have sometimes argued that God must be just, but in respect of loving anything within

---
[1] John xiv. 23.

the province of creation His will can give the decision, and is just as free to decide one way as another. Such argumentation collides with the Johannine declaration. If love is not as deep, as intrinsic, as essential, as anything in the ethical nature of God, then John made a mistake. For if language has any clear sense, the affirmation that "God is love" must signify that love is fundamental to His ethical nature, and that no attribute or activity is more essential. Indeed, taken by itself the Johannine sentence might be construed as subordinating all other divine attributes to love. But probably there was no distinct intent to weigh God's love against His righteousness or holiness. If less emphasized than the former, the latter receives still a distinct tribute.[1] The thought to which we are pointed is that in the deepest depth and highest height of the Godhead love is present.

The term Father is applied to God in a multitude of instances in the Johannine writings. In the majority of these it designates the relation between God and the Son of God. In some instances the term is given a broader application. Thus in the address to the Samaritan woman God is referred to as the Father, to whom all true worshippers will pay their ascriptions.[2] That God holds a fatherly relation to men generally is not formally stated anywhere in the Johannine writings. It may be said also that the stress which they place upon spiritual rebirth as a condition of a filial standing and their blunt designation of sinners as children of the

---

[1] 1 John ii, 29, iii. 7.
[2] John iv. 23. See xv. 16, xvi. 23; 1 John ii. 1, iii. 1; 2 John, 3, 4.

THE JOHANNINE THEOLOGY 335

devil look like a negation of the conception of universal fatherhood. But, on the other hand, God's love for the world and costly provision for the salvation of every one that can be persuaded to accept His gracious offers argue for such a disposition as may well be associated with divine paternity. The truth seems to lie in a qualified affirmation of universal fatherhood. According to the illustration used in another connection, God overlooks neither the man in the sinner nor the sinner in the man. The one is a subject for His fatherly compassion; the other, for His displeasure and rebuke. Only with the extirpation of his better capacities does a man descend wholly to the plane of wrath. John has not indeed said just this; but if we put together what he says on the love and on the wrath of God respectively the result seems to be essentially as stated.

In dealing with the person of Christ John does not attempt, any more than did the author of the Epistle to the Hebrews, to construe in Him the relation between the human and the divine. He contents himself with recognizing both the one and the other. His consciousness of the former is indicated in the first place by his representation that the Son of God came in the flesh.[1] In his terminology, as well as in that of other New Testament writers, the flesh denotes more than mere bodily substance.[2] By itself, however, it does not include an indubitable reference to every constituent of manhood, to the $\pi\nu\epsilon\hat{\upsilon}\mu\alpha$, as well as to the $\psi\upsilon\chi\acute{\eta}$. Accordingly a completer sign of conviction of Christ's

---

[1] John i. 14; 1 John iv. 2.   [2] John iii. 6.

humanity is furnished by the picture which the evangelist gives of human experiences, emotions, and elements of consciousness in his Master.[1] This order of statements has been taken advantage of by a few recent writers on biblical theology for exhibiting the Johannine teaching as being agreeable to their humanitarian predilections. But their construction stands as little chance of winning the general assent of scholars as did the Socinian of an earlier day. Critics as little constrained by the bonds of orthodoxy as Pfleiderer and Holtzmann make no question but that a transcendent or essentially divine rank and character are assigned to the Johannine Christ.[2] And no wonder; for, let the revelation on the human side be what it may, it is still true that it is like asking a man to deny the sight of his eyes to set him to discover in the Johannine writings only a human Christ.

Among the tokens that Christ is to be thought of as standing essentially on the plane of divinity are the following : (1) A suggestion is given that He is above the creaturely sphere, and ranks as a kind of *alter ego* of the Father, in that the characteristic Johannine terms which are used to define the one are used to describe the other also. If God is defined as light, the Son also is called the true light, the source of illumination to men as well before as in His incarnation.[3] If God is represented as the absolute life, the Son is said also to have

---

[1] John iv. 6, 34, xi. 33-38, xii. 27, xiii. 21, xix. 28-30, xx. 17.

[2] Holtzmann, Lehrbuch der neutestamentlichen Theologie; Pfleiderer, Urchristenthum. Compare Grill, Untersuchungen uber die Entstehung des vierten Evangeliums; Réville, Le Quatrième Évangile, son Origine et sa Valeur Historique; Loisy, Le Quatrième Évangile.

[3] John i, 4, 9, viii. 12, ix 5

life in Himself, to be the life, and thus to be competent to quicken as many as He may please.[1] If God is described as the true, the Son is called the truth.[2] The representation runs precisely as though the latter were regarded as the substantial image of the former, one in whom are repeated the divine perfections. (2) Titles are ascribed to Christ which belong to a divine range. In the prologue to the Gospel He is declared not only to have been with God but to have been God. In repeated instances He is called the Son of God. This title He shares with no other; for it is a peculiarity of the Johannine writings that believers are never called sons of God. As having experienced spiritual rebirth they are τέκνα θεοῦ, but the term Son (υἱός) is reserved to their Lord and Master. This fact could hardly have come about by accident, and may be regarded as testifying to John's sense of the uniqueness of Christ's sonship. The use of the term μονογενής witnesses still further to the extraordinary sonship of Christ.[3] Likewise the context which often goes with the filial title, testifying as it does to an extraordinary consciousness of copartnership with the Father, argues for a transcendent kind of sonship. No ordinary filial bond gives a basis for such declarations as these: "The Father loveth the Son and hath given all things into His hand... My Father worketh until now, and I work.... The Father judgeth no man, but He hath given all judgment unto the Son, that all may honor the Son even as they honor the Father.... He that hath seen me hath seen the Father.... All

---

[1] John i. 4, v. 21, 26, xiv. 6.   [2] John xiv. 6.
[3] John i. 14, 18; 1 John iv. 9.

things whatsoever the Father hath are mine."[1] In this line of statements an ethical oneness with the Father may be contemplated; but more than that is implied. Mere identity of a human with a divine will, so long as a proper creaturely consciousness remains, never provides for such an order of statements. The conclusion is enforced that back of the ethical union of Christ with the Father a transcendent connection in the order of being must be predicated. (3) Functions and attributes are ascribed to Christ which associate Him with a divine sphere. As the Logos He wrought in creation. All things were made by Him; and without Him was not anything made that hath been made.[2] The prerogatives of resurrection and judgment belong to Him.[3] In His consciousness of a transcendence of temporal limitations He is able to speak of a glory which He had with the Father before the world was,[4] and also to declare, "Before Abraham was, I am."[5] He reads the secrets of men's hearts and forecasts the future as though the barriers to ordinary vision were transparent to his glance.[6] He promises His disciples that He will do whatsoever they shall ask in His name.[7] Even so momentous a thing as the mission of the Holy Spirit He conditions upon His own agency, promising to send this other Advocate to further by His witness the work which He Himself had founded.[8] (4) The practical worth of divinity is ascribed to Christ in the measure of spiritual

---

[1] John v. 17, 21–23, xiv. 9, xvi. 15.
[2] John i. 3.
[3] John v. 21–29, xi. 25.
[4] John xvii. 5.
[5] John viii. 58.
[6] John ii. 24, 25, vi. 64.
[7] John xiv. 13, 14.
[8] John xv. 26.

dependence upon Him which is affirmed of men. He is the bearer of eternal life, the source of true freedom, the sole way of access to the Father. The disciple can do nothing apart from Him. If a man abide not in Him he is cast forth as a branch and is withered.[1]

As may be gathered from the foregoing, the Johannine christology is on essentially the same plane as that of the later Pauline Epistles and the Epistle to the Hebrews. A few statements pertaining to the first may seem, it is true, to come nearer to an affirmation of the equality of the Son with the Father than do any propositions in the other writings. Here will be recalled in particular the declaration, "I and my Father are one";[2] also the expression, "that men may honor the Son even as they honor the Father."[3] But the former sentence, though indirectly pointing to a transcendent nature as testifying, along with kindred utterances, to an order of consciousness which belongs alone with such a nature, has probably a direct reference rather to ethical than to metaphysical oneness. It is not therefore an unequivocal expression of equality. The second expression taken by itself bespeaks equality; but it is to be noticed that the equal honor is to be rendered to the Son on the score of an office which He receives from the Father. Thus the connection assigns a certain preeminence to the Father. The like is true of other passages which give an exalted view of the Son's prerogatives. In the midst of the highest expressions of His self-consciousness the Son acknowledges a certain dependence upon the Father.

---

[1] John iii. 36, viii. 36, xiv. 6, xv. 5, 6; 1 John v. 11, 12.
[2] John x. 30.   [3] John v. 23.

This in no wise militates against the fact of His being the eternal Son. Why should not He who was in the bosom of the Father, as He trod the earth in human form and sought to win men to the Father, give an ideal expression of the spirit of sonship, exhibiting Himself in no sort of isolation from His source, but as ever and perfectly devoted to the paternal will? Even for one eternally and metaphysically the Son of God divine discretion would, as it seems to us, dictate just this bearing. It is not to be denied nevertheless that the total representation of John involves a certain aspect of subordination in the position of the Son. In some sense the Father is made the deeper and more ultimate spring in the Godhead, while the Son is the organ of universal manifestation.

V.— The Holy Spirit.

As in the Pauline Epistles, so also in the writings of John, the province of Christ's pneumatic nature and that of the Holy Spirit are not closely discriminated. The universal function of the Logos in the rational creation, as the bearer of light and life, is such as might very naturally be associated with the Holy Spirit.[1] On the other hand, gifts and powers which might be regarded as involved in the pneumatic nature pertaining to Christ's personality are apparently referred to the Holy Spirit; for it is said that to the Son God "giveth not the Spirit by measure."[2] Once more, in immediate connection with the promise to send the Spirit Christ adds, "I will

---

[1] John i. 4.   [2] John iii. 34.

not leave you desolate, I come unto you,"[1] as though the coming of the former might be identified with His own coming.

Still doubt is not to be entertained as to the intent of John to assign a distinct standing to the Holy Spirit. No more is it to be doubted that in his references the Spirit is contemplated as a personal agent. He is placed over against Christ as another Comforter ($\pi\alpha\rho\acute{\alpha}\kappa\lambda\eta\tau\sigma$), another Advocate or Helper, as the name might also be rendered.[2] Furthermore the Spirit is represented as witnessing to Christ, and as glorifying Him by declaring the message relating to His person and work.[3] The Spirit is thus in the office of representing the Son distinguished from Him much as the Son is distinguished from the Father whom He represents without excluding His presence from the sphere in which the representation occurs. That in one or another connection the Son seems to accomplish what is otherwise made a function of the Holy Spirit may be explained in part by the instrumental position of the latter. As sending the Spirit to continue the work visibly inaugurated by Himself, the Son may be said to do what is done through the Spirit. In performing such functions as witnessing, teaching, and convicting of sin, righteousness, and judgment, the Spirit appears in a personal character. The application of neuter pronouns to Him involves no denial of this character. When closely associated with the neuter substantive $\pi\nu\epsilon\hat{\upsilon}\mu\alpha$ the pronouns naturally follow its gender. They are not, however, made conformable in every instance. The original text shows clearly

---

[1] John xiv. 18.   [2] xiv. 16.   [3] xv. 26, xvi. 13, 14.

enough that, apart from the pressure of grammatical propriety, the preference of the speaker or narrator was for the masculine form of the pronouns to denote the Spirit.[1]

The language of the fourth Gospel implies an economic subordination of the Holy Spirit to the Father and the Son. Respecting His metaphysical relations within the Godhead it offers no direct statement. The metaphysical sense that has been put into the clause, "which proceedeth from the Father,"[2] is based on a dogmatic predilection. The words are more naturally understood of a procession, or sending forth, into the sphere of action, than of an eternal mode of subsistence. The fact that παρά is employed here, the same preposition which is used in stating the going forth of the Son to fulfill His mission, supports the economic sense. As the uniform language of the ancient creeds illustrates, the technical doctrine of procession requires for its suitable expression the use of the preposition ἐκ. It is noticeable also that the Greek fathers in citing the Johannine sentence evince a disposition to substitute ἐκ for παρά.[3]

A peculiarity in the Johannine exposition of the work of the Holy Spirit is the stress which is placed upon the production in men of a Christ consciousness. In the conversation with Nicodemus the Spirit is indeed mentioned as the agent in regeneration,[4] and in the interview of the risen Christ with His disciples promise is given

---

[1] John xiv. 26, xv. 26, xvi. 13, 14.   [2] xv. 26.
[3] Westcott, The Gospel According to St. John, p. 225. Compare Dods, Expositor's Greek Testament, I. 833.
[4] John iii. 3–8.

that they shall be assisted by the Holy Spirit in the guidance and discipline of the Christian brotherhood.[1] But the main stress falls upon the idea that it belongs to the Spirit to induct men into evangelical truth, to carry forward the teaching function which Christ fulfilled during His visible ministry, to glorify Christ in the thought of men by taking of the things of Christ and declaring them, in a word, to transfuse into the minds and hearts of men a vital Christ consciousness, a consoling and transforming sense of union with Him notwithstanding His recession from the sphere of the outward vision.[2] In view of this larger and more effective impact it was expedient for Christ to go away. By withdrawal from the narrow sphere of sense observation He was all the better prepared to become a universal power in men.

VI. — The Work of Christ.

In no other New Testament writings is so much made of the revealing office of Christ as in those of John. In various ways the sentiment is emphatically expressed that through Him a saving enlightenment is ministered to men. He is compared in His office to the illuminating agent in nature. He is the true light which lighteth every man, the light of the world in following whom men escape from darkness and have the light of life.[3] His presence in the world serves to make visible the glory of the only begotten of the Father.[4] He is the

---

[1] John xx. 23 [2] xv. 26, xvi. 7–15; 1 John ii. 20, 21.
[3] John i. 9, viii. 12. [4] John i. 14.

manifested truth and the manifested life.[1] The true knowledge of God is eternal life;[2] and this knowledge is mediated through Christ. The unseen Father is declared through the incarnate Son and glorified by Him.[3] So perfectly are the mind, will, and purpose of God reflected in Him that he that hath seen Him can be said to have seen the Father.[4] His economy is an economy of truth as well as of grace.[5] To this end came He into the world, that He might bear witness to the truth.[6] He is a bearer of life as a messenger of truth. His words are words of eternal life.[7] While His flesh is described as the bread given for the life of the world, the explanation is added, "It is the spirit that quickeneth; the flesh profiteth nothing: the words that I have spoken unto you they are spirit and are life."[8] The message of truth is thus identified with the meat which the Son of man giveth and which abideth unto eternal life.[9] A like efficacy is assigned to His message in the declaration to the disciples, "Already ye are clean through the word which I have spoken unto you."[10] According to some commentators a kindred significance belongs to the comprehensive statement that the blood of Christ cleanseth from all sin,[11] the reference here being not so much to the remission of guilt, as to the elimination of the sinful disposition, and this being effected by the manifested love and righteousness of God in Christ, for which the blood is the symbol. As

---

[1] John xiv. 6; 1 John i. 2.
[2] John xvii. 3.
[3] John i. 18, xvii. 4.
[4] xiv. 9.
[5] i. 17.
[6] xviii. 37.
[7] vi. 68.
[8] vi. 63.
[9] vi. 27.
[10] xv. 3.
[11] 1 John i. 7.

THE JOHANNINE THEOLOGY

we conceive, it is not necessary to exclude a reference to remission, and we maintain only that it is quite consonant with the Johannine way of thinking to associate cleansing with the blood of Christ on the ground that it is a message-speaking blood, the bearer to men's hearts of an order of truth in which purifying and renovating virtue resides. In line with the ruling conception of Christ as the revealer of saving truth, we have the further representation that through the instrumentality of the Spirit He continues in the glorified state His enlightening office. The Spirit sent in His name, as was noticed above, has the work of vitalizing in men's souls the revelation given in and through Him. In short, according to the Johannine representation Christ came into the world as a truth-radiating personality, and fulfilled in large part His saving office as a bearer and impersonation of truth.

Closely related to the foregoing point of view, indeed capable of being included under it, is the Johannine representation of the work of Christ, and especially of His death, as the supreme specimen of loving self-sacrifice. The parable of the good shepherd emphasizes the fact of this self-sacrifice. A specially significant expression of its efficacy is contained in the words, "Verily I say unto you except a grain of wheat fall into the earth and die, it abideth by itself alone; but if it die, it beareth much fruit."[1] This sentence might be styled a statement of the law of the reproductive power of self-sacrifice. According to the connection it applies both to Christ and His disciples, and sets forth the

---

[1] John xii. 24.

great truth that all spiritual fruitage is conditioned upon the deed of willing self-devotement. A like sentiment may be regarded as underlying the prophetical declaration. "And I, if I be lifted up from the earth, will draw all men unto myself."[1] It witnesses to the practical potency of the loving self-sacrifice manifested in the self-delivery of the Son of God to the ordeal of the cross.

The Johannine teaching represents still further that Christ fulfills the great end of His incarnation by bringing men into vital connection with Himself. Coming with all the wealth of His personality into the human sphere He imparts from His own higher life to those who are drawn into fellowship with Himself. In description of this mystical and efficacious union He is able to say to his disciples, "I am the vine, ye are the branches; he that abideth in me and I in him the same beareth much fruit."[2] A like conception is contained in the declaration, "God gave unto us eternal life, and this life is in His Son. He that hath the Son hath the life; he that hath not the Son of God hath not the life."[3]

As compared with the Pauline theology the Johannine does not so fully centre the attention upon the death of Christ. It is less emphatically a theology of the cross. The idea of revelation comes to the front, and in conformity therewith large account is made of the life of the Redeemer. It is manifest too that John was less inclined than Paul to dwell upon the judicial aspect of Christ's work. Most of what the former says is in line

---

[1] John xii. 32.   [2] John xv. 5.   [3] 1 John v. 11, 12.

with the moral-influence and mystical theories of atonement. Still, it needs to be acknowledged that in the background of the Johannine representation there is a sufficiently distinct recognition of essentially the same objective phase of atonement as appears elsewhere in the New Testament. This is especially noticeable in the Epistle. Nothing in the Pauline writings more clearly implies that the universal dispensation of grace is based upon Christ's work than does the Johannine declaration that He is the propitiation (ἱλασμός) for the sins of the world.[1] A kindred view with respect to the saving office of the Redeemer is implied in the affirmation that He is with the Father as an advocate for the one who has sinned,[2] as also in the statement that forgiveness of sins takes place for His name's sake.[3] In the Gospel there is no formal assertion of such an objective value in Christ's work as is indicated by the term propitiation; but the idea which belongs with that term is implicitly recognized in the designation of Christ as "the Lamb of God,"[4] in the representation that He was to die for the people,[5] in the assertion of the necessity of His death,[6] in the description of His death as a voluntary offering or sacrifice,[7] and in the declaration that access to the Father is solely through Him.[8]

VII. — THE INITIATION AND UNFOLDMENT OF THE NEW LIFE.

By limiting the attention to a few sentences of the Johannine writings one may get much the same im-

---

[1] 1 John ii, iv. 10.   [4] John i. 29, 36.   [7] John x. 17, 18
[2] 1 John ii. 1.   [5] John xi. 50–52.   [8] John xiv. 6
[3] 1 John ii. 12.   [6] John iii. 14.

pression of determinism, or divine election, as a few sentences of the Pauline epistles are fitted to convey. Christ is represented as conditioning the ability of men to come to Himself and to believe His message upon the effectual working of the Father. "All that which the Father giveth me," He says, "shall come to me." "No man can come to me except the Father which sent me draw him." "Glorify thy Son, that the Son may glorify thee: even as thou gavest Him authority over all flesh, that whatsoever thou hast given Him, to them He should give eternal life." "The works that I do in my Father's name, these bear witness of me. But ye believe not, because ye are not of my sheep."[1] But, on the other hand, there are sentences which give an emphatic impression of the universality of divine grace. The saving purpose of God is represented as reaching out to the world. The Son is sent to be the Saviour of the world. He is the propitiation for the sins of the whole world. He is lifted up in order that He might draw all men unto Himself. The burden of His complaint against the unbelieving is, "Ye will not come unto me that ye may have life."[2] If then the apostle is to be reconciled with himself, the former order of expressions must be understood, not as implying an arbitrary division of men into opposing classes, but simply the truth that men reach the attitude of faith only as they are led up to it by a special divine preparation. Combining the two orders of expressions we obtain the conclusion that men

---

[1] John vi. 37, 44, xvii. 1, 2, x. 25, 26. See also vi. 39, 65, ix. 39, xii. 38–40; 1 John ii. 19.

[2] John iii. 16, v. 40, xii. 32; 1 John ii.2, iv 14.

are at once deeply dependent upon the divine working and free to cooperate with or to resist it.

Salvation, or the sum of benefits brought by Christ, is frequently described in the Johannine writings by the phrase "eternal life."[1] As the phrase is used in both the Gospel and the Epistle, it denotes the inward enrichment and enduring blessedness which come from union with the Father through the Son. Doubtless we shall not be in error if we impute to the compendious expression a meaning closely akin to that which is contained in the Synoptical expression, "the kingdom of God," or "the kingdom of heaven," taken in its more subjective application.

In speaking of the attainment of salvation it is characteristic of John to pass by the terms descriptive of relationship, and to employ those descriptive of nature. He stands in contrast with Paul, in that he enters into no discourse upon justification or adoption. It is the interior character of the child of God rather than the filial standing or relationship that he emphasizes. His leading thought is that of being born anew (or being born from *above*, as some prefer to render ἄνωθεν), or being begotten of God.[2] The new bent, disposition, or life potency signified by these terms, he regards as the product of the mysterious working of the Holy Spirit. Of any sacramental agency in connection with the change he has very little to say. A possible reference to baptism appears indeed in the words addressed to Nico-

---

[1] John iii. 15, iv. 36, vi. 54, 68, x. 28, xii. 25, xvii. 2, 3; 1 John i. 2, ii. 25, v. 11, 13, 20.

[2] John i. 12, 13, iii. 3–8; 1 John ii. 29, iii. 1, 2, 9, iv. 7, v. 1, 4, 18.

demus.[1] But it is to be noticed that the reference occurs in a sentence designed to illustrate the meaning of a misunderstood term; and hence may be regarded not so much as emphasizing the instrumentality of water as intimating by its means that the new birth denotes a cleansing or purifying as well as a renewing of its subject. In any event the passage as a whole makes the instrumentality of water quite subordinate to the agency of the Spirit. It contains no statement that the working of the Spirit is tied to the rite of baptism; on the contrary it virtually denies this notion. The supposition that the new birth can be attached at pleasure to an external occasion is discountenanced by the declaration: "The wind bloweth where it listeth, and thou hearest the voice thereof, but knowest not whence it cometh, and whither it goeth: so is every one that is born of the Spirit."

The first of the statements in the fourth Gospel respecting the new birth makes it dependent upon faith.[2] In this statement, too, is contained the Johannine idea that faith has in Christ its proper object. Of course it was not in the mind of John to dissociate the Father from the Son as an object of believing apprehension. But treating of the Son as the bearer of salvation he speaks mainly of faith as directed to His person and work.[3] In a number of instances the connection suggests that by faith he means only a mental assent to a given order of facts. It is evident, nevertheless, when

---

[1] John iii. 5. [2] John i. 12, 13.
[3] John iii. 15, 16, 18, 36, vi. 29, 40, vii. 38, viii. 24, xx. 29, 31; 1 John iii. 23, v. 1.

we glance at his total representation, that faith stood with him for an ethical bearing as well as for an intellectual conviction. In the sixth chapter of the Gospel he makes the believing on Christ equivalent in its efficacy to eating His flesh and drinking His blood — terms which signify a most thorough appropriation of Christ as a ground of religious satisfaction and a spring of spiritual life. The criticism also which was passed upon the Pharisees, to the effect that they were in no condition to believe as seeking glory one of another, indicates that faith is inclusive of a moral disposition.[1] In short, it is not to be doubted that in the Johannine conception faith involves a self-committal which brings into intimate fellowship and affinity with its object.

Along with faith John magnifies knowledge, depicting it in some instances as a source of salvation, in others as a proof or result of a regenerated nature.[2] In his estimate of the true *gnosis* he vies with the most appreciative utterances of Paul as contained in the Epistles to the Colossians and Ephesians. It would be a mistake, however, to suppose that in this he was rendering any tribute to a speculative grasp of truth. The knowledge that he commended is that practical knowledge which is dependent upon the religious disposition, which comes through inner conformity to Him who is the truth. Doubtless he thought of it as including a vital heartfelt assurance of divine favor and love.[3]

The distinctive attributes and tests of Christian char-

---

[1] John v. 44.
[2] John vii. 17, viii. 31, 32, xvii. 3, 17; 1 John ii. 3, 4, 20, 21, 27, iii. 6, iv. 7, 8.   [3] John xiv. 21, 23.

acter, as set forth by John, are righteousness and love. He pictures the Christian as one who has totally renounced sin, and whose relation to Christ and to God excludes it absolutely. "Whosoever abideth in Him sinneth not: whosoever sinneth hath not seen Him, neither knoweth him ... Whosoever is begotten of God doeth no sin, because his seed abideth in him: and he cannot sin, because he is begotten of God."[1] This is description according to the unqualified type. It pictures the ideal to which the Christian in perfect fidelity to his calling must conform. That a margin of possible deflection from the ideal has to be recognized was not ignored by John. He speaks accordingly of a gracious provision for the forgiveness of sins that are not unto death,[2] and represents Christ as saying that even the fruit-bearing branch needs pruning in order to attain unto its best capacity of fruitfulness.[3]

No words could surpass in emphasis those with which John insists upon love as essentially descriptive of the Christian. He carries up the demonstration of its necessity to the highest possible point, in defining God as love and describing Christians as those who are begotten of God. Being in fellowship with the infinite personal Love and bearing His likeness they can but live the life of love, paying a full-heart tribute both to God and to the brother. The great historic incentive to this love is the manifestation of the love of God in sending His Son. Among the inward benedictions which it brings at the stage of perfection is the expulsion of all fear.[4]

---

[1] 1 John iii. 6, 9. [2] 1 John ii. 1, 2, v. 16, 17. [3] John xv. 2.
[4] John xiii. 34, xiv. 21–24, xv. 9, 10, 12, 13, xvii. 21, 26; 1 John ii. 9–11, iii. 10–12, 14–18, iv. 7–21, v. 1, 2.

VIII.— THE CHRISTIAN BROTHERHOOD.

Church constitution receives no attention in the Johannine writings. The word Church is not so much as mentioned, except in the third Epistle. Elsewere there is reference only to a brotherhood or flock of Christ. Stress is placed upon the unity appropriate to this brotherhood;[1] but no official bonds of unity are specified.

A nearly equal silence is maintained in respect of ordinances. Mention is indeed made of the fact that the disciples of Jesus baptized,[2] but at that stage the ceremony could have had no distinct ecclesiastical association such as belonged to it from the day of Pentecost. It was a token of repentance in preparation for the kingdom.[3] Of baptism as a proper church rite no word is spoken by John. Even if the mention of water in the discourse on the new birth is to be understood of Christian baptism, it is only its import for individual experience, not its ecclesiastical function, that comes into account. The reference to water in 1 John v. 6 does not call for consideration here, as it concerns only the baptism of Christ at the initiation of His ministry.

No unequivocal reference to the eucharist is found in the Johannine writings. It may be granted that at the time the evangelist penned the sixth chapter of the Gospel it was natural that some of its terms should suggest to his mind the sacrament of Christ's body and blood. But the discourse of this chapter has no direct bearing

---

[1] John x. 16, xvii. 21, 22; 1 John ii. 19, iii. 14–18.
[2] John iii. 22, iv. 1, 2.   [3] See Matt. iv. 17; Mark i. 14, 15.

on the subject of the eucharist. In the first part of the discourse the same office precisely is ascribed to faith which in the second part is ascribed to the eating of Christ's flesh and the drinking of His blood. Moreover, the concluding declaration (verse 63) takes the acts described as eating and drinking entirely out of the category of material transactions, and identifies them with a spiritual function. It is necessary therefore to regard the discourse as a figurative and graphic means of enforcing the spiritual appropriation of the whole message of divine truth in Christ. As Westcott remarks: " The people had eaten of the loaves ; that which it was their highest blessing to do was to eat the Son of Man. This eating is essential to all, inasmuch as without it there is no life and no resurrection. And further, this eating leads necessarily to life in the highest sense ; it has no qualifications (such as eating worthily); it is operative for good absolutely. It follows that the eating cannot refer primarily to the holy communion ; nor again can it be simply prophetic of that sacrament. The teaching has a full and consistent meaning in connection with the actual circumstances, and it treats essentially of spiritual realities with which no external act, as such, can be coextensive. The well-known words of Augustine, *crede et manducasti*, "believe and thou hast eaten," give the sum of the thoughts in a luminous and pregnant sentence."[1]

With the progress of sacerdotalism in the Church there was a tendency to utilize the reference to remitting and retaining sins in John xx. 23 in behalf of a priestly func-

---

[1] The Gospel According to St. John, p. 113.

tion of absolution. But this interpretation savors of gratuitous exaggeration. The words in question were spoken to the company of the disciples. There is nothing on record which requires us to suppose that they were addressed exclusively to the apostles or to any circle of officials. The parallel reference in Luke xxiv. 33–36 indicates that others besides the twelve were included in the company upon which Christ pronounced His benediction, and to which He pledged the assistance of the Holy Spirit. It was not then a special sacerdotal prerogative which the words of Christ described, but a function of the Christian body as such. Speaking ideally, or on the supposition that the Christian body would be fully submitted to the guidance of the Holy Spirit, He affirmed that in establishing rules of conduct and administering discipline over its members, it would but execute the divine will. Its binding and loosing upon earth, to use the Synoptical phrase, would correspond with that in heaven; in other words, the adjustment of the relations of men to the brotherhood would reflect their real relations to the kingdom of God. If in place of the brotherhood as a whole one prefers to regard the apostles as contemplated in the promise, the meaning is still remote from the sacerdotal theory of a judicial prerogative in the priest over the confessing penitent. There is no question here of remitting or retaining sins in the eminent sense, but only in the secondary sense of that power of passing judgment which belongs to religious society when fulfilling to the best its vocation. Certainly it is the unequivocal dictate of reason that no human society, or set of officials, can forgive sins in the eminent sense, since the divine judgment is absolutely final in determining the status of the individual as approved or condemned, and it is absurd to suppose that any human sentence can either get ahead of the divine judgment or control the same. The best that the human sentence can do is to follow and give effect, in the accessible relations of a given subject, to the divine judgment. This end the optimistic and idealizing words attributed to Christ contemplated as about to be realized in the Christian brotherhood.

IX. — Eschatology.

Some of the Johannine representations seem well-nigh to cancel the antithesis between the two worlds, and to take away all occasion for contemplating a future crisis. Thus eternal life is frequently spoken of, not as a remote inheritance, but as a present possession. "He that believeth on the Son hath eternal life."[1] "He that eateth my flesh and drinketh my blood hath eternal life."[2] "The witness is this, that God gave unto us eternal life, and this life is in His Son."[3] Again there are references to the coming of Christ which seem to identify it, not with the visible inauguration of a dispensation radically diverse from the present, but with a spiritual advent to men still living in the common earthly relations.[4] Still further, there are sentences which picture judgment, not as the event of a future day, but as an ordeal that is now being visited upon one class of men, and for another class has been put entirely away.[5] Once more, in various connec-

---

[1] John iii. 36. [2] John vi. 54. [3] 1 John v. 11.
[4] John xiv. 18, 23. [5] John iii. 18, 19, ix. 39, xii. 31, v. 24.

THE JOHANNINE THEOLOGY 357

tions the resurrection is given a present and spiritual application, and the disciple is spoken of as if instated here and now in an order of life which makes physical death practically of no significance.[1]

Expressing the sense of the foregoing we may say that the apocalyptic element, or the thought of the outward crisis, is not prominent in the Johannine teaching. Its favorite point of view is that of the spiritualism which makes minor account of distinctions of time and place and centers its contemplation upon the relations of the soul to God and upon the fruition of the life that is lifted up into close fellowship with Him. Still the apocalyptic element is not wanting. The ordinary postulates of New Testament eschatology evidently lay in the background of John's mental picture of the future. In at least one instance he makes an unequivocal reference to the coming of Christ in the sense of a distinct manifestation at a special epoch,[2] and there are other probable references to an advent of the like kind.[3] He speaks also, or represents Christ as speaking, of a last day and of a resurrection and a judgment associated with that day.[4] On these topics there is apparently a combination of the ideas of process and consummation. "As the future resurrection seems to be viewed as an element, and, in some sense, as the consummation of the Son's bestowment of life upon mankind, so the future judgment appears to be regarded as the culmination of a process of judgment which is inseparably connected with

---

[1] John v. 24, 25, viii. 51, xi. 25, 26.
[2] 1 John ii. 28.   [3] John xiv. 3, xxi. 22.
[4] John v. 28, 29, vi. 39, 40, 44, 54, xii. 48; 1 John iv. 17.

the presence and effect of divine light and truth in the world."[1] That the consummation of judgment will leave some men outside the pale of eternal life was manifestly the thought of John. His recognition of a sin unto death — that is, an offence, or series of offences, against the light so aggravated as to cancel religious sensibility — testifies to that effect.[2]

As compared with the Apocalypse, the Johannine writings here considered are distinguished by reticence on the heavenly life. The many mansions of the Father's house, the being with Christ and beholding His glory, the seeing God or Christ as He is and being like Him — these few phrases include the whole message that is delivered respecting the inheritance in store.[3] The brevity of the message, however, does not prevent its being exceedingly rich in content.

X.— Conclusion.

The opinion has sometimes been expressed that the Johannine type represents the goal of doctrine in the New Testament, and is fitted to serve as the ultimate Christian theology. This opinion, it strikes us, cannot be accepted without very considerable qualification. With all its excellencies the Johannine type is not a substitute for other New Testament types. The Synoptical teaching fulfills an important function in its greater wealth of ethical detail. It has also some special features as respects the characterization of God

---

[1] Stevens, The Johannine Theology, p. 347.
[2] 1 John v. 16. [3] John xiv. 2, xvii. 24; 1 John iii. 2.

for which the Johannine teaching does not compensate. Lofty as is the latter, it has a tinge of vagueness and mysticism. The Synoptical description of the heavenly Father as exercising a minute and tender providence, and as generously welcoming the returning prodigal, provides for a more homelike feeling in the divine presence than is fostered by John's less concrete representations. No less is there room for the Pauline type alongside the Johannine. The former, if it does not reach deeper than the latter, does excel in variety of ethical and religious content. Moreover, it ministers in a superior degree an incentive to world-conquering enterprise. Paul was a man in whom missionary aspiration was at a maximum. He could almost wish himself accursed from Christ for his brethren, his kinsmen according to the flesh. He counted himself a debtor both to the Greek and the Barbarian. He was ever anxious to lay new foundations for the Gospel and to voice through a widening circle the call to men to be reconciled to God. And thus, as bearing the stamp of his spirit, his epistles are naturally a perennial source of missionary incentive. With the Johannine writings it is different. The love of God is indeed represented as going out to the world, and the inference may be drawn that Christians should follow the divine precedent. Nevertheless, it is true that in general the world in these writings is set over against Christians as a kind of alien domain. Love for the brotherhood is fervently inculcated, but very little is said which conveys any impression of an obligation of outreaching affection for the unevangelized world. The Johannine teaching opens the door upon a beautiful and transfigured life of intimate fellowship with God and of pure love to the children of God. Herein it fulfills a high office. But it needs certainly to be supplemented by the Pauline teaching with its larger infusion of missionary ardor or spirit of world-conquering enterprise. The truth is, no one of the New Testament types is to be elected as giving by itself the complete doctrinal standard. One may excel another in important respects, but it is by their united contributions that the full-orbed truth of the new dispensation is made to shine upon the minds and hearts of men.

INDEX

Abbot, E., 304, 316
Abbott, T. K., 182
Acts, Book of, 124 f., 140 ff.
Adeney, W. F., 259
Adoption, 238, 349
Advent, the second, 117 ff., 169, 258 ff., 356 f.
Allegorizing, the Alexandrian, 22, 29 f.; the Pauline, 194 f.
Alexandrianism, 20 ff., 272, 321
Alogi, the, 303
Angelology, 20, 99, 208, 282 f., 331
Antitheses, Pauline, 213 ff.; Johannine, 325 ff.
Apocalypse of John, 130 ff., 158 ff.
Apocryphal Gospels, 52 ff.
Apostles, their office, 109 ff., 142 f.
Assurance, 241 f., 351
Atonement, 11, 12, 19, 105 ff., 146 f., 165 f., 228 ff., 286 ff., 343 ff.
Augustine, 203

Bacon, B. W., 78, 181 f., 187 f., 259, 278
Baldensperger, W., 12
Baptism, 113 ff., 148 ff., 255 ff., 296, 350, 353
Baruch, Apocalypse of, 9, 14, 18, 38
Beyschlag, W., 67, 203, 236, 278, 298
Binding and loosing, 110 ff., 354 ff.
Bishops, 143, 167, 254 f., 268
Bousset, W., 13, 18, 74, 90, 139, 259

Briggs, C. A., 58
Bruce, A. B., 80, 236, 256, 273

Charles, R. H., 13, 16, 100
Chase, F. H., 124, 278
Church, the, 107 ff., 140 ff., 157, 167 f., 252 ff., 295 f., 353
Christology, 18 f., 31, 56 ff., 99 ff., 144 ff., 162 ff., 219 ff., 284 ff., 335 ff.
Clement of Alexandria, 54, 145
Clement of Rome, 145
Colossians, Epistle to the, 31, 179 ff.
Conception, the supernatural, 56 ff.
Cone, O., 220, 231, 236
Corinthians, Epistles to the, 177, 179
Cremer, A. H., 231

Dalman, G., 59, 89, 100
Deacons, 143, 254 f., 268
Demonology, 20, 98 f., 209, 283, 331
Denney, J., 222, 231, 293
Devil, the, see *Satan*
Didache, 145
Divorce, 251 f.
Dods, M., 342
Drummond, J., 24 ff., 35, 305, 309

Ecclesiasticus, 18, 21, 36, 89
Egyptians, the Gospel according to the, 53
Elders, 143 f., 157, 255, 268, 295
Election, see *Predestination*

361

INDEX

Enoch, Book of, 9, 12 f., 15, 38, 100

Ephesians, Epistle to the, 31, 179 ff.

Eschatology, Jewish, 14 ff., 20, 27; Christian, 95, 117 ff., 169 f., 258 ff., 297 ff., 356 ff.

Essenes, the, 6 ff.

Eucharist, the, 115 f., 148, 257 f., 296, 353 f.

Eusebius, 48 ff., 54, 307 f.

Evangelists, 254

Ezra, Fourth Book of, 9 f., 14, 18

Faith, 81 f., 155, 167, 187, 239 ff., 294 f., 350

Family, the, 250 ff., 295

Fatherhood of God, 89 ff., 153 f., 201 f., 334 f.

Findlay, G. G., 185

Flesh, as opposed to spirit, 97 f., 213 ff., 281, 329 f.

Galatians, Epistle to the, 177 f.

Garvie, A. E., 205, 231

Gifford, E. H., 231

God, conceptions of, 11, 23, 87 ff., 153, 199 ff., 278 ff., 331 ff.

Godet, F., 222, 231, 236, 264

Gould, E. P., 77

Grace, as contrasted with law, 217 ff., 265

Grill, J., 35, 336

Handmann, R., 53

Harnack, A., 50 ff., 128, 183, 188, 274, 276, 278

Haupt, E., 120, 182

Hawkins, J. C., 50, 124

Hebrews, Epistle to the, 32 f., 270 ff.; Gospel according to the, 52

Heinrici, C. F. G., 208

Hesse, F. H., 188

Hippolytus, 59

Hirscht, A., 134

Holtzmann, H. J., 7, 14, 125, 128, 203, 228, 236, 278, 336

Hort, F. J. A., 150

Ignatius of Antioch, 308

Irenæus, 132, 307

James, epistle of, 36, 126 ff., 153 ff., 275 f.

Jesus, His nativity, 56 ff.; His self-consciousness as a subject of development and source of teaching, 59 ff.; His witness respecting His own person and office, 99 ff. See *Christology*

John, question of his indebtedness to Alexandrianism, 33 ff., 321; evidences as to his authorship of the fourth Gospel, 300 ff.; sources, characteristics, and teachings of this Gospel, 318 ff.

Josephus, 11, 15, 17

Jubilees, Book of, 9, 18, 38

Judgment, the, 122, 159, 170, 265, 297, 356 f.

Jude, Epistle of, 37, 278

Julicher, A., 49 f., 115, 178 f., 278

Justification, 156, 167, 235 ff., 293, 349

Justin Martyr, 14, 55, 59

Kaftan, J., 236

Kattenbusch, F., 115

Kautzsch, E., 13

Kennedy, H. A. A., 259, 266

Kenosis, Doctrine of the, 224 f.

INDEX

Kingdom of God, or of heaven, 73 ff., 253
Klopper, A., 78
Knowling, R. J., 148

Lambert, J. C., 114 f., 258
Lange, J. P., 231
Lagrange, M. J., 12
Law, the, 10, 79, 126, 127, 155, 217 ff.
Lightfoot, J. B., 49, 182, 316
Lipsius, R. A., 222, 231, 236
Lobstein, P., 58
Logia, the, 48 ff.
Loisy, A., 336

McGiffert, A. C., 188, 272
Man, his nature and condition, 18, 30, 93 ff., 154, 209 ff., 280 ff., 324, 329 f.
Marriage, 250 f., 267 f.
Mary, the Virgin, 168
Mayor, J. B., 127, 129
Ménégoz, E , 33, 273, 290
Messiah, Jewish doctrine of the, 11 ff., 18, 25, 229; Messiah Ben Joseph, 12
Meyer, H. A. W., 222, 231, 236, 298, 303
Millennial reign, 169 f.
Moffatt, J., 50, 51, 119, 259, 278
Morality, as related to religion, 68 ff.
Moule, H. C. G., 182

Nitzsch, F., 236

Origen, 54
Olshausen, H., 231

Papias, 48, 309 f.

Pastoral Epistles, 186 ff., 266 ff.
Pastors, 254 f.
Paul, the apostle, question of his indebtedness to Pharisaism, 17 ff., to Alexandrianism, 28 ff.; sources of his theology, 188 ff.; his teachings, 199 ff.
Peabody, A. P., 316
Peake, A. S., 273, 289
Peter, the apostle, 109 ff., 143, 255; First Epistle of, 270 ff.; Second Epistle, 276 ff.; so-called Gospel of Peter, 54
Pfleiderer, O., 19, 28 f., 177, 221, 228, 336
Pharisaism, 8 ff., 18 ff., 69
Philemon, Epistle to, 179, 184
Philippi, F. A., 231
Philippians, Epistle to the, 179 f.
Philo, 21 ff.
Plumtre, E. H., 278
Poor, blessing upon the, 83 f.
Porter, F. C., 139
Prayer, 92, 168
Predestination, 17, 85 ff., 203 ff., 242 f., 347 f.,
Preexistence of souls, 25, 26
Prophets, 254

Quartodecimans, 304 f.

Ramsay, W. M., 161 f.
Rauch, C., 139
Reconciliation, see *Atonement*
Regeneration, 76, 156, 238 f., 293, 349 f.
Renan, E., 184
Repentance, 81 f., 294
Resurrection, 15, 27, 121 f., 261 ff., 297 f., 356 f.; of Christ, 234, 292

Retribution, future, 122, 265 f., 297, 358
Revelation, Book of, see *Apocalypse*
Réville, J., 336
Ritschl, A., 231
Robertson, A., 151
Ropes, J. A., 55

Sabatier, A., 87
Sadducees, 5, 6
Salmon, G , 183
Salmond, S. D. F., 183, 207
Sanctification, 243 ff , 293 ff., 352
Sanday, W., 115, 222, 231, 236
Satan, 98, 161, 209, 330 f.
Schmidt, N., 101
Schmiedel, P. W., 125
Schultz, H , 7
Sharman, H. B., 78
Siegfried, C., 28, 33, 35
Smith, W. R., 271
Sin, 96, 154, 211, 281, 326 ff.
Somerville, D., 41
Son of God, 102, 221, 284, 336 f.
Son of Man, 99 ff.
Spirit, the Holy, 105, 147 f., 164 f., 221 f., 226 ff., 340 ff.
Spitta, F., 130, 278
Stanton, V. H., 53, 54, 305, 309
State, obligations to the, 249, 295

Stevens, G. B., 99, 118, 167, 231, 236, 259
Suetonius, 162
Swete, H. B., 55
Synoptical Gospels, 39 ff.

Tacitus, 137
Teachers, 254
Tennant, F. R., 212
Terry, M., 134, 231
Thessalonians, Epistles to the, 172 ff.
Tholuck, F. A. G., 231
Tongues, speaking with, 151 f.
Toy, C. H., 208

Von Soden, H., 182, 271, 278

Weber, F., 9, 12, 26
Weiss, B., 220, 236, 259, 278, 298
Weizsacker, C., 125, 139
Wellhausen, J., 7
Wendt, H. H., 317
Wernle, P., 50
Westcott, B. F., 273, 325, 342
Wisdom of Solomon, 21, 24 f., 28 f., 89, 145
Wrede, D. W., 176

Zahn, T., 127, 186, 269, 278, 309

www.ingramcontent.com/pod-product-compliance
Lightning Source LLC
Chambersburg PA
CBHW072132220426
43664CB00013B/2216